Representative democracy in Britain today

Politics Today
Series editor: Bill Jones

Representative democracy in Britain today

Colin Pilkington

Manchester University Press

Manchester and New York

distributed exclusively in the USA by St. Martin's Press

Published by Manchester University Press
Oxford Road, Manchester M13 9NR, UK
and Room 400, 175 Fifth Avenue, New York, NY 10010, USA

Distributed exclusively in the USA
by St. Martin's Press, Inc., 175 Fifth Avenue, New York,
NY 10010, USA

British Library Cataloguing-in-Publication Data
A catalogue record for this book is available from the British Library

Library of Congress Cataloging-in-Publication Data
Pilkington, Colin.
    Representative democracy in Britain today / Colin Pilkington.
        p. cm. – (Politics today)
      ISBN 0-7190-4817-6. – ISBN 0-7190-4818-4
      1. Democracy – Great Britain   2. Representative government and
    representation – Great Britain.   3. Great Britain – Politics and
    government.   I. Title.   II. Series: Politics today (Manchester,
    England)
    JN900.P55   1997
    321.8′0941 – dc20   96-34391
                                                             CIP

ISBN   0 7190 4817 6 *hardback*
        0 7190 4818 4 *paperback*

First published in 1997

00 99 98 97   10 9 8 7 6 5 4 3 2 1

Typeset in Great Britain
by Servis Filmsetting Ltd, Manchester

Printed in Great Britain
by Bell & Bain Ltd, Glasgow

Contents

V   Democratic deficit

Preface

While they were talking, the ship reached Portsmouth. The water-side was crowded with a host of people who were gazing intently at a stout man kneeling on the deck of a warship, with his eyes bandaged. Four soldiers stood opposite him who, with the utmost composure, fired three rounds each into his head, at which the crowd dispersed, apparently quite satisfied. Candide asked who the stout gentleman was who had so ceremoniously been disposed of.

'He was an admiral,' they told him. 'But why execute this admiral?' he enquired. 'In this country,' came the answer, 'we find it pays to shoot an admiral from time to time to encourage the others.'

> *The execution, in March 1757, of Admiral Byng, – held*
> *accountable for the loss of Minorca to the French.*
> From *Candide* by Voltaire, Chapter XXIII

This book was conceived at the end of 1994, when a tide of sleaze was submerging the government, concern was being expressed about the growth in the number of quangos, heads of the privatised industries were being described as 'pigs with their snouts in the trough', the Home Secretary was subject to no fewer than nine guilty verdicts by the High Court and the nature of parliament and government was under review by both Nolan and Scott. The original intention was to write about this as evidence of a decline in ministerial accountability but the catalogue of concerns grew ever longer until the matters I had listed for discussion extended into almost every corner of political life. In the end it became apparent that the subject could only be covered adequately by examining what must be called the crisis in representative democracy as it exists in Britain today.

In an article dealing with the BSE crisis over beef, and New Labour's response to the (European Union) EU ban, the social democratic thinker, David Marquand, claimed to see a divide in the development of liberal democracy, 'On one side is the myopic, profit-driven, public-interest-denying culture which has always been latent in British capitalism, and which has swept all before it in the last fifteen years. On the other is the regulatory culture associated with the social capitalisms of mainland Europe'.[1] What has to be considered therefore are the many ways in which the form of democracy existing in Britain today diverges from the idealised picture presented at the end of the nineteenth century, a view which lauded Britain as being the cradle of democracy and guardian of liberty, and the British parliament as being the Mother of Parliaments and role model for all would-be democracies.

This book therefore begins by considering the meaning of the concept of liberal democracy and examining the historical process by which the British version of that concept came into being. It then goes on in turn to examine four areas in which the ideal may be considered as having become somewhat tarnished:

1 The democratic control and regulation of finance and the economy, by which accountability should literally mean the accounting of government to the people for the raising and use of public funds.

2 The concept of representation and the representative nature and probity of our representatives, including the legitimacy of their acting on behalf of the people.

3 The accountability of government ministers for their actions and mistakes, and the means by which government institutions might be held to account.

4 The democratic deficit represented by the unelected, the unaccountable, the secret and the remote nature of government and the constitution.

The book is intended for the student of politics, or the general reader with an interest in current affairs, and is not meant to be a partisan or polemic work. However, I trust that it will make students think again about arguments over the British constitution and political system that have been put forward for some time by bodies such as Charter 88. Above all I trust it will lead to a realisation that mere adjustments or fine tuning to parts of our constitutional structure, such as reforming the electoral system, are not enough; and that the time is ripe, as we approach the new millenium, for a complete revamp of the constitution, root and branch.

My thanks for support and encouragement go as always to Dr Bill Jones, as editor of the Politics Today series. I should also like to pay a valedictory tribute to Richard Purslow who played a major part in the formulation of this book before his departure from Manchester University Press: his contributions to the proposed outline I drew up were invaluable. A grateful acknowledgement is due to many members of the Politics Association, but I am particularly indebted to Glynnis Sandwith of PARC (Politics Association Resource Centre). Practical assistance was given by Dennis Harrigan and other members of the NEAB (Northern Examinations and Assessment Board) team examining government and politics. I also have to say that I received much useful guidance as to what students actually need from their resource materials from those candidates whose work was submitted to me as examiner. Indeed, I should like to pay tribute to one student in particular. For his highly competent and merciless evaluation of the worth, usefulness and readability of resource material I salute the work of Matthew Forrester, of Leftwich County High School in Northwich, Cheshire. Matthew was only sixteen and a year eleven student when he wrote his critique but his conclusions were very logical, very incisive and very mature, such as to give this academic writer considerable pause for thought as to how far what he had to say had any relevance or meaning for the average student for whom he was supposed to be writing.

Colin Pilkington
May, 1996

Notes

1 David Marquand, 'Time to take sides', the *Guardian*, 28 May 1996.

Abbreviations

AMS	additional member system
C and AG	Comptroller and Auditor General
COR	Committee of the Regions
DTI	Department of Trade and Industry
EC	European Community
EGO	extra-governmental organisation
EP	European Parliament
EU	European Union
FMI	Financial Management Initiatives
FPTP	first-past-the-post
GCHQ	Government Communication Headquarters
GDP	gross domestic product
GMS	grant maintained school
IMF	International Monetary Fund
IRO	integrated regional office
LEA	Local Education Authority
MEP	Member of the European Parliament
MP	Member of Parliament
NAO	National Audit Office
NDPB	non-departmental public body
NEAB	Northern Examinations and Assessment Board
NEC	National Executive Committee
NHS	National Health Service
NUM	National Union of Mineworkers
OMOV	one-member-one-vote

OPSS	Office of Public Service and Science
PAC	Public Accounts Committee
PARC	Politics Association Resource Centre
PC	Plaid Cymru
PCA	Parliamentary Commissioner for Administration
PCC	Press Complaints Commission
PESC	Public Expenditure Survey Committee
PIRC	Pension Investment Research Consultants
PLP	Parliamentary Labour Party
PR	proportional representation
PSBR	Public Sector Borrowing Requirement
SIs	statutory instruments
SMP	Scottish Member of Parliament
SNP	Scottish National Party
STV	single transferable vote
TEC	training and education council
TGWU	Transport and General Workers' Union
vfm	value-for-money

I

Introduction – historical background

1

What is democracy?

No one pretends that democracy is perfect or all-wise. Indeed, it has been said that democracy is the worst form of government, except all those other forms that have been tried from time to time.

Winston S. Churchill

The task of Parliament is not to run the country but to hold to account those who do.

William Ewart Gladstone

The word 'democracy', like so many political terms, including the word 'politics' itself, comes from the Greek. It is one of the strange paradoxes of history that the concepts and theories by which we describe political organisation in the modern world were developed in communities that have nothing whatsoever in common with anything we know or can conceptualise today. We call Greek communities of the Classical era city-states but they were not states as we would recognise them. Even the more important of them, such as Athens or Sparta, covered a very small geographical area and were populated by little more than about 20,000 inhabitants: hardly more, in size and complexity of structure, than over-grown villages. Economically, the Greek states were poor in comparison to the contemporary empires of Egypt or Persia. Temperamentally they were quarrelsome and unlikely to co-operate for mutual aid and security. Indeed, as one political theorist has put it, 'the human and economic limitations of the average Greek city were such that it is difficult at first sight to see why reflection upon its problems could remotely concern or interest the social thinkers of later ages'.[1]

The truth is that, despite what one might think, Greek thought is still relevant to political theory. Poor and fragmented as the Greek city-states were, they were pre-eminent in political study and experimentation. The number and variety of Greek city-states meant that the political philosophers of the time could observe what was the equivalent of a series of laboratory experiments into the best way in which society can be ordered and organised. When someone such as Aristotle concluded that democracy was the most desirable form of government it was a conclusion based on first-hand knowledge of a wide range of alternatives. The governance of society has never been so intensively studied as it was at that time, meaning that we have a vast body of theoretical knowledge built up by the Greeks through which we can consider the justification for, the faults of, and the threats to, modern democracy, despite the differences between our worlds.

It is necessary to be cautious, however, and it must be realised that the democracy we are discussing in this book is not, and cannot be, what the Greeks meant when they used the term. The size and complexity of today's society is so different from that of the Athens of Pericles that the democratic institutions we have in place today must of necessity be radically different from their Grecian forebears.

The Greeks had two words for government. There was *archeia*, from which we get the English ending '-archy', as in monarchy, oligarchy or even anarchy. Secondly there was *kratia*, from which we get our ending '-cracy', as in democracy or aristocracy. Although they were both terms for systems of government there was a subtle difference between them. 'Archy' had the implication of 'powerful leadership', while 'cracy' is better rendered by the word 'authority'. As a result, the word 'oligarchy', meaning 'government by a few', carries the implication of a rule imposed by the few on the many, by force if necessary. Whereas 'democracy', the rule of the 'demos' or 'people', carries the connotation not only of 'rule of the people, by the people' but also of 'rule of the people, in the interests of the people and with the consent of the people'. It is this concept of government by consent, and of popular consent lending legitimacy to government, that is more important to our understanding of democracy than the mechanics of how the people as a whole can be involved with government in a participatory sense.

Limitations on true democracy

An idealised view of democracy, sometimes called 'true democracy' or 'direct democracy', would envisage a governmental and legislative process in which all members of society are involved, and in which all decisions are arrived at by mutual and unanimous agreement. In fact, such a process is of necessity an ideal that is not achievable in the real world. Even in the small city-states of Ancient Greece it was impossible for all members of society to be involved: there have always been those who are excluded from the democratic process. In Athens, half the population was automatically excluded because women were not thought capable of the reasoned judgement necessary for political participation: an attitude widely held until recent times and never quite removed from some people's thinking. Children, slaves and residents who were not native-born citizens were also disbarred from the Athenian Assembly. Among those entitled to attend the Assembly, a form of indirect democracy evolved whereby the Assembly as a whole chose an electoral college which in turn elected the officials who would direct the day-to-day functioning of the state. The procedure was, in effect, the birth of representative democracy. Routine administration would be dealt with, not by the people as a whole which would be too unwieldy a process for efficient administration, but by a small and efficient group who nevertheless represented the people as a whole. That small group would be democratic rather than oligarchic in that they would be chosen by the Assembly and could, as easily, be dismissed by the Assembly. Furthermore, the ranks of office-holders were not part of any closed society:

any member of the Assembly was automatically eligible for selection to hold office.

Despite the relative openness of Athenian government it was, nevertheless, the case that the right to participate in government was a selective process, and a right for which a would-be participant had to qualify. The Greeks thought that every form of government had its benevolent aspect and its corrupt face – the benign and paternal monarch could become an oppressive tyrant; the enlightened elite of the aristocracy could become a self-interested and repressive oligarchy. The fear of Athenian philosophers such as Plato or Aristotle was that rule of the people could quite as easily become rule by the unthinking masses. It is a fear that has persisted and we must remember that, despite a modern-day belief in the inherent goodness of the democratic ideal, democracy has largely been distrusted by history.

> For most of human history it [democracy] has been treated by intellectuals and – less surprisingly – political leaders with contempt: democracy meant rule by the untrained ignorant mob . . . it entailed determining what was right by counting heads, rather than by consulting standards of truth, morality or reason.[2]

Equally as unrealistic as universal participation is the possibility that all members of society will agree with one another and that decisions can be arrived at by unanimous consent. Decisions are usually made with the agreement of the majority, determined by some form of ballot. For many people their understanding of the term 'democracy' is limited to the concept of accepting the decisions of a majority of the population; a process known simply as majoritarianism. Yet majoritarianism has its very real dangers, as was recognised by Plato when he talked of the 'tyranny of the majority', by which large sections of the population can be forced into courses of action that are anathema to them, simply because they represent a minority in the population as a whole. As Jay says, 'voting can be an instrument that polarises the citizen body by separating them into victors and vanquished'.[3] Typical of the innate unfairness of majoritarianism is Britain after 1979, when a Conservative administration maintained itself in government despite never having the support of more than about 40 per cent of the electorate.

True democracy, in the sense of direct participation in government, probably never existed. But, according to Greek political philosophy, as epitomised by Aristotle, that was not important. It is not the mechanics of a political constitution that matter but the purpose of that constitution. Popular support in a democracy is the source of the government's legitimacy; it does not dictate the arrangements through which that government functions.

> Democracies can be mere examples of mob-rule or representative of the general prudence and wisdom . . . of the population. If the proper end of government is the pursuit of the good life, only governments which consider this common interest have the right, or morally satisfactory, constitution. Only authority exercised in pursuit of this common interest is just.[4]

In other words, in Abraham Lincoln's famous definition of democracy as 'government of the people, by the people, for the people', the most important of these three defining characteristics of democracy is '*for* the people'.

Natural law and the Age of Reason

The embryonic democracies of the Greek city-states were submerged by the imperialism, firstly of Alexander's Macedonia and then of Rome. And, when the Roman Empire faded, its place as a universal political entity was taken by a Roman Catholic Church in which 'order', as laid down by God, was the overriding value. As we shall see in Chapter 2, there were some surprisingly democratic institutions existing in the Middle Ages, even at the height of the feudal system, but anything that we could understand as being democratic was subordinate and largely irrelevant to a view of a divinely ordained hierarchical structure that was maintained by the Church and which it would be blasphemous or heretical to question. The theologians who represented what political theory there was in the Middle Ages, developed the concept of a universe governed by natural law, which was in effect God's law and to which all creation, including kings and emperors, was subject.

As the Middle Ages drew to an end, the medieval concept of a divine order and hierarchy embracing all of humankind was usurped during the Reformation by the theory known as the Divine Right of Kings. Protestant leaders such as Luther or Calvin were unwilling to offend kings and princes and stressed the importance to their followers of obeying the civil power because that power had been ordained of God. Monarchs were perceived as being God's representatives on earth, by birth and by annointment at their coronations. And this special relationship with God placed the monarch above and beyond the law. Kings, as epitomised by Louis XIV of France who most significantly stated that 'l'état c'est moi', became absolute monarchs who were, in the Greek meaning of the term, tyrants. It was the reaction to this development, the desire of people to be free from tyranny and to make the king as equally answerable to the law as his subjects, which led to the re-examination of democratic ideas in the seventeenth and eighteenth centuries.

Originally, critics of the Divine Right used two arguments to justify their criticism, both still contributory to our ideas of democracy:

1 Conscience: individuals should not be forced into doing something which is against their deeply-held beliefs.
2 The rule of law: everyone in society must accept natural law, including the rulers. If rulers refuse to abide by natural law their subjects are not obliged to obey them.

These two viewpoints led to the secularisation of the natural law theory. The concept of natural law was superseded by the concept of natural rights which gave rights to all the people, not just the monarchs, and which also provided for sanctions against those who offended against natural law, even if they were monarchs. Initially the key figure in this development was the French philosopher, René Descartes (1596–1650), who put forward the proposition *cogito ergo sum* (I think therefore I am).

This statement, which might seem so commonplace to us, was, in fact, revolutionary at the time and represented the rebirth of individuality. According to medieval ideas, humankind was not supposed to think for itself in analysing social and political organisation: God's will, as revealed and interpreted through the Church, should be accepted without question. Descartes made it clear that humans had the right and ability to work out their own salvation through rational thought. The latter part of the seventeenth century and the first three-quarters of the eighteenth century are together known as the Age of Reason. It is during this time that theories of rationality laid down the basis of a liberal democratic tradition that still has a great deal of influence today. The Age of Reason also saw the practical application of liberal democratic theory, most obviously in the Declaration of Independence and the Constitution of the United States of America.

The prophet of liberal democracy was the English philosopher, John Locke, who published his *Two Treatises on Government* in 1690, at a time when England was going through the turmoil of expelling James II in the so-called Glorious Revolution. Locke accepted the idea, common among thinkers of the Age of Reason, that society was the product of a contract between ruler and ruled for the mutual satisfaction and security of all. Locke's definition of this contract and its implications can be summarised under three headings:

1 Individuals are born free, equal and possessed of rational thought.
2 Individuals enter into a political community in order to safeguard their natural rights through the rule of law.
3 Authority is by the consent and agreement of the people, rulers who forfeit that consent can legitimately be removed.

The natural rights which are at the centre of Locke's thesis were said to be 'Life, Liberty and the enjoyment of Property'. For the period they were revolutionary ideas and, almost a century later having been further developed by Paine and Maddison among others, they culminated, almost unaltered, in one of the most famous revolutionary documents ever published.

We hold these truths to be self-evident, that all men are created equal, that they are endowed by their creator with certain inalienable rights, that among these are Life, Liberty and Happiness. That to secure these rights, Governments are instituted among men, deriving their just powers from the consent of the governed.[5]

Balanced government

Locke had argued that the powers of the monarch should be limited by dividing the executive arm of government from the legislature. This suggestion was very much developed by the French jurist, Charles Louis de Montesquieu, who published his *l'Esprit des Lois* in 1748. For Montesquieu the greatest curb on tyranny was to prevent the concentration of power into too few hands. He therefore considered the three powers of government:

1 The Executive, being the power to frame policy and carry out the law;
2 The Legislature, being the power to make laws;
3 The Judiciary, being the power to enforce the laws and punish those who break them.

For tyranny in a state to be avoided, these three powers must be separated and kept separate. Ironically, Montesquieu claimed to base his ideas on the system existing in Britain, despite the fact that Britain did not have, and never has had, true separation of powers. His ideas were, however, adopted enthusiastically by the founding fathers of the United States. In *The Federalist*, a collection of papers written by individuals concerned in the drafting of the US Constitution, James Maddison wrote that 'the accommodation of all powers, in the same hands, may justly be pronounced the very definition of tyranny'. In the US Constitution the powers are indeed separated, with the executive (President), legislature (Congress) and judiciary (Supreme Court) not only being separate bodies but having the ability to control and limit the powers of one another.

[The government] should not only be founded on free principles, but in which the powers of government should be so divided and balanced among several bodies of the magistracy, as that no one could transcend their legal limits, without being effectually checked and restrained by the others.[6]

Maddison believed not only in the separation of powers but in an additional series of checks and balances that would both constrain and compensate for executive power. The Federalists advocated a system of government that was divided vertically into executive, legislature and judiciary and horizontally into layers of state and federal government, together with a wide variety of interest groups and organisations, including political parties. In the nineteenth century Alexis de Tocqueville attempted to explain why, of the two countries that had gone through a popular revolution in the late eighteenth century, the United States had retained its democracy while France had reverted to tyranny. And de Tocqueville ascribed the democracy of the United States to this diversity of often-competing centres of power and influence, which is known as pluralism.

Thinkers of the liberal tradition, beginning with Locke, were more concerned with removing or limiting the powers of tyrants to be concerned with the actual form of government which replaced that tyranny. As long as laws were just and equitable, and paid due respect to the natural rights of the people, those laws would be obeyed no matter who was responsible for making them. Locke did express the opinion that the ideal form of government should be decided by a majority in a representative parliament while Rousseau, in his *Social Contract* (1762), said that all members of a society should share a common responsibility in making the laws of that society because everyone in that society has an interest in the workings of those laws. But generally, at that time, liberal thoughts on representative democracy did not extend to the concept of popular participation. Eighteenth-century Britain, despite a very aristocratic or oligarchic form of government, claimed to be a representative democracy, but that representation was geographical rather than popular: as indeed, in theory, it still is.

Calls for universal voting rights that would transform representative democracy into popular democracy did not emerge until the nineteenth century. In most countries which had, or which developed, a liberal democratic constitution, the right to vote was subject to qualification through ownership of property or level of education or, in most countries, by sex. Even those who, like John Stuart Mill, believed in universal suffrage for both men and women nevertheless believed in weighting those votes by favouring the literate and better-educated voters with more votes than the illiterate and uneducated.

Even the growth of socialism in the nineteenth century did not champion the extension of voting rights to the community at large. Early socialists such as Saint-Simon were basically elitist and paternalist in their thinking: the duty of government was to look after the poorest members of society through an embryonic welfare state. However, the poorest members of society could not participate in a governmental process they were incapable of understanding; conduct of government would be in the hands of the educated, the *Savants* as Saint-Simon called them. Nor did Marxism advocate the extension of voting rights, because Marx saw parliaments as bourgeois institutions which the theory of communism was dedicated to sweep away, along with all the other apparatus of the State. Between the revolution and the dawn of pure communism, government would take the form of a 'dictatorship of the proletariat' which never sought to be democratic in the tradition of liberal democracy. It was only with the revisionist ideas of the late nineteenth century leading to the development of social democracy that socialist parties finally embraced the democratic tradition.[7]

The orthodox view of democracy

Academic historians in nineteenth-century Britain developed a view of history, based on the liberal tradition that was known as the 'Whig interpretation of history'. That interpretation found such widespread acceptance as to become the normal and universally accepted view of historical development. So normal indeed that the Liberal Tradition described in the Whig

Interpretation acquired the value judgement of being the ideal system of government for a developed society. Firmly established in Western Europe, the United States and former British Dominions, the idea of democracy has been promoted by the former imperialist powers in the emergent post-colonial nations; an acceptance of democratic government has become a pre-requisite of membership in certain international groupings and to qualify as a recipient of aid; and democracy is the touchstone by which the West has accepted links with countries of the former Soviet Union.

This orthodox view of democracy, and specifically repre-sentative democracy, has a number of common, basic character-istics:

- Government is through elected representatives who are not elected to express directly the views of their constituents but to apply their independent judgement of the national interest on behalf of their constituents.
- Participation in decision-making has to be earned and those thought of as not being competent to exercise political judge-ment are excluded from voting. This selectivity has been used in the past to exclude women and the working class and is still used for classes of the population like children, the mentally disturbed and those guilty of criminal acts.
- A balanced constitution with such a system of checks and bal-ances as was advocated by Maddison should maintain the del-icate balance between the extremes of autocratic rule on the one side, and mob rule on the other.
- A democratic society is a pluralist society and a major func-tion of government is to harmonise the conflicting interests which exist in that society in order to create a consensus.
- The government must undertake to maintain the natural civil rights of the individual members of society, ensuring the right of all citizens to be heard and not giving any individual or group of individuals unfair preference over any other.

Bound up with the traditional view of a liberal democracy is the concept of natural rights which must be protected by a prop-erly democratic government. Many States, particularly those which acquired a democratic constitution in rebellion against autocracy, lay so much stress on the rights of the individual that they have written a Bill of Rights into their constitutions. Other States, however, including Britain, do not have a written constitution and therefore no written guarantee of their rights. Nevertheless the liberal tradition that every individual has certain inalienable rights is made manifest in two supranational documents. The United Nations General Assembly adopted a Universal Declaration of Human Rights in December 1948, laying down guidelines for the whole world. Two years later, the recently-founded Council of Europe drafted the European Convention for the Protection of Human Rights and Fundamental Freedoms, now signed by more than thirty countries and reinforced by the European Court of Human Rights in Strasbourg.[8] The Convention has sixty-six articles with an additional ten protocols, but at heart it remains based on the rights described by Locke as 'Life, Liberty and Property', or by Jefferson as 'Life, Liberty and the Pursuit of Happiness'.

Some of the main provisions of the European Convention, which can be taken to represent fundamental democratic rights, are:
- The right to life and liberty.
- Freedom from arbitrary arrest and the right to a fair trial.
- Freedom from slavery, torture or inhuman treatment.
- Freedom of expression, thought, conscience and religion.
- Freedom of peaceful assembly and association.
- Freedom of movement.
- Peaceful enjoyment of possessions.
- The right to education.
- Free expression of the people's wishes in the choice of legislature, including free elections by secret ballot.

Elitism

The universality of the liberal and pluralist democratic state, and the apparently universal acceptance of democracy as the most desirable form of government, should not blind us to the fact that there are still those who are not totally convinced by the arguments in favour of democracy. We have seen that, as far back as Plato, there have been those with their doubts about democracy, who believe that democracy is mob rule and who consider that government should be in the hands of an educated elite. The view of the elitist is that the vast majority of people do not have the ability or the interest to become involved in government and so democracy is always going to fail, because the expertise of the so-called 'ruling classes' is what is really required to run the country.

- The general mass of the public is too large and too inefficient to govern their own affairs and tend to leave it to the experts.
- Large numbers of people cannot make effective decisions and need some competent individual or group of individuals to take charge of the decision-making process.
- The average man or woman in the street is apathetic and indifferent towards the political process. Consider how many people cannot even be bothered to vote in elections.
- The administration of a country has to be bureaucratic and bureaucracy is by its very nature hierarchical, with different tiers of management and with the very best on top and in charge.
- If you leave all your decisions to what has been decided by the majority then you are creating the tyranny of the majority. The majority will always choose the compromise decision, which is usually the lowest common denominator, which leads to mediocrity in the standard of administration.

The arguments advanced by the elitists do not necessarily invalidate the arguments for democracy but are listed here to remind us that a general acceptance of the desirability of democracy does not automatically mean that it is the only possible form of government, nor that it is held in equal esteem by all political scientists.[9]

Notes

1 Charles Vereker, *The Development of Political Theory*, Hutchinson University Library, London, 1957.

2 Richard Jay, 'Democracy', in R. Eccleshall, V. Geoghegan, R. Jay and R. Wilford, *Political Ideologies*, Unwin Hyman, London, 1984.

3 *Ibid.*

4 Vereker, 'Development', page 29.

5 Preamble to the American Declaration of Independence (1776).

6 James Maddison, *The Federalist*, papers XLVII and XLVIII. The extract here is quoted from an edition edited by Beloff and published by Blackwell, 1948.

7 A very good summary of the liberal democratic tradition is in 'Ideology and the liberal tradition' by Bill Jones, in B. Jones (ed.) *Politics UK*, (2nd edition), pages 105–17, Harvester Wheatsheaf, Hemel Hempstead, 1994.

8 Duncan Watts, 'Europe's Bill of Rights', *Politics Review*, April 1994, page 12.

9 For a discussion of pluralism, elitism and other theoretical perspectives the reader should consult P. Dunleavy and B. O'Leary, *Theories of the State*, Macmillan, London, 1987.

2

The growth of the democratic ideal in Britain

Magna Carter was therefore the chief cause of Democracy in England, and thus a *Good Thing* for everyone (except the Common People).

Sellar and Yeatman, *1066 and All That*

The humourous work *1066 and All That* is a parody of all those half-remembered fragments that make up the average person's knowledge of early and medieval history. The passages relating to parliament are a reminder of the ways in which we half-understand that the roots of British democracy go back a very long way in time. A closer and more academic study rapidly shows that the *1066* view of history is not only false but that events which are supposed to underpin our democracy, such as Magna Carta, actually have a meaning almost diametrically opposed to accepted belief. Yet there were developments in the twelfth and thirteenth centuries that may not have laid down the foundations of democracy but which certainly laid down the intellectual environment within which democracy could flourish. No matter what the truth of the situation, there is a tradition in the English-speaking world that we are a free people with a history of freedom stretching back into the remote past. Even in the corruptly oligarchic eighteenth century, historians and political thinkers could talk of Britain's 'Ancient Liberties'; Europeans like Montesquieu could take England as their model for an ideal political regime; and the American revolutionaries could base

their claims for independence on Magna Carta and their historical rights as Englishmen.

The Rule of Law

It has to be said that this chapter on the development of representative democracy in Britain is more concerned, at least before
1603, with developments in England. The United Kingdom
parliament at Westminster is a direct descendent of the medieval
English parliament and, although there may have been
contributions made by Scotland, Wales and Ireland, they are
essentially peripheral to the development of the British system
we know today.

The kings of Anglo-Saxon England had their *Witangemot*, or
'meeting of wise men', represented by the magnates and leading
churchmen of the kingdom. After the Conquest, Norman kings
inherited the *Witan* and turned it into the Grand Council, out of
which the king selected his close advisers, or Privy Council. The
important point to remember about the Norman kings is that
they were natural administrators and bureaucrats. By placing
the feudalism of Normandy within the framework of an Anglo-
Saxon administration, William the Conqueror and his son,
Henry I, created a far more centralised political system than was
usual in contemporary Europe; a system that was extremely efficient and which considerably strengthened royal power.

The effective state created by Henry I was temporarily lost
during the anarchy of Stephen's reign, when a divided and
warring royal administration failed to prevent local magnates
from creating centres of power through which they could challenge royal supremacy. It is in reaction to the anarchy that we got
two important developments – the legal system created by Henry
II and the Great Charter of Liberties granted by Henry's son,
John.

Henry II did not create a new legal system; he merely adopted
elements that had been tried by his grandfather and great-
grandfather, turning them into an administrative framework
which still underlies the principles of British law. Henry restored

the prestige and authority of the royal courts through the use of:
- Itinerant judges who toured the country on pre-arranged circuits, ensuring that royal justice was regularly available in even the most remote shires of the kingdom.
- Juries were used to swear that a crime had occurred; to provide local evidence; and to determine guilt or innocence. As early as 1164 it was established that a jury should consist of 'twelve of the more competent men'.[1] By the reign of Henry III trial by jury had completely replaced trial by ordeal as a means of deciding a man's guilt or innocence.
- The issue of writs to transfer cases to the king's courts from shire, hundred or manor courts.

By providing royal courts available to everyone, free from bias, and by providing trial by sworn jurors, the king's courts gained a reputation for true and fair justice. By the end of Henry II's reign 'royal justice was taking to itself all serious pleas, both civil and criminal, and leaving to the shire, hundred and manor courts only petty offences against public order and minor local disputes between individuals'.[2] This forms the basis for two mainstays in the British view of justice:

1 *Sovereignty.* Within a sovereign power there has to be one authority which is responsible for all law and justice, free of external interference. Henry II did not succeed fully because the Church claimed the right to try members of the clergy in its own courts. In all other respects England had one, unified, legal structure.

2 *Rule of Law.* There was one royal law administered to all the king's subjects in all parts of the kingdom, without regard to local loyalties or favouritism. This is not to say that, in practice, bias and injustice did not continue to flourish for centuries thereafter. But the principles of equality before the law and impartial justice had been established.

Magna Carta

As the quotation from *1066 and All That* shows, one of the few things everyone remembers from primary school history is that our democracy is based on Magna Carta. When a copy of the charter was exhibited at the New York World Fair in 1939, the American press described it as 'the ever-living fountain from which flow those liberties which the English-speaking world enjoys today'.[3] Yet, serious examination of Magna Carta will show that it was reactionary rather than democratic in its purpose.

Granted by King John in 1215, Magna Carta was imposed by the baronage of England who had taken up arms against the king. Their aim was to clarify feudal law in the face of what they saw as John's disregard of royal duties and obligations and, as a result, most of the provisions are totally irrelevant in modern terms. Large sections deal with the intricacies of feudalism, while other sections deal with temporary matters such as relations with Prince Llewellyn of Wales. Those sections which justify Magna Carta's reputation as the safeguard of our liberties, are those which assure freedom from arbitrary taxation, arrest or imprisonment. The two clauses which are held to be the most important are:

> (12) Scutage and aids [i.e. taxation] shall only be levied in our kingdom by common counsel of our kingdom [i.e. through a parliament].
> (39) No freeman shall be arrested, imprisoned, dispossessed, out-lawed, exiled, or deprived of his standing, nor shall we proceed against him by force, except by the lawful judgment of his peers and according to the law of the land.[4]

The charter was re-issued in 1217 and 1225 and made statute law by Edward I in 1297. Magna Carta was much quoted in the thirteenth and fourteenth centuries as the basis of English law and liberties but it became out-dated by the fifteenth century and was largely forgotten. It was re-discovered in the seventeenth century and used by parliament in its quarrel with the king. It is to this revival of interest, aligning Magna Carta with Locke's belief in curbing the powers of a tyrant, that we owe our present-day estimate of its importance.

Parliament

Just as it easy to over-estimate the importance of Magna Carta, so is it easy to exaggerate the relevance of medieval parliaments. A statue to Simon de Montfort stands outside the Houses of Parliament, as though this thirteenth-century Earl of Leicester were the founder of English democracy. As with Magna Carta, De Montfort was fighting for the rights of nobles against the too-restrictive hand of royal government. The fact that both Magna Carta and de Montfort's parliament sowed the seeds of an English constitution, was an unintended by-product.

Barons in revolt against Henry III imposed the Provisions of Oxford in 1258. These created a form of limited monarchy, with real power in the hands of a small council nominated by the barons, and this council chose to emphasise the legislative functions of parliament. With time, however, the king, and his son Edward, clawed back much of the power they had lost at Oxford. The hard-core around de Montfort was left with little support from the baronage, but considerable support among the commons, the knights and gentry of the shires and the citizens of England's main towns and cities. When de Montfort summoned a number of parliaments to his aid in 1264 and 1265, he made up for declining support among the nobility by including members of the commons for the first time.

From that time on, it became normal to summon representatives of the commons to parliaments, although it was midway through the next century before it became standard practice. The pattern for parliaments was set by the so-called Model Parliament of 1295, to which Edward I summoned not only earls, barons, archbishops, bishops and heads of monastic foundations, but also two knights from every shire, two representatives from each city, two burgesses from every borough and proctors representing the ordinary clergy, two from every diocese. So many were called that they could not sit together in one place and the practice grew that the commons sat apart from the lords.

At some time in the fourteenth century, possibly as early as

1320, a book was written called *Modus Tenendi Parliamentum* or 'How to hold a Parliament'. It is not certain who wrote this work but it is probably by William Ayreminne, clerk to parliament between 1316 and 1324. 'How to hold a Parliament' is not necessarily how parliaments were conducted in the fourteenth century but how the writer thought they ought to be.

'How to hold a Parliament' established a principle linking taxation and representation which is at the heart of our modern concept of representative democracy. In that sense the book is as important to the development of democracy as is Magna Carta. As Bagley and Rowley say, the commons' claim to be the sole voter of taxes suited the aspirations of far more English people than a coterie of rebellious barons. The crucial clause is number twenty-three, dealing with the question of 'Aids' (grants of taxation) to the king.

> everything that has to be affirmed, annulled, granted or denied, or otherwise done by Parliament, should be granted by the Commons of Parliament . . . namely the proctors of the clergy, the knights of counties, and the citizens and burgesses, who together represent the whole commons of England. This is not true of the magnates, each one of whom attends Parliament only in his own right as an individual, and not as the representative of anyone else.[5]

The ability to withhold taxes from the king was always the principal weapon in parliament's efforts to curb royal power and the right of parliament to determine taxation was granted at a very early date. The need for parliamentary consent to direct taxation was granted in 1340 and that for indirect taxation (largely customs duties on wool) in 1362. Because the wool trade was a major source of tax revenue in fourteenth-century England, and most wool merchants were represented in the House of Commons, it became a parliamentary convention that only the commons could approve the granting of taxation.

The commons in parliament used their financial power for the first time in 1376, when they refused to allow Edward III any more money for his war with France. 'The Commons said they were tired of these continual demands for money . . . because it was clear that the king would have plenty of money if the kingdom were governed properly but it would never do well while wicked officials carried out the business of government.' [6] The commons elected a knight of the shire, Peter de la Mare, to act on their behalf; de la Mare thus becoming the first Speaker of the House of Commons. Under the leadership of their Speaker the commons impeached the king's ministers and for a time the king was placed under the guidance of a special council.

Parliament had discovered its ability to challenge and punish any members of the government who might not be doing their job properly. Twice, in 1386 and 1388, parliament impeached the advisers of Richard II, executing some of them and placing the king under the control of a council chosen by parliament. In 1399, Henry Duke of Lancaster (Shakespeare's Bolingbroke) seized power as Henry IV, deposing Richard II. But, having taken the throne by force, Henry legitimised his actions by getting the approval of parliament.

> Parliament began on September 30 and, when Henry of Lancaster went in . . . Sir Thomas Percy shouted 'Long Live Henry of Lancaster, king of England' at which all the lords, bishops and commons shouted 'Yes, yes, we want Henry to be king.' A list of all the evil things King Richard had done was read to parliament and when this had been done the Recorder of London read out King Richard's sentence. 'It is ordered by the clergy, lords and the commons of England that John of Bordeaux, also known as Richard of England, be sentenced to imprisonment.[7]

Of course, the parliamentary motion was a sham, lending respectability to a military *coup d'état*: a device used by many twentieth-century dictators. Yet the fact that Henry IV felt such a course of action to be worthwhile showed that he believed parliament could legitimise the actions of a monarch by its consent. Three hundred years before Locke wrote his treatise, England was moving towards the belief that the people had the right to remove a bad ruler and that the people's representatives in parliament should exercise that right in their behalf.

Another pre-echo of Locke's work is found in Scotland. In

1320 fifty-three Scottish lords, assembled at Arbroath Abbey, wrote to the Pope supporting Scottish independence from England and the right of Robert Bruce to be king. The Scots combine two of Locke's ideas:

1 That the duty of a ruler is to defend the liberty of his subjects.
2 That a ruler who fails in this duty can, and should be, removed.

> Yet if he (King Robert) should give up his task, and agree to make us or our kingdom subject to the English, we should drive him out as our enemy and a betrayer of his own rights and ours, and we would make some other man King who could defend us; for, as long as a hundred of us remain alive, never will we be brought under English rule. It is not for glory, riches or rewards that we fight, but for freedom – which no honest man gives up except in death.[8]

Democratic trends in the Middle Ages

Medieval England was not a democratic society, and yet there were elements which accepted the theory of legitimacy through representation. We have described how the principle of representation gained acceptance in parliament. But at a local level that principle operated even more strongly. In the towns and cities every working man who had served his time as an apprentice had to belong to the relevant guild or trade association and the city's corporation or ruling body was made up of leading members of those guilds. Through their guild, therefore, every citizen was represented on the city's ruling body. In the villages, decisions such as the division of land in the large-field system, or the use of common grazing, were made by villagers meeting together and they elected their own leader in the reeve, who represented their interests with the lord of the manor and in the manor court.

Of course, these harbingers of democratic decision-making were more theory than practice. In the cities it was the rich and powerful leaders of the merchant guilds who ran the council rather than ordinary guild-members. And in the villages, the supposedly elected reeve was often a placeman imposed by the lord of the manor. Despite this lack of democratic purity the principle remained and allowed later reformers to claim a democratic tradition in English life that stretched back over the centuries.

Another factor that crept into English political life was an element of egalitarianism. The uprisings of 1381 that later were mistakenly called 'the Peasants' Revolt' were markedly different from similar uprisings in France or elsewhere. Particularly in the risings of Kent and Essex, which led to the occupation of London, there was surprisingly little in the way of motiveless killing and random pillage. Most men in the ranks of the rebels were there in protest at the unfair poll tax of 1380 or at the Statute of Labourers which limited the freedom of serfs. But, beyond these simple grievances, there was a small body of men around leaders such as Walter Tyler and Jack Straw who had a definite political purpose.

History books are written by the victors and it is impossible to know objectively what the losers thought and felt. Since the rebels lost in 1381, history has depicted them as an unthinking mob, with ideas that were confused, destructive or wildly incredible. Yet Tyler's control of his mob of thousands, marching from Canterbury to London in just three days, shows an extraordinary administrative skill and the man must have had a shrewd political brain. We know of demands about such things as the abolition of villein status and serfdom, but equally significant is the demand made by Tyler at his last meeting with the king, claiming that 'all men should be equally free and no legal status should differentiate one man from another, save the King alone'.[9] The rebels had nothing but contempt for parliament, and their cry of 'For the King and the True Commons' meant that parliament should represent the ordinary common people of England, not the middle-rank gentry who actually sat there.

The ideology behind Tyler and his rebels was provided by the renegade priest, John Ball. Again, his words were only written down by his enemies and we cannot be certain as to what he actually did say. But there is a fairly full account of a sermon he preached to the rebels outside London for which he took as his text a simple rhyme then in common use:

When Adam delved and Eve span,
Who was then the gentleman?

From that basic statement of equality Ball went on to develop an argument that has very interesting parallels to many later theories:

> In the beginning all men were created equal but slavery was introduced through the greed of wicked and unjust individuals, against the will of God. If God had intended some men to be serfs and others to be lords, He would have made that clear from the start. Englishmen! Cast off the yoke you have worn too long and win the freedom you want. Take heart and act like the good husbandman in the gospel who gathered the wheat into his barn but tore up and burned the weeds that choked the crop. England's weeds are the oppressive rulers. So tear them up and do away with them – evil lords, unjust judges and lawyers. When they are disposed of all men will enjoy equal freedom, all will have the same nobility, rank and power.[10]

The Revolt of the Commons was put down and arguments for wider and fairer representation of the people in parliament were forgotten for some time. Nevertheless, the growth of parliamentary institutions that would later assist in the development of representative democracy continued. The practice of petitions being presented to the king by parliament for his approval slowly changed into the legal preparation of petitions as bills, which, once having been passed by parliament and approved by the king, became statutes. By the mid-fifteenth century it was established that statutes had necessarily to receive the consent of the commons in order to become law. In theory at least, parliament, and the House of Commons in particular, was becoming the legislature of England.

Representation for the shires was determined by electors, defined in 1429 as 'freeholders of land worth more than two pounds a year'. These Members of Parliament (MPs) were supposed to be knights but more often were just prominent local men or retainers in the households of local magnates. The burgesses in parliament were elected by various means but in fact were usually chosen by a small oligarchy within the borough's governing body. However, since parliamentary business was held to be tedious by the richer and more powerful burgesses, MPs tended to be quite humble citizens and were often paid for their attendance in parliament. The reality of MPs being chosen by richer and more powerful men of influence was a factor that would persist until the Reform Act of 1832. While it may seem undemocratic to us, it must be realised that, in the eyes of their contemporaries, these members of the House of Commons were seen as truly representative, even if they were not elected by universal suffrage.

The development of parliament was delayed in the fifteenth century by the Wars of the Roses; a time when people wanted a strong ruler to give them peace, rather than weaken the monarchy by curbing royal power. The Tudors provided strong rule but they did not call many parliaments and, when they did so, that parliament was under strict royal control. Yet, despite being managed by the monarch, parliament gained in influence. Statute law, approved by parliament, became the normal form of legislation and MPs gained the right of free speech through the granting of parliamentary privilege.

The foundation of the Church of England under Henry VIII and the Dissolution of the Monasteries removed the religious orders from the House of Lords and prevented the Pope from intervening in English sovereignty. The Reformation also deprived churchmen of their role in the administration of government and the sixteenth century saw the growth of a new lay bureaucracy of civil servants and administrators. Executive government powers were moving out of the hands of the nobility and clergy into a new middle class of public servants.

A constitutional monarchy and a Bill of Rights

The seventeenth century saw the culmination of the struggle between king and parliament. The dispute between Charles I and his parliament was like a continuation of the Barons' Wars and, as such, was part of a struggle that had been going on for four hundred years! This phase was more bitter because Charles I had discovered the Divine Right of Kings, while most MPs were Nonconformist in religion, enabling both sides to adopt positions with the fervour of religious conviction. To one side, the parliamentarians were attempting to curtail the king's God-given rights. To the other side, the king was attempting to tax and rule without the consent of his people as expressed through parliament.

On one point the student should be very clear. Because the parliament was fighting to limit what it saw as tyrannical power and because the execution of Charles I resulted in the formation of a republic in England, there is a temptation to believe that parliament was fighting for democracy. But this was not the case. There were radicals and democrats on the parliamentary side such as Gerard Winstanley's 'Diggers' or John Lilburne's 'Levellers', who advocated the re-distribution of land and abolition of the House of Lords, but they were opposed by Cromwell and the parliamentary leadership and suppressed by the army.

The true movement towards democracy comes not from the English Civil Wars but from their aftermath in 1688 when James II was driven out and the throne was offered to William and Mary, in return for the granting of a Bill of Rights. That Bill of Rights, granted in 1689, was primarily concerned with securing the protestant succession but it did encompass the supremacy of a freely elected parliament and thereby accepted a constitutionally limited monarchy. Since 1689 there has not been a year when parliament has not met. In another landmark in the transfer of power, the year 1707 saw the last occasion when a monarch felt able to refuse the Royal Assent to a bill that had passed through parliament.

Another product of the 'Glorious Revolution' of 1688 was the birth of political parties. They were hardly what we understand by the term 'parties', being more factions or interest groups formed by influential families, their friends and hangers-on. The coterie around Lord Shaftesbury, anti-Catholic and believers in civil liberties, who had forced the expulsion of James II, formed themselves into the Country Party; nick-named Whigs by their opponents, after a band of Scottish gypsies. Those who remained loyal to the legitimate Stuart succession formed the Court Party, nick-named Tories, after a gang of Irish bandits. For a century and a half the two parties remained mere associations of interest and influence but they did allow for some organisation at election time in favour of national interests and it did allow for the formation of administrations made up of like-minded individuals with a common programme.

The Bill of Rights left the monarch few powers except those residual rights and privileges embodied in the royal prerogative. The prerogative was lost to the monarch due to the accession of the House of Hanover. George I did not speak English and both he and George II were more interested in the affairs of Hanover than those of Britain. As a result, the reins of government passed increasingly into the hands of the king's ministers and the royal prerogative was exercised by government ministers acting in the name of the king. It was the birth of Cabinet Government under the guidance of a Prime Minister that was the final transfer of power from the monarch to a parliament representing the people.

Reform and suffrage

Parliaments and governments of the eighteenth century were in the hands of an oligarchy, with the unrepresentative House of Lords supreme and the House of Commons elected by patronage and corruption. Representation was largely unchanged from the fourteenth century: each county electing two members, regardless of size. The situation in the boroughs was dubious to say the least, particularly in those boroughs which had declined in population and importance since the Middle Ages. Many towns were known as 'pocket boroughs' because they had a mere handful of electors who were in the pocket of some wealthy patron who bought their votes to put his placemen in parliament. Some boroughs had no electors at all, like the original site of Salisbury, Old Sarum, which retained its borough status after the population moved away and returned two MPs for a field inhabited only by sheep.

By the standards of the time, eighteenth-century Britain was regarded as democratic. Parliament was regarded as representative in that different interests and different geographical areas were represented, while concepts such as representation of the people and proportionality were alien to contemporary thought. Yet elsewhere, in the American and French Revolutions, there were those who promoted the rights and liberties of the people as a whole. A radical movement for reform did begin, in protest at the hardships produced by the Napoleonic Wars and the Industrial Revolution, but the upper classes feared that concessions to the working class would result in the excesses of the French Revolution. Radical movements were ruthlessly put down in violent incidents like the Peterloo Massacre of 1819. Reform when it came was the result of middle-class protest.

The Industrial Revolution created a wealthy, entrepreneurial middle class. Businessmen and mill-owners saw themselves as the source of national prosperity and a force for the modernisation and revitalisation of Britain. Yet these important individuals had no say in government and the sprawling new industrial towns and cities were virtually without representation. The middle classes gained support from Utilitarians such as Bentham and Mill, who called for a more representative parliament based on a fairer and more rational electoral system.

The Great Reform Act of 1832 represents the first major change in parliamentary representation for centuries. The rotten boroughs of the eighteenth century were swept away and parliamentary seats given to the large urban areas, while representation in the shires was made to relate to population size and distribution. The vote was given to owners of property worth £10 a year, granting the suffrage to the wealthier middle classes, but still excluding the working class.

Chartism

The working classes and their radical supporters felt betrayed by the Reform Act. The House of Commons may have expanded but it had been for the benefit of the prosperous middle classes only and there was a feeling, akin to that of Wat Tyler, John Ball and the rebels of 1381, that the House of Commons should represent the true commons. Working-class groups set up clubs for political and social reform; known as Hampden Clubs after the parliamentary leader of the Civil War period. These working men's clubs helped draw up *The People's Charter*, which demanded a voice for the working class in parliament, as well as protesting about unemployment, rising prices and the iniquities of the Poor Law. Although hoping to gain their ends by parliamentary means, the Chartists were not averse to more extreme methods: 'We will have the charter, peaceably if we can, forcibly if we must'.[11] The Charter was presented to parliament as a petition in May 1839 and rejected by them in June.

The Chartist Movement, now increasingly in the hands of those who favoured violence, struggled on for another ten years as a series of strikes and riots firmly repressed by the authorities, who were ready to use the army to put down any protest. Petitions to parliament were presented in 1842 and, most famously in 1848, the 'year of revolutions'. Their petitions rejected on both occasions, the movement, having lost much of its early respectability, slowly faded away; ceasing to exist, even in name, after 1858.

The People's Charter was as concerned with economic and social reform as it was with political issues but it did contain six positive demands for democratic reform.

(1) *Universal male suffrage*: the first extension of suffrage was the Representation of the People Act of 1867 which, under the threat of further unrest, extended the vote to all urban householders. The suffrage was extended to rural constituencies in 1884. The percentage of adult males entitled to vote rose from 20 per cent in 1832, to 33 per cent in 1867 and to 67 per cent in 1884.[12] It was 1918 before the remainder of the working class were enfranchised. What the Chartists did not think to ask for was female suffrage, although this created a protest movement every bit as committed as Chartism. Women over thirty were granted the vote along with rural working class males in 1918. It was 1928 before women over twenty-one were given

the vote, and 1969 before the voting age was reduced to eighteen for both sexes.

(2) *Secret ballot*: making the vote secret was granted in 1872 with the intention of making bribery or intimidation ineffective.

(3) *Payment of MPs*: the independence of MPs from outside influence was not possible while they were open to financial inducements; and lack of money obviously militated against working-class members. It was the growing presence of Labour Party MPs which led to the payment of MPs in 1912 (£400 a year).

(4) *Abolition of property qualifications for MPs*: as with the payment of MPs this reform was supposed to remove the disadvantage felt by would-be members without private sources of income. Instituted in 1710 the property qualification for shire members was £600 and that for borough members, £300. The property qualification in the shires was higher because MPs for the counties were still theoretically 'knights of the shire'. The property qualifications were removed in 1858.

(5) *Constituencies of equal size:* the ideal was for all votes to have equal value, which was not possible while representation was on a pattern fixed in medieval times. Change began with the abolition of the rotten boroughs in the 1832 Reform Act, but continued through a series of Redistribution of Seats Acts. There is now a Boundary Commission which regularly reviews the size of constituencies in order to keep them at an average population of 66,000. However, constituencies in Scotland and Wales are smaller than those in England because the Redistribution of Seats Act of 1944 provided a minimum number of parliamentary seats for those two countries.

(6) *Annual parliaments:* this is the one demand of the Chartists that has not been granted. It was believed in the early nineteenth century that MPs would be more accountable for their actions if they had to present themselves for re-election every year. Even the most diehard reformers, however, acknowledged that no government could construct a proper programme if the entire parliament had to endure a general election every twelve months. The most which parliament would concede was a

reduction in the life of a parliament from seven to five years in the Parliament Act of 1911.

Political parties

The trigger for the growth of political parties was the Reform Act of 1867. The virtual doubling in the size of the electorate meant that better organisation was needed in order to ensure the election of preferred candidates. At the time there were two political parties in existence which had emerged from the relatively informal groupings of Tories and Whigs. In the 1840s Robert Peel had given the name of Conservative Party to the Tories but had immediately split them over the Corn Laws, that half of the party dedicated to reform going off to join the Whigs. Whereupon the Whigs and Peelite Tories combined to form a new party known as the Liberal Party. These two embryonic parties were then developed by Disraeli for the Conservatives and by Gladstone for the Liberals. The personalities of the two men ensured that both parties would have a coherence based on a strong national leader; it also ensured the development in British politics of confrontational bi-partisanship.

Disraeli and Gladstone encouraged strong party organisational structures to encourage the selection and support of suitable candidates among the ever-increasing numbers of eligible electors. Registration societies were set up across the country as forerunners of constituency parties. Their aim was to identify supporters and ensure that as many as possible were registered to vote and turned out to vote in elections. These local parties were controlled by national associations – the National Union of Conservative Associations and the Liberal Federation. Both parties began to hold annual conferences for enthusiastic party members.

The growth of mass political parties had two implications for representative democracy, one positive and one negative.

1 The growth of constituency parties meant that anyone could become involved in the political process, providing a practical form of popular participation.

2 The growth of political parties in parliament meant that governments were formed along party lines, with automatic support for a government formed by the party leader. This reversed the check placed by parliament on the power of the executive and began the process whereby Lord Hailsham could later say that Britain was governed by an 'elected dictatorship'.

The growth of political parties and the foundation of governments on an electoral majority in the House of Commons helped shift the balance of power in parliament from the Lords to the Commons. After the Reform Act, in 1839, the Duke of Wellington was the first to refuse the premiership on the grounds that a prime minister should be a member of the House of Commons. Peers continued to form governments, down to Lord Salisbury who was premier at the turn of the century, but the practice died out in the twentieth century as the volume of important legislation originating in the Commons increased. There was a moment in the 1920s when the Conservatives contemplated making Lord Curzon prime minister, and there were those in 1940 who would have preferred Halifax to Churchill as premier in wartime. By 1963, however, when Lord Home was chosen to succeed Macmillan, it was a condition of his accepting office that he should renounce his peerage and secure a seat in the Commons.

Despite the shift of power to the Commons, the Lords retained their right to veto any legislation passed by the Commons. This was a handicap to the development of democratic government because not only were the Lords MPs through heredity rather than the choice of the people, but they provided a natural Conservative majority and successive Liberal governments had considerable difficulty in passing their legislation. This difficulty became a crisis when the Lords refused to accept Lloyd George's Budget of 1909 with its social welfare provisions. Two elections, in January and December 1910, were fought on the issue and, in 1911, the Parliament Act removed the Lords' ability to reject a money bill and left them only delaying powers over other public bills; that delay being for two years originally but reduced to one year by the Parliament Act of 1949.

Institutions other than parliament

The process of democratisation in the nineteenth century which manifested itself in parliament through the extension of the suffrage, the growth of political parties and a diminution of the power of the Lords, can also be discerned in other political institutions over the same period, notably in local government and the civil service.

Local government had existed from the earliest times, certainly at parish or borough level where councils and their ratepayers were chiefly responsible for the upkeep of roads and oversight of the Poor Law. The rapid expansion of towns, both in area and population as a result of the Industrial Revolution, led to problems which forced local councils into new areas of responsibility and organisation. The threat of disease, especially the great cholera epidemics, led to a need for clean water, sewage disposal and drainage. The crime-ridden dark alleyways of the growing cities required street lighting and policing. Growing unemployment in the towns placed immense strains on a Poor Law that was originally intended to relieve the rural poor.

In towns and cities parish councils were replaced by boards of leading citizens who looked after a range of services – water, sanitation, lighting, police, hospitals, schools, workhouses, etc. After the Reform Act of 1832 this *ad hoc* structure of local authorities was rationalised, particularly by the Poor Law Amendment Act of 1834 and the Municipal Corporations Act of 1835. In 1888, the Local Government Act extended the new organisation to the counties. Throughout the country every citizen had at least one local government authority to look after the needs of that citizen's local area. It was the heyday of municipal pride as can be seen by the impressive Town Halls that dominate the major industrial cities and many individuals found an outlet for their political ambitions in the local arena, as can be seen from the prominence gained by the Chamberlain family in the politics of Birmingham.

Until the mid-nineteenth century, civil servants were employed in a wide variety of government offices and departments, recruited by patronage, influence and even purchase: often seen as suitable employment for those younger sons of the aristocracy who had failed to gain a place in the Church or the Army. In 1853 the government set up an enquiry into the efficiency of the civil service, headed by Sir Stafford Northcote and Sir Charles Trevelyan. The latter was the nephew of Lord Macauley who had recently re-organised the Indian Civil Service (ICS), and it is therefore not surprising that the Northcote–Trevelyan Report, issued in 1854, should model itself on what were seen as the strengths of the ICS. The report called for a unified Home Civil Service, recruited through competition and promoted on merit, providing a professional, neutral and anonymous service that would administer the affairs of government without prejudice or favour.

Summary

This has been a long, perhaps over-long, look at the history of representative democracy in Britain, and England in particular. It might also be said that I have spent a disproportionate amount of time considering the Middle Ages. It is, however, important that we make the point as to the antiquity of Britain's democratic traditions. For those campaigning for a greater say in political affairs for the common people, whether a seventeenth-century parliamentarian, a nineteenth-century Chartist or a twentieth-century trades unionist, the appeal has always been to the ancient rights and liberties of the British people. The purpose of this historical survey has been to show just how ancient those rights and liberties are.

Ideas of justice under the rule of law, of the freedom of the individual from arbitrary tyranny, of fairness and equity, these ideas have been with us since Magna Carta in the thirteenth century, and even then the people were appealing to liberties they believed had existed in an earlier age. What of the govern-mental and parliamentary framework which is able to deliver democratic principles? That too is remarkably long-established: the framework of our present system can be discerned in the book 'How to hold a Parliament' of 1320. Yet, the very antiquity of British political institutions may lead us to question the extent to which Britain is still a satisfactory model of representative democracy.

In a state such as Britain, without a written constitution, there is an inertia against disposing of outmoded institutions and patterns of government tend to be amended rather than reformed. If the history of British democratic institutions seems to prove how old those institutions are, it also shows how little they have changed. A respected political journalist has described the constitution of modern Britain as 'handed down virtually intact from the settlement of 1688, with universal suffrage bolted on'.[13] Therefore, if the structure of the State is little altered since 1688, which was hardly a time of true democracy, then can we trust that structure to deliver a form of democracy such as we would wish to have today?

The aim of this book, therefore, is to examine the political structures and processes of today in relation to the democratic ideal to which we aspire and which, according to all that history, we should have. And we should ask ourselves how far the present structures live up to their historic ideals, or by how much the present situation has moved or regressed from that ideal.

Notes

1 Clause 1, Assize of Clarendon (1166).
2 J. J. Bagley and P. B. Rowley, *A Documentary History of England (1066–1540)*, Penguin, Harmondsworth, 1966
3 Quoted by Bagley and Rowley, *Documentary History*, page 91.
4 From the British Museum Cotton MS. Augustus II, 106, quoted in full by Bagley and Rowley, *Documentary History*, page 53.
5 Quoted by Bagley and Rowley, *Documentary History*, pages 186–7.
6 Froissart, *Chronicles*. The extracts quoted are freely adapted from the translation by G. Brereton in Penguin Classics, 2nd edition, London, 1978.
7 *Ibid.*
8 *The Declaration of Arbroath 1320*. There is a very good facsimile edition, with translation, produced by the HMSO, London.

9 Quoted in Sir Charles Oman, *The Great Revolt of 1381*, Oxford 1906; re-printed by Greenhill Books, London, 1989.

10 Adapted from the account in *Chronicon Angliae*, quoted at length in Oman, *The Great Revolt*, pages 51–2.

11 An interesting survey of the Chartist Movement is included in chapter 6, J. F. C. Harrison, *The Early Victorians 1832–51*, Weidenfeld & Nicolson, London 1971. Revised edition published as paperback by Fontana, London, 1988.

12 Figures are as quoted by John Kingdom, *Government and Politics in Britain*, Polity Press, Cambridge, 1994, page 167.

13 Will Hutton, *The State We're In*, Jonathan Cape, London, 1995, page 4.

II

Economic democracy

3

Checking the accounts

It is inseparably essential to the freedom of a people and the undoubted rights of Englishmen that no taxes be imposed upon them but by their own consent.

Assembly of South Carolina, 1764

'My other piece of advice, Copperfield,' said Mr Micawber, 'you know. Annual income twenty pounds, annual expenditure nineteen nineteen six, result happiness. Annual income twenty pounds, annual expenditure twenty pounds ought and six, result misery.'

Charles Dickens, David Copperfield (chapter 12)

I think it has been made clear in the historical background material that the ability of the House of Commons to control the supply of money to the executive was the key to the growth of democratic accountability. Therefore it should come as no surprise if we regard the economy as the place to start in a survey of present-day representative democracy. At its simplest it can be expressed as – the government takes our money as taxpayers: it is only right that we should ask them to account for how they have spent our money.

During her years in government Margaret Thatcher was fond of comparing herself and the management of the national economy with a prudent housewife balancing the household budget between the conflicting demands of income and expenditure. She was not the first politician to do so. Over a century previously Gladstone reorganised public finance, using good housekeeping practice, into a twelve-month budgetary cycle which included a series of institutions for the parliamentary control of that budgetary process. Under the Gladstonian system the government's management of finance was divided into three functions, all of which would have been familiar to a Victorian head of household:

1 *Government spending*: future expenditure is very carefully planned and the amount of money needed to continue, and possibly increase, governmental provision is carefully estimated.

2 *Government revenue*: careful consideration is given to the ways and means whereby the money to meet those estimates can be raised.

3 *Scrutiny of government finances*: checks are made to ensure that all the money expended is spent correctly, with no waste, keeping costs as low as possible and ensuring as far as possible that expenditure does not exceed income so as, ultimately, to give value for money.

These three functions have established themselves in an annual cycle, the most public manifestation of which is the Budget, in which the Chancellor of the Exchequer surveys the economic situation nationally and internationally, summarises the amounts of money that are needed by the government in the coming year and lays down the ways and means by which he proposes to raise those amounts of money.

The budgetary process

The first part of the budgetary process is provided by the estimates procedure, sometimes known as 'the spending round', by which all the spending departments of the government submit estimates to the Treasury of the amounts they believe they will require in order to continue their function in the coming year. Of the spending departments the largest in terms of expenditure is Social Security, closely followed by the three Departments of

Health, Education and Defence. Many of the larger departments, in particular the Department of the Environment, have many of their functions, including expenditure, carried out by other bodies such as local government. Unusual in the structure are the regional departments: the Offices for Wales, Scotland and Northern Ireland. In those divisions of the United Kingdom it is the regional Office rather than the Whitehall Department that is responsible for services such as education, health, housing and transport. An agreed proportion of public expenditure for the country as a whole is allocated each year to the Scottish, Welsh and Northern Ireland Offices for distribution to the public bodies concerned.

There was once a more leisurely time in parliament when each department's estimates were debated separately, but in the more crowded world of the late twentieth century the estimates are normally voted together except for a few areas where expenditure is delegated to other bodies such as local government. In fact the estimates for any one year are voted on over a period of two and a half years because a certain proportion is advanced before the start of the financial year in 'votes on account' and there is a supplementary 'excess vote' well after the close of the financial year so as to authorise unforeseen expenditure. Since the 1960s the estimates procedure has been guided by, and also known as, the Public Expenditure Survey Committee (PESC), which produces a five year over-view of the estimates as an aid to financial planning.

The central platform of the Budget is the Finance Bill which incorporates the legislation authorising both the expenditure required by the estimates and the forms of taxation or revenue measures proposed by the Chancellor. Until recently the Budget was only one of two financial statements made by the Chancellor during the course of a year: a discussion of the estimates being given in the Autumn Statement in November and the measures to be taken to pay for them being announced as the spring Budget in the following March or April. It was Norman Lamont, in his Budget of March 1993, who announced that, as of November 1993, both statements would be made at the same time, in the autumn. The original division was created by the constitutional convention that, while the House of Commons has the sole right to approve the raising of taxation, the government has the right to determine its spending priorities free from parliamentary interference. However separating the two statements meant that spending ministers in particular failed to recognise the link between revenue and expenditure. Bringing the two statements together was meant to make it clear to government ministers that they could not have low taxation and high public spending at the same time.

Since 1993 the unified Budget has been in November, with the Finance Bill following in January. The bill is debated exhaustively, the committee stage for the main taxation measures being taken on the floor of the House of Commons, in what is known as a Committee of the Whole House, although the more routine matters that make up the bulk of the bill are taken by a normal standing committee. Discussion of the Finance Bill takes longer than any other parliamentary procedure, with the possible exception of the debate on the Queen's Speech, requiring anything up to four months to pass through parliament, even though the House of Lords has no power to amend or delay a Money Bill for more than a month. During that length of time there is therefore ample opportunity for the issues to be debated at length by the House of Commons, although it is very rare for major amendments to be made to a Finance Bill: defeat of the government over VAT on fuel in December 1995 being the first reversal on a major budget measure for eighteen years, and these defeats only happened on either occasion because of the reduced size of the government's majority.

Control and checking of the budgetary process is in the hands of the Public Accounts Committee (PAC), established by Gladstone for the purpose in 1861. This is a select committee of the House of Commons made up of fifteen MPs, their membership proportional to party representation in the House but with a senior Opposition MP as chair. The PAC is possibly the most important and powerful of the select committees; and is certainly the most hard-working, meeting twice a week, for two to three hours each time, throughout each parliamentary session. The PAC is assisted in its work by the National Audit Office (NAO) under the control of the Comptroller and Auditor General (C and AG).

Expenditure

Since 1945, with the establishment of the Welfare State and increased government involvement in the economy, the amount of money spent by government bodies at all levels has increased immensely. Amounting to around 10 per cent of national income at the turn of the century, public expenditure rose rapidly after the Second World War, to reach nearly 50 per cent by the 1990s. The scale of spending has increased so much that parliament itself is no longer responsible for, nor able to control, the full extent of that spending. A proportion of spending has been delegated to local government and other bodies, and only the 80 per cent of spending which is the direct responsibility of government departments – known as *supply expenditure* – is voted on by parliament. And such is the control of the executive over the legislature that even this limited power is seldom exercised. 'Parliament no longer regards itself as bound to limit spending and restrain taxation *per se*; its decisions on fiscal issues, like others, are determined by the political priorities of the party in power.'[1]

During the so-called post-war consensus in British party politics both Conservative and Labour governments adhered to the economic policies of John Maynard Keynes, a Liberal economist whose work in the 1930s was devoted to eliminating the problem of high unemployment. Keynes was an advocate of *demand management*, by which any downturn in the economy would be overcome by government intervention to create demand and thus: 'the long boom of western capitalism saw public expenditure being used for the quite new purpose of managing the national economy'.[2] Sometimes known as 'spending one's way out of recession' the key to demand management was high public expenditure by the government, which meant that, for the boom years of the 1950s and early 1960s, government departments could have almost as much money as they wanted in the annual spending round. In the process the Gladstonian ideal of balancing the books was lost and quite normally the government would spend in excess of projected government revenue, leading to *deficit budgeting*. Under a deficit budget the government will make up the difference between income and expenditure by borrowing from the money markets, building up the Public Sector Borrowing Requirement (PSBR). The growth of the economy was such in those years that governments would counter criticism of deficit budgeting by saying that the deficit could easily be made good by increased productivity and natural economic growth.

This free-for-all approach to expenditure went against the nineteenth-century principles advocated by Gladstone and still pursued by the Treasury. The annual struggle between Treasury and spending departments over the size of estimates proved to be counter-productive and led to short-termism, the same battles were fought year after year with no allowance for long-term planning. After criticism of the Treasury in parliament a committee was set up under Lord Plowden, a former Treasury civil servant, to recommend ways in which public expenditure might be rationally planned. The recommendations of the Plowden Committee resulted in the establishment of the PESC, a body made up of senior departmental officials which had the task of forecasting the trends in economic growth and the need for public expenditure over a period of five years.

During the 1970s the economic climate that had encouraged demand management was collapsing, its collapse precipitated by the oil crisis of 1973. By 1976, when James Callaghan became Prime Minister, the Keynesian approach was no longer viable and the Prime Minister told the Labour Party Conference: 'We cannot now, if we ever could, spend our way out of a recession'.[3] The Callaghan government, with Denis Healey as Chancellor, became the first to apply monetarist rather than Keynesian principles to the budgetary process but this was a mere forerunner to the strict monetarist ideas of the Thatcher administrations first elected in 1979. The guiding principle of Thatcherism was hostility to public spending and the whole estimates procedure was therefore once more reformed, in order to create a much stricter approach that would curtail the prodigality of the spending departments.

The estimates procedure begins with discussions between the Treasury and officials of the various government departments, in which the overall sum of public money likely to be needed by each department is discussed. The result of these meetings is a report from the PESC to the Chief Secretary to the Treasury which he takes to the Cabinet for agreement and which forecasts the overall extent of public expenditure over a projected three-year period. Following that Cabinet meeting, the 'spending round' begins in earnest with a series of what are called *bilaterals*, when individual spending departments meet face-to-face with Treasury ministers in order to put forward their bids for next year's budget. The discussions are confrontational, with each minister fighting hard for his or her corner and the Treasury fighting equally as hard to limit expenditure. The outcome for the spending minister is important since the success of a ministerial career is measured by the minister's effectiveness and, in the eyes of his or her civil servants, a minister's effectiveness lies in his or her ability to extract money from the Treasury. This attitude was satirised in the BBC television programme *Yes, Minister* when the senior civil servant, Sir Humphrey Appleby, defines the role of a government minister as seen by the civil service: 'His duty is to fight in Cabinet for the money *we* need to do *our* job.' The process bears a distinct resemblance to barter in the marketplace, with the original bid from the department set millions of pounds above reasonable expectation and the Treasury's first offer as many millions below what is required; subsequent haggling allows bids and offers to converge in a process described by Kingdom as 'having more in common with a north African *souk* than a rational decision-making process'.[4]

Estimates agreed in the bilaterals are passed to a Cabinet subcommittee chaired by the Chief Secretary to the Treasury, which collates the estimates to be passed to full Cabinet for approval. If any spending minister cannot agree with the Treasury during the bilaterals there is an appeals procedure in the form of a committee known as the *Star Chamber.* This committee was first constituted under the 1974–79 Labour government but it was revitalised by Margaret Thatcher who originally appointed William Whitelaw to oversee disputes over estimates. The Star Chamber consists of a senior Cabinet minister who heads a small group of senior Cabinet colleagues, who are themselves either non-spending ministers or ministers whose estimates had been settled. The membership is not fixed but may change each time the group is convened. The Star Chamber hears the contrary arguments of both the department concerned and the Chief Secretary and then rules on the size of the departmental allocation. Ministers who are still dissatisfied are entitled to take their complaint before the full Cabinet but, with the Cabinet unwilling to undermine the authority of the Star Chamber, they very seldom receive any satisfaction there.

An idea of what went on in Cabinet meetings when cuts in departmental estimates were sought is given by Joel Barnett, Chief Secretary to the Treasury in Callaghan's government between 1976 and 1979: 'On defence I had asked for [cuts of] £50 million, and was helped enormously by Fred Mulley, the Secretary of State. Fred spoke at such great length that the Prime Minister left the Cabinet Room – I assume for the toilet – and was still speaking when he returned. Jim then put pressure on Fred and I got £30 million, rather more than I expected . . . Cabinet democracy works in strange and mysterious ways.'[5]

The scrutiny of expenditure

There is very little public or parliamentary input into the estimates procedure. Many interest groups will lobby the relevant government departments before the spending round begins, so as hopefully to influence departmental bids. This is particularly true of public sector trades unions wanting to know that sufficient funds are made available for pay increases to their members, but it is equally true of other interest groups like the motoring and road haulage groups, attempting to ensure that the Transport Minister will maintain the road-building programme, and so on. There is no evidence as to what, if any, effect lobbying by outsiders has on the government because the whole process 'is somewhat obscure and more or less closed to public scrutiny'.[6] It has been estimated that less than 200 people are privy to discussion of the estimates across the whole range of government departments. Despite this air of secrecy there is intense interest by the press in the estimates procedure, especially in areas like health or education in which the public have an interest in wanting the minister concerned to get as much money as possible. Stories do appear in the newspapers about the size and nature of cuts being demanded by the Treasury or the lengths to which some ministers are willing to go to fight their corner. But there are suggestions that many of these press reports are deliberately leaked as part of the bargaining process: 'It is very likely that the Press is used, through inspired leaks, as one of the battlegrounds on which departments try to improve their chances of success.'[7] A minister fighting a rearguard action against cuts in his or her budget will try to work up public opinion through the press in the hope that the government will release more funds so as to allay hostility from the electorate.

Parliamentary control of expenditure is far less rigorous than might be expected, given the historic importance of money matters to parliamentary control of the executive. Time devoted to expenditure by the Commons has been further reduced by the amalgamation of the Autumn Statement and the Budget which has meant the disappearance of the annual February public expenditure debate. Elements of expenditure that are considered by parliament fall into two categories.

(1) *Information statements* – which include all statements about government policy, including the Financial Statement made by the Chancellor in the Budget. Debates on these matters do not deal with specific sums of money but consider the government's expenditure plans as a whole. As a means of controlling government expenditure, debates on economic policy are not particularly effective, partly because the subject matter is too

complex and specialised in nature for most MPs, and partly because debates on general economic policy are regarded as votes of confidence and it is unlikely that any member of the government party will vote against policy statements. Such debates therefore tend to become unfocused opposition attacks on government policy in general without any detailed examination of specific proposals.

(2) *Authorisation measures* – which amount to voting on supply estimates. There was a time when each department's estimates were voted on and parliamentary control could mean the actual refusal to grant supply. Between 1858 and 1872 estimates were voted down on seventeen occasions but control in that sense has long ceased to exist.[8] To cope with such issues there were traditionally something like twenty-nine days known as 'supply days' set aside each year for discussion of supply estimates. But, as time went by, the convention grew that supply days were granted to the Opposition for debates on subjects chosen by the opposition parties, as against the other days when the government party set the agenda. It may well have been that matters of supply were debated on supply days but it was more often the case that subjects other than finance and the economy were discussed. As of 1983 the system changed and twenty days a year were officially designated 'Opposition Days' for general debates initiated by the opposition parties. Eight days for debates on supply estimates were suggested by the Procedure Committee but ultimately just three days were set aside for this purpose, the actual estimates to be considered being chosen by a Liaison Committee made up of the chairs of certain select committees.

If the system for scrutinising the estimates seems to lack any real teeth, much the same is true of the parliamentary bills which make money available for the continued running of government before the estimates are approved (votes on account) and for the appropriation of money to the equivalent of the government's current bank account (Consolidated Fund bills). Again, there is very little real discussion of substantive matters, with the bills virtually 'going through on the nod'. Parliament's own watchdog is critical of this. The Commons

Procedure Committee said, in a report of 1978: 'It is clear to us that the present financial procedures of the House are inadequate for ensuring control over public expenditure and . . . has long since ceased to exercise detailed control over public expenditure in any but the formal sense of voting the annual estimates and approving the Consolidated Fund and Appropriation Bills.'[9]

The possibility arises for MPs to raise the matter of expenditure in questions in the House of Commons, whether to the Prime Minister or any other minister. The effectiveness of Question Time as such is questionable: it is seen by the public as being largely a form of adversarial point-scoring exercise and ministers have become adept in evading the crucial point of any oral question aimed at them. Written questions can be more searching and more effective in getting at the truth but they form an exchange that takes place outside the public's view and, since a written answer seldom gets much airing beyond the pages of Hansard or the MP's local constituency newspaper, they have very little impact on the deliberative process. A very few MPs, such as Labour's Tam Dalyell, have made an art form out of pursuing a contentious issue through questions in the House, but on the whole they can not be regarded as a serious means of challenging the executive over economic management.

To a certain extent MPs have only themselves to blame for losing the ability to control government expenditure. As long ago as 1977, Ann Robinson of the Study of Parliament Group was saying that the sheer weight of legislation passed by parliament in the late twentieth century means that detailed scrutiny of the financial implications of such legislation is impossible. Furthermore, such legislation will often commit government to long-term – even indefinite – expenditure that cannot be altered later. 'So much of the expenditure is in the form of "relatively uncontrollable" long-term commitments that, even if the House did have the ability to tinker with estimates, such changes as it could make would be marginal.'[10]

It might be expected that parliamentary scrutiny of expenditure might be better carried out by parliamentary committees. The first select committee to oversee public expenditure was set up as long ago as 1807 with the specific aim of making economies in the amounts paid out in salaries and fees to public servants. A direct descendent of this committee was the PAC established by Gladstone in 1861 but this was largely concerned with a *post hoc*, value-for-money survey of sums expended and, as such, will be examined later in this chapter. In 1912 an Estimates Committee was established to consider the annual departmental estimates and, for most of the twentieth century apart from two short periods when it was in abeyance during the World Wars, the Estimates Committee remained alongside the PAC as one of only two major select committees in the House of Commons. In 1971 the Estimates Committee was replaced by the Expenditure Committee which had a wider remit in that it could examine all government spending rather than just the departmental estimates and was involved in the five-year projections of the PESC. The Expenditure Committee was in fact a federal structure made up of six sub-committees, each with its own area of competence; these six being sub-committees for defence and external affairs, trade and industry, education and arts, social services, environment and general.

During the 1970s dissatisfaction was expressed as to the effectiveness of select committees in parliament and a Procedure Select Committee was set up in 1976 to review the situation and to suggest possible reforms. The report of the committee in 1978 advocated a system of interlocking select committees so established that for the most part each committee shadowed the workings of a specific government department. The same report recommended that these departmental select committees 'will concentrate much of their attention on consideration of the Estimates and other expenditure projections'.[11] The recommended pattern of select committees was established by the Conservative Leader of the House, Norman St John-Stevas, in June 1979, taking the six sub-committees of the Expenditure Committee as a model for the departmental structure. The actual number of select committees established varies with time and according to the government in power but the largest number achieved was in the Commons elected in the 1992 general election which saw sixteen departmental committees and thirteen non-departmental committees. An obvious result of the 1979 reforms was the disbanding of the Expenditure Committee and the transfer of its ability to scrutinise estimates to the relevant departmental select committee.

In theory at least the establishment of departmental select committees should have increased the ability of MPs to scrutinise government spending. And certainly there has been some success in forcing some departments to improve their procedures and in making the public more aware of certain aspects of departmental affairs. And yet, compared with the hopes expressed in 1979 that the select committees would enhance the democratic accountability of government, the outcome as far as control of estimated expenditure is concerned has not been particularly noteworthy.

(1) Select committees have proved unwilling to become too involved in financial matters; partly because too much of the economic detail is over-technical for those MPs who are members of the committees. According to Likierman[12] the average amount of available time spent by the select committees in discussing departmental estimates throughout the 1980s has only been around 5 per cent.

(2) Select committees always discuss things after the event. The estimates discussed by the committees have already been formulated, agreed and approved. Therefore the procedures of the committees have no place in the decision-making process, from which they are, in any case, disbarred by the constitutional convention that only the Crown can propose expenditure.

(3) Select committees can report and criticise but they do not necessarily lead to action. The government may announce that it has taken note of a committee's report but it is under no obligation to act on that report. Very few major recommendations made by select committees have been accepted by government. Nor is there any obligation on the part of parliament to debate committee reports.

(4) Select committees are supposedly non-partisan in party political terms and on many issues the committees have shown

themselves to be remarkably free of party bias and have refused
to divide on party lines, enabling them to produce unanimous
reports, whether critical of the government or not. On economic
matters, however, where the government party feels itself to be
particularly vulnerable, there is a tendency for committee
members to revert to party loyalties and fail to present a united
front.

(5) Select committees find that obscure and complicated economic issues do not have as high a profile in the press and broadcast media as other more controversial matters. It is therefore a
matter of priorities in maintaining the standing of a committee
and in the context of public visibility economic matters rate very
low.

The Budget

The Chief Secretary to the Treasury is responsible for the estimates procedure but the general guidance of the economy and
the framing of financial proposals is very much in the hands of
the Chancellor of the Exchequer, although the chancellor will
pay considerable attention to the workings of the PESC under
the Chief Secretary. The overall economic strategy for the
country is evolved by the Chancellor, as leader of the Treasury
team, with the consultative assistance of the Bank of England.
The importance of the economy is such that the Prime Minister
is bound to take a keen interest in the development of economic
policy: traditionally the Prime Minister has the title of First Lord
of the Treasury and ranks in Cabinet as a Treasury minister.
Most prime ministers are very close to their chancellors and a
connecting door between numbers 10 and 11 Downing Street
enables them to meet unofficially at frequent intervals. Just occa-
sionally the Prime Minister of the day disagrees with the
Chancellor and this can disturb the smooth running of financial
affairs. In 1989 the then chancellor, Nigel Lawson, was totally at
odds with Margaret Thatcher, particularly over the European
Exchange Rate Mechanism and the relationship between the
pound and the deutschmark. In an attempt to curb her

Chancellor, Margaret Thatcher announced in October that her former personal economic adviser, Sir Alan Walters, would return from the United States to resume his duties. Lawson immediately presented the prime minister with an 'either-he-goes-or-I-do' ultimatum and, when she refused to dismiss Walters, Lawson resigned very publicly in a gesture that was later seen as the first step to Margaret Thatcher's own departure. As John Smith said for Labour, 'No Chancellor can carry out his arduous duties without full support of the Prime Minister'.[13] And the converse – that no Prime Minister can continue long without the support of their Treasury team – is equally true.

The workings of the Chancellor of the Exchequer and the general financial strategy of the government are scrutinised by the Treasury and Civil Service Select Committee which publishes about ten reports each year dealing with the various financial and economic statements made by Treasury ministers. This committee has been one of the few to make a significant impact in the Commons through publication of critical reports. During the early 1980s the Select Committee flourished under the chairmanship of Edward du Cann, who combined the task with being chairman of the 1922 Committee of Conservative backbenchers. Despite being thought a friend of Margaret Thatcher, du Cann used the Treasury Select Committee to criticise the government's economic policy through: 'a series of critiques, some of them quite damaging, of monetarism in all its aspects. He even permitted a draft report, highly critical of the state of the economy, to be published in the middle of the 1983 election.'[14] These actions infuriated the Prime Minister but, like so many reports of the select committees, they were ignored by the Prime Minister and had no effect on government policy.

The Chancellor of the Exchequer presents each year a Financial Statement on the state of the economy which, since 1993, has been amalgamated with the Autumn Statement on estimated expenditure. This is then followed by the chancellor's financial proposals for raising the necessary revenue. The whole thing is known as the Budget and it is one of the great set-pieces of the parliamentary year, ranking alongside the State Opening of parliament. It is, however, the proposals on tax which receive all the attention. While the purpose of taxation is to raise the money needed for public expenditure, there is always a hidden agenda as well.

(1) Governments of any party have always regularly heralded the approach of an election by a tax-cutting 'give-away' Budget but the Conservative governments after 1979 used the cutting of income tax as part of their general strategy to provide incentives to the so-called 'Enterprise Culture'.

(2) Taxation can be a tool of social policy, as in Lloyd George's so-called 'People's Budget' of 1909: 'Lloyd George as Chancellor needed to raise £16 million in extra revenue to finance the government's planned social programme . . . [and he] determined that the money should come principally from the rich.'[15] Taxation therefore has a function, for the Labour Party in particular, in the redistribution of wealth, by which money is taken from those with an ability to pay in order to provide more equal services for those in the lower income brackets.

(3) Excise duties on tobacco, alcohol, petrol and betting have for some time been known as 'taxes on sin' and the raising of these duties can always be disguised as action against anti-social behaviour, whether it is discouraging cigarette smoking or providing the incentive for a move from leaded to unleaded petrol: 'such taxes on "vice" could even be regarded as slightly morally uplifting'.[16]

By convention, Budget proposals are voted automatically because many of the measures, such as rises in excise duty, have to come into force immediately in order to prevent panic buying and evasion through stock-piling. However, the measures are then debated item by item during the Finance Bill, a process that stretches over many months. It was one of the criticisms of the Procedure Committee report of 1978 that the Commons almost never seeks to challenge a government's financial proposals. Since financial measures can be regarded as an issue of confidence in the government, the measures are heavily whipped and, as long as the government retains a majority, represent the extent to which parliament has become a rubber stamp for the decisions of the executive. For MPs to vote decisively against a Budget measure there are certain pre-conditions that have to be in place:

- The government should be a minority government or have a very small majority.
- There should be a vocal group of dissident MPs on the government benches who are ready to rebel against instructions of government whips.
- The proposed measures should be seen as potentially very unpopular with the electorate.

In 1993, in Norman Lamont's last Budget, it was proposed to raise VAT for the first time on fuel in the form of gas and electricity, services that had been zero-rated until then. The proposal was that a rate of 8 per cent would be imposed in November 1993, with a second rise to 17.5 per cent in November 1994. The proposed tax was very unpopular because it was seen as a regressive tax imposed on a necessity. The unpopularity was compounded by the fact that the very people who could least afford the new tax – the old and infirm – were the very same as those who most needed the heat and light provided by gas and electricity. The first rise to 8 per cent went through the Commons despite vigorous campaigning by the Opposition. But, a year later, the situation had changed. The government had lost a series of by-elections in what had previously been safe Conservative seats in the south of England – Newbury, Christchurch and Eastleigh – all seats with an ageing population and a high proportion of pensioners in the population and in all of which the issue of VAT on fuel therefore played a major part. Because of these and other by-elections the government's overall majority had been reduced to thirteen from the twenty-one it had been at the time of the 1992 general election. This was compounded by the presence of nine Conservative MPs who rebelled over the issue of Europe and had had the party whip withdrawn, not to mention a disinclination of Ulster Unionist MPs to support the government in the aftermath of the Downing Street Declaration. When the second part of the VAT rise was introduced in the Budget of November 1994 it was rejected by an alliance of Opposition and rebel government MPs.

Such a defeat on a Budget measure is rare for a government party and was unheard of during the 1979–93 period, despite the unpopularity of many Thatcherite economic measures. The last such serious defeats had taken place during the Labour government of 1974–79, the most serious of these being the Rooker–Wise Amendment passed in June 1977 by the Labour MPs Jeff Rooker and Audrey Wise to enforce the automatic indexing of personal tax allowances. This amendment to the Budget was extremely damaging to the Labour government, costing them £40 million in that financial year, when they were in the midst of an economic crisis, Chancellor Denis Healey having had to call in the International Monetary fund (IMF) to bail out the UK only a short time before. But the conditions for a backbench rebellion on the Budget were present in 1977, as they were in 1994. The Callaghan government was slipping into a minority position and would shortly rely on the Liberals to sustain them in the Lib-Lab pact, while many on the left wing of the Labour Party were ready to rebel against their own government which had had to abandon socialist principles in order to introduce monetarist measures at the behest of the IMF.

The accounting procedure

As has been seen, there is very little parliamentary check on the expenditure or budgetary procedures of the executive, unless a majority is prepared to precipitate a general election by defeating the government on an issue of confidence. And yet this is not necessarily important, even in a democratic sense, since very few MPs, let alone the public they represent, have the economic expertise to handle detailed control over the management of the economy. As one commentator says: 'In Britain it is ministers who have unambiguously to shoulder responsibility (insofar as any politicians do) for fiscal policy and economic failure. Parliamentary interference would inevitably result in the blurring, if not the destruction, of any clear locus of responsibility for economic management.'[17] Indeed Adonis is not alone in comparing favourably the situation in Britain with that in the

United States where it seems that there is a crisis every year because of the refusal by Congress to approve the Budget submitted by the President. Although done in the name of democracy this example of a representative legislature challenging the executive is not particularly democratic, but rather serves the electoral interests of both sides. Congress can avoid the responsibility or blame for passing unpopular taxation measures, while the President can blame Congress for any failure in the execution of economic policy.

If concern is largely about democratic control of the economy that concern need not focus on either expenditure nor revenue but rather on the nature of checks into the effectiveness of the government in raising and spending public funds. The important area therefore is the accountancy procedure, checking on the need and effectiveness of revenue-raising measures and on whether the electorate has received value-for-money from government expenditure. The principal vehicle for this remains the PAC, the oldest surviving select committee, established by Gladstone in 1861, and still probably the most important as well as the most effective. The PAC's remit covers two categories:

1 The PAC scrutinises the accounts of government departments and agencies to ensure that money voted by parliament was indeed spent according to its intended purpose.

2 The PAC examines the effectiveness of public expenditure in achieving 'value-for-money' (vfm).

The PAC is made up of fifteen MPs who are chosen in proportion to the representation of the various parties in the Commons, but with a chair who by convention is always drawn from the Opposition, and is usually someone who had been a Treasury minister when in government. The PAC is assisted in its work by an officer of the Commons whose office can be traced back to at least the year 1314, although the current involvement of the officer was decided by the Gladstone reforms in 1866: this is the C and AG. The C and AG has a dual function in that he is both the officer who sees to the transfer of funds to the departments from the Consolidated Fund for the purpose of carrying out agreed expenditure, and in addition is the person responsible for auditing the accounts of government departments and agencies. This latter work was originally carried out by the Exchequer and Audit Department on behalf of the C and AG but, as of 1983, the National Audit Act reorganised the C and AG's department to form the NAO, with ultimate responsibility being taken by a nine-member Public Accounts Commission, which should not be confused with the PAC. These structures are intended to ensure that the C and AG and NAO are totally independent of government, being servants of the Commons and not the Crown. The National Audit Act of 1983 also widened the remit of the NAO to take in more than the mere check of government department spending that had been the task of the Exchequer and Audit Department and the NAO has responsibility for all public spending plus financial oversight of bodies such as the National Health Service and even non-governmental state bodies such as the Commissioners of the Church of England.

There are about 900 staff in the NAO, all graduates and chartered accountants. They are not civil servants, their salaries being paid directly out of the Consolidated Fund and therefore not subject to regulation by either government or parliament. The C and AG is appointed by the Queen on the joint recommendation of the Prime Minister and chair of the PAC and can only be removed from office by a joint motion of both Houses of Parliament. Both C and AG and NAO are truly independent and pride themselves on their freedom from undue influence by any vested interest. The NAO has to conduct around 500 audits of public bodies each year, as well as about 40 vfm reviews. All NAO reports go to parliament by way of the PAC and are published to ensure that interested members of the public have access to information on the financial probity of the government. It is a freedom of information only tempered by the inability of many people to understand the technical details of departmental accountancy.

The PAC meets twice a week throughout each parliamentary session. They have the right to look into any of the accounts submitted by the C and AG from the NAO and, if the NAO has found anything worth further examination, the PAC will summon the accounting officer of the relevant department to appear before them, where he or she is exhaustively questioned about any faults or discrepancies. Even more important are the vfm reports which may well turn up examples of malpractice or inefficient administration worthy of a special enquiry conducted by the PAC. It was a PAC enquiry that unearthed the massive waste of public funds when the De Lorean car plant was set up in Northern Ireland, and another such report revealed the cynical way in which the finances of Rover Cars and the Royal Ordnance were underpinned so as to make the organisations suitable for privatisation, only for British Aerospace to make a profit of £650 million from asset-stripping the privatised concerns.[18] In more recent years the PAC has increasingly concerned itself with the accountability of the various quangos and agencies set up by the government, as will be seen later in this book.

In many ways the PAC is the most efficient of the select committees in acting as a watchdog over the economic activity of government:

- The reports published by the PAC can gain a lot of coverage in the press, particularly if there is the hint of a potential financial scandal. The government will do a great deal to avoid the adverse publicity that would follow if they ignored any concerns expressed by the PAC.
- Compared to other select committees, the PAC can better represent itself as non-party and disinterested because, unlike those others, the PAC is not concerned with policy but with administrative practice and the implementation of policy.
- The PAC meets with little hostility from the influential Treasury ministers because the PAC shares with the Treasury a somewhat parsimonious approach to public spending based on 'economy, efficiency and effectiveness'.

Summary – the effectiveness of parliamentary scrutiny

The National Audit Act of 1983, with its reform of the duties and powers of the PAC, C and AG and the NAO, has considerably strengthened the technical ability of parliament to scrutinise the financial aspects of government, but there are still many weaknesses.

(1) Economic, financial and fiscal information is not generally available, except for that information released by the Treasury. Parliament is therefore dependent for information on the very body it is supposed to be scrutinising.

(2) Despite the efficiency of the PAC it still does not have one sub-committee to take on some part of the burden of work. Public expenditure has increased many times over since the Gladstonian reforms of the 1860s but the structures set up by Gladstone in those reforms have hardly altered, and certainly have not increased since then. The PAC simply does not have the time to cover the whole extent of public expenditure and therefore has to be selective in just what is examined.

(3) The departmental select committees which should be examining the spending and efficiency of their departments find that there is very little interest or political capital in the routine examination of expenditure. To use modern parlance, there are not many 'sound-bites' available to the MP concentrating on economic accountability.

(4) Accountability is becoming even harder to achieve as reform of the civil service through the 'Next Steps' initiative hives off departmental activities and responsibilities into a proliferation of semi-autonomous government agencies.

Notes

1 Andrew Adonis, *Parliament Today* (2nd edition), Manchester University Press, Manchester, 1993, page 179.
2 John Kingdom, *Government and Politics in Britain*, Polity Press, Cambridge, 1991, page 392.
3 Quoted by Kingdom, *Government and Politics*, page 394.
4 Kingdom, *Government and Politics*, page 387.
5 Joel Barnett, *Inside the Treasury*, André Deutsch, London 1982. This anecdote and other extracts by Joel Barnett, together with extracts from another book by a former Chief Secretary, Jock Bruce-Gardyne, *Ministers and Mandarins*, Sidgwick & Jackson, London,

1986, are to be found in Andrew Likierman, *Public Expenditure*, Penguin, Harmondsworth, London, 1988, pages 44–7.

6 M. Burch and B. Wood, *Public Policy in Britain*, Martin Robertson, 1983, page 138.

7 Likierman, *Public Expenditure*, page 44.

8 *Ibid.*, page 159.

9 Quoted in Adonis, *Parliament Today*, page186.

10 Ann Robinson, 'The House of Commons and public expenditure', in S. A. Walkland and M. Ryle (eds), *The Commons in the Seventies*, Fontana, London, 1977, page 131.

11 Quoted in Likierman, *Public Expenditure*, page 160.

12 *Ibid.*

13 Paul Nettleton, the *Guardian*, 1 November 1989.

14 Hugo Young, *One of Us*, Macmillan, London, 1989, page 244.

15 Kingdom, *Government and Politics*, page 201.

16 David Childs, *Britain since 1945, A Political History* (3rd edition), Routledge, London, 1992, page 246.

17 Adonis, *Parliament Today*, page 187.

18 Geoffrey Lee, *Privatisation*, in Bill Jones (ed.), *Political Issues in Britain Today* (3rd edition), Manchester University Press, Manchester, 1989, page 157.

4

Regulation of industry and finance

Capital allocation lies at the heart of the free enterprise economy, and both the investing institutions and the banks must expect their performance in that role to be the subject of external scrutiny.

Stephen Dorrell, as financial secretary to the Treasury in 1993

We still go to our bank managers for loans and advice, comfort and succour, but to whom do bank managers go when they need a bit of comfort and succour? To head office? Oh, come on. Going to a bank's head office for tenderness is rather like going to the Devil for moral guidance.

The Times columnist, Miles Kington

If, as has been shown in the previous chapter, there is very little control over economic policy in the parliamentary context, this is even more the case as far as extra-parliamentary institutions are concerned. There are three institutions, or bodies, which can be said to have considerable influence within the economic sector but which, on examination, prove to be largely unaccountable. They are:

1 The Treasury, which is theoretically accountable to the public through government ministers, but which all too often acts as though it is the superior body to which government ministers are themselves accountable. As Will Hutton says of the Treasury, 'the channels of accountability have become constitutional fictions'.[1]

2 The Bank of England, which is supposedly answerable to parliament through the Chancellor but which, in fact, primarily identifies with and represents the financial institutions of the City of London.
3 The supposedly regulated boards of the privatised utilities, which in theory represent the concept of a share-owning democracy, but which emphasise the undemocratic division between control and ownership in industrial and financial organisations.

The Treasury

The Treasury is a small but very influential part of the civil service. Indeed, alongside the Cabinet Office, the Treasury can be said to run the civil service. Certainly, the most able and most influential of civil servants tend to gravitate towards employment within the Treasury and, in the promotion stakes, the senior positions in all government departments tend to be filled by civil servants who have spent some of their formative years there.

Basically, the Treasury can be said to have three broad functions:

1 It is the principal source of advice on economic policy for the Chancellor of the Exchequer and all government ministers, including the Prime Minister.
2 It is the institution responsible for the control of public spending.
3 In conjunction with the Bank of England, the Treasury controls the financial markets through mechanisms such as the level of interest rates or the exchange rate for foreign currencies.

Critics of the Treasury claim that, where it should be leading the development of economic policy, it serves in fact only to stifle the initiatives of other government departments. The small, enclosed and essentially elitist world of the Treasury engenders the growth of what is known as 'the Treasury view', an approach to policy initiatives that is conservative, highly orthodox and primarily concerned with preventing the spending of public money. Hutton calls the Treasury, 'the embodiment of the book-keeping nightwatchman view of the state'.[2] Civil servants expressing the 'Treasury view' manage to imbue the department's attitude with the rather sanctimonious air of holding the moral high ground, as exemplified by the anonymous Treasury official who is quoted as saying, 'Parliament is incapable of exercising its financial responsibilities. We must do it for them.' It is in this context that we can see the Treasury's view of democratic accountability as being akin to the children's nurse who tells her charges: 'Nanny knows best what is good for you.' Roy Jenkins, as a former Chancellor, said that the Treasury was 'open and democratic only in the sense that Whig society in 1780 was so'.[3]

Public expectations of government tend to focus on the spending of money. Politicians are elected on the basis of their party manifesto at election time and can be said to have been mandated by the electorate to spend public money in fulfilling their promises. All too often the government is told by the Treasury that the money needed to carry out their promises is not there. In their memoirs, Labour politicians such as Richard Crossman, Barbara Castle and Tony Benn repeatedly relate how the spending programmes of Labour governments were thwarted by the advice of senior civil servants in general, and Treasury officials in particular. To the extent that the Treasury blocks expenditure that the electorate has been shown to want, the Treasury can be said to be opposed to the will of the people, and is thereby incompatible with representative democracy. The constitutional theory is that government departments are accountable to the electorate through ministerial responsibility: but how far can a minister be said to be responsible when, as the testimony of the Labour ministers mentioned above shows, ministerial wishes can be set aside by the contrary advice of officials?

Another criticism levelled at the Treasury is that it is far too much in thrall to the City of London. Social and welfare issues, and even expenditure on manufacturing industry, are all subordinated to the monetarist and deflationary tenets held by the

Treasury in support of the money markets. The outcome of this attitude is an almost obsessional concentration by the Treasury on the PSBR. As economists such as Will Hutton have argued,[4] this has led to an over-centralisation of government through too wide a definition of what is meant by 'public sector'. Everything from buying paper clips for a school office to building a battleship is regarded as public expenditure and the borrowing of money for that expenditure is strictly controlled by the Treasury, in the desire to keep the PSBR under control.

This can have unfortunate effects. Institutions such as the Post Office, which are regarded as being within the public sector, are encouraged by the government to be commercially minded and to be directly competitive with privately owned enterprises. The Post Office, however, cannot invest in developing its own services in the same way as a private firm might invest because, where the private firm would look to the banks or financial institutions for a commercially negotiated loan to pay for that investment, the Post Office is not allowed to borrow money without stringent conditions imposed by the Treasury. In effect the Treasury blocks access to the money markets for enterprises within the public sector.

October 1994 saw the publication of the 'Fundamental Review of the Treasury' which sought to extend the 'Next Steps' review of the civil service to Treasury affairs. Proposals in the review included the shedding of 30 per cent of senior positions, from assistant secretary level up, with an obvious knock-on effect for junior grades. The Treasury would also give up the detailed scrutiny of other government departments, the control of civil service pay, and would cut back the Treasury's involvement in economic forecasting. It was claimed that the intention was to adopt a more strategic and flexible view of public spending, with the ultimate aim of reducing government misuse of the Treasury as a tool of government economic policy.[5]

According to Will Hutton, the reorganisation of the Treasury is part of a process by which the administration of government is increasingly handed over from departments, which are accountable to the electorate through their ministers, to execu-

tive agencies and semi-autonomous bodies, which are accountable only to themselves on operational issues.[6] The result of
reform in the Treasury would be to make an already remote
government department even less democratically accountable.
On behalf of the Opposition, Gordon Brown, the Shadow
Chancellor, believed that a major institutional change was
required in the ethos of the Treasury. According to Brown, the
Treasury was too narrow in its thinking, with its concentration
on controlling inflation and public spending, resulting in a very
conservative and reactionary economic policy. In a major speech
laying down the policy guidelines for the forthcoming election,
Brown stated that Labour would like to see the Treasury become
more involved with the issues of employment, investment and
growth, turning the Treasury from being a simple finance ministry into an 'engine for growth'.[7]

The Bank of England

The Bank of England is a close partner of the Treasury in the
management and manipulation of the economy. It is Britain's
central bank and essentially its task is 'to act as the government's
banker and the instrument of its financial policies, raising
money day by day so that the government can pay its bills and
also managing the state's foreign exchange reserves and its currency policy . . . the Bank has become a high profile adviser on
interest-rate strategy'.[8] Unlike Germany's Bundesbank, the
Bank of England is not independent but was one of the first
institutions to be nationalised by the 1945 Labour government,
coming under government control in 1946. Yet the Bank is
famously free from government restraints, claiming that the
ethics of financial security and probity demand a confidentiality
that borders on total secrecy, 'keeping out any prying eyes from
Parliament, the media, and even the government'.[9]

   The Bank is staffed by its own officials who are not civil servants but are recruited directly and paid rather more than most
public servants. The duties and responsibilities of these officials
and the workings of the Bank are administered by the Court, a

body made up of eighteen directors. Of these eighteen, six are themselves Bank officials, including the men holding the top two jobs, the Governor and Deputy-Governor. The Governorship of the Bank of England is possibly the most important position in the gift of the Prime Minister. Although supposedly non-political, the Governor is a major world figure, not only in international finance but also in international politics, able to speak on equal terms to the heads of foreign governments and representing Britain at international economic conferences such as the regular meetings of the G7 countries.

Since the last war, the Governor, who is nominated by the Prime Minister, has been recruited to the position from either a major merchant or clearing bank. During the 1980s, Margaret Thatcher was determined to appoint a Governor who would suit her own particular version of financial rectitude and, in a highly controversial move, nominated a former head of the National Westminster Bank, Robin Leigh-Pemberton. This was such a blatantly political appointment that it created a storm in the cosy Treasury–Bank world and left Margaret Thatcher's successor, John Major, determined to play safe when the time came to appoint a successor to Leigh-Pemberton. In a break with tradition John Major made an internal appointment, nominating Eddie George, a man who had made his career as an official of the Bank.

Of the other twelve directors of the Bank's Court, six are representatives of the City's financial institutions and six supposedly represent different interest groups. The latter are almost always representatives of industry and are, in practice, usually prominent industrialists. At one time it was considered obligatory for one of the six to be a trade unionist but it was always a token position and, when the union position became vacant in 1994, the government refused to nominate a replacement union representative. Of the eighteen directors a majority are linked to the interests of the City, financial institutions and money markets and this bias is reflected in the location of the Bank of England on Threadneedle Street in the heart of the City of London. It is widely accepted that the Bank of England will always side with the banking sector of the economy at the expense of industrial capital: the thrust of Bank policy is always towards high interest rates, bad news for those willing to invest in industrial expansion.

In one important aspect of public accountability the Bank of England has been seen to fail quite spectacularly in recent years and this is in the supervision and regulation of the banking industry. In 1991 the investment bank BCCI collapsed, ruining many investors, including public bodies like the Western Isles Council in Scotland: the creditors of BCCI being left with the possibility of regaining little more than thirty pence in the pound. A judicial enquiry into the BCCI collapse described the role of the Bank of England as 'a tragedy of errors, misunderstandings and failures of communication'.[10] Yet, despite the widespread criticism which should have led to reform, things were little better when the old-established merchant bank, Barings, collapsed in early 1995 as a result of highly speculative dealing in the Asian markets on the part of one of Barings' investment managers. A newspaper editorial said at the time that, 'whatever else Barings has done, it has raised profound questions as to the regulatory efficiency of the Bank of England in supervising the banks. How could a single dealer have got away for so long risking all a bank's capital . . . and how could the Bank of England have allowed it to breach so many rules?'[11]

In the report on the Barings' collapse, published in July 1995, it was revealed that the Bank of England had turned a blind eye to Barings' over-exposure to risk. There was supposed to be a requirement that Barings would not exceed the placing of more than 25 per cent of their capital in risk investment but, because of 'old boy network' links between Bank of England personnel and senior directors from Barings, that requirement was relaxed until Barings had committed 73 per cent of their capital in the Far Eastern markets that ultimately collapsed. Critics in the Labour Party and elsewhere were somewhat scathing about the effectiveness and accountability of a financial regulator which permitted 'the illicit transfer of £827 millions to a rogue trader'. In the wake of the report the Chancellor of the Exchequer,

Kenneth Clarke, leapt to the defence of the Bank of England and praised it as being one of the best regulatory systems in the world. And yet, as the same newspaper pointed out, 'Following Johnson Matthey and BCCI, this [Barings] is the third major systemic banking failure that the Bank has been involved in'.[12]

The question was asked as to whom the Bank of England was responsible for this seeming dereliction of duty? The accountability problem with supervising the banking system is that the body responsible for regulating that system is the Banking Supervision Board; which is in turn, of course, dominated in its membership and functioning by the Bank of England. The question, as it so often is, is how well can the regulators function when the ones who must be investigated and censured by them are themselves? Equally important for the Bank is the question as to how the Bank can possibly remain as the City's watchdog when the real ambition of the Bank of England is to become the source of monetary policy for the economy, while taking on the role of an independent central bank. The desire of the Bank of England to boost its regulatory function by being seen as the properly accountable regulator of the financial market was continually thwarted in the early 1990s by crises in the financial world which threw doubt on to the extent of the Bank's grasp of events in the City. These crises not only involved the bank collapses detailed above but also the continuing troubles of the Lloyds insurance syndicates and the virtual collapse of credibility in the personal pension scheme market.

Failures by the Bank of England in regulating the financial markets have put into serious doubt the efficacy of the Bank if it were to realise its ambition to become a central bank independent of government control, on the same lines as the German Bundesbank. And yet, it is a development advocated by so many politicians, economists and financiers that it has become regarded as an inevitable and desirable progression. The essence of independence would be that the Bank of England would be given sole discretion on monetary policy: which in effect would mean that the Bank, and the Bank alone, would have the power to set interest rates without reference to the government. The proposal was strongly advocated by Nigel Lawson in 1988 while he was Chancellor of the Exchequer but was ruled out by Margaret Thatcher for fear that such a move would be seen as an admission of failure on the part of the government economic team.

A powerful lobby of financial and City interests has been advocating the move towards an independent bank for some time and pointing out that, if Britain were to agree to join a single European currency, the independence of the Bank of England would then have to be granted automatically as a prerequisite of membership. There are, nevertheless, equally powerful City voices which are wary about granting the Bank too much independence and who particularly feel that control of interest rates cannot be divorced from the remainder of government economic policy: 'Can one really place a *cordon sanitaire* around monetary policy and divorce it from the rest of economic policy? Does not monetary policy itself have political and social dimensions that cannot simply be left to technicians? Is it not ultimately a negation of democracy, whatever the inbuilt safeguards for accountability, to try to do so?'[13]

During 1993 the Chancellor, Kenneth Clarke, in cooperation with the new Governor of the Bank of England, Eddie George, introduced measures to increase the transparency of Bank affairs and thereby introduce a degree of accountability for the formulation of economic policy. These measures centred on the minutes of the monthly meeting between governor and chancellor being published for the first time, allowing the general public to see where the responsibility lay for crucial decisions on such matters as interest rates. Unfortunately for the credibility of the Bank of England the result was a very public exposure of flaws in the Bank's financial judgement.

During the summer of 1995 the minutes of these monthly meetings showed repeatedly that the Governor wished to raise interest rates to combat a possible rise in inflation and constantly urged this policy on the Chancellor. On 5 May Eddie George said that, 'without an interest rate rise, the authorities could be faced very quickly with a loss of credibility'; on 7 June he repeated his warning, saying, 'Interest rates need to be raised sooner rather than later'. On each occasion the Governor's requests were denied by the Chancellor who believed that inflation could be restrained without any change in interest rates. By the autumn the Chancellor was justified in the stand he had taken by a downturn in the economy which suggested that, if interest rates had been raised, the economy could have been in trouble as a potential recession threatened. On 18 September, Eddie George admitted that he had been wrong and that the economy had survived inflationary pressures without departing from a low interest rate policy. Opponents of an independent central bank cited this as evidence that a Bank of England free of political control and free to ignore the wishes of the Chancellor would have chosen to increase interest rates in a move that would eventually have proved damaging, an implication which obviously undermined the case for Bank independence.

Moves have been made towards granting some independence to the Bank of England. In December 1993 the Commons Treasury and Civil Service Select Committee came down in favour of more freedom for the Bank, albeit not quite as much as is enjoyed by the Bundesbank. In a report supported by members from all parties, with Labour's Diane Abbott the only dissenting voice, the committee recommended that the Bank of England should have control over monetary policy in general, and interest rates in particular. But the governor would be required to report to the committee at regular intervals and there would therefore be some measure of parliamentary control. In particular, the committee felt that the government should retain the right to over-ride the Bank's decisions on inflation targets if such targets were seen as unrealistic in the light of general government policy.

In the early summer of 1995, with doubts about the independence of the Bank having been raised by the dispute between Clarke and George, the Labour Shadow Chancellor, Gordon Brown, attempted to clarify the Labour Party's stance. This was an attempt by Labour to follow the guidance of the Treasury Committee by granting some measure of autonomy to the Bank of England while maintaining some form of democratic control through parliament. During an important speech in the City,[14] Brown made five important points:

1 The Bank should have an advisory monetary policy committee, with a membership made up of the Governor, Deputy-
   Governor and six directors.
2 This committee should be answerable to the Treasury select
   committee in parliament.
3 There should be wider representation for industry and the
   regions on the Bank's Current Court.
4 Any Bank report on monetary policy should be vetted by
   independent economic experts.
5 Meetings between the Governor and Chancellor should be
   programmed for a year in advance.

The response of Eddie George to these proposals was largely to welcome them. The position of the Bank of England in his view was that the Bank probably had as much independence at the moment as was necessary and anything which helped the demo-cratic process through greater transparency could only be welcome. 'Even if we [the Bank of England] actually determined interest rate moves', he told a Spanish newspaper, 'it would still be healthy if that were done in a very transparent and open way.'[15]

Control and Ownership

When the Thatcher government began the process of privatisa-tion one of the main elements in the political agenda was the intention of simplifying requirements for the purchase and sale of shares, removing many of the costs involved and breaking the cartel-like grip of a small circle of stockbrokers. By removing the mystique surrounding the process of share ownership, the idea was to extend the proportion of society involved in the buying and selling of shares and thereby involving an ever-larger number of people in the concept of capitalism. The sale of council houses in the early 1980s was said to have created a property-owning democracy and the selling-off of nationalised utilities was intended to create a matching share-owning democracy. In the early privatisations such as British Telecom the sale and issue of shares were specifically engineered to favour the small investor. When British Gas was privatised a deliberately 'down-market' approach through the 'Tell Sid' advertising campaign stressed the fact that the ownership of shares was now open to anyone, of any social class, and that millions of people now owned shares who would not have dreamed of the possibility only a few years previously.

Thatcherite supporters of privatisation laid great stress on this populist vision of the process and considerable emphasis was given to popular capitalism being a more realistic alternative to socialist public ownership for the involvement of the people in the democratic ownership of industry. Many of the public accepted the rhetoric and really did believe that the ownership of large sections of industry had been wrested from bureaucratic control and placed in the hands of the people. In May 1995, the failure of an attempted small shareholders' revolt, at a General Meeting of British Gas shareholders, led to the realisation that spreading the ownership of shares had very little to do with democracy and that in industry there is a considerable difference between ownership and control.

The test case for shareholder democracy came at the Annual General Meeting of British Gas, the privatised utility. At the end of 1994 there had been a public outcry at what was seen as an excessive pay rise awarded to the chief executive of British Gas, Cedric Brown. In what was claimed as a necessary move to bring the chief executive's pay into line with what 'market forces' dictate for other large enterprises, Brown's salary was increased by 75 per cent (from £270,000 to £475,000). This might have been justified by the improved performance of British Gas over recent years if there had not been signs that British Gas was slowing down economically. As if to rub salt in the wound, the same week that saw Cedric Brown's pay rise by 75 per cent saw a reduction of as much as 15 per cent in the pay of 2,600 gas showroom workers, who also had to accept reductions in holidays and overtime entitlement.[16] Within a few weeks resentment at British Gas grew even further when it was revealed that Mr Brown was eligible for a performance bonus that could be worth 125 per cent of his salary. There was also the question of Richard Giordano, the non-executive chairman, who was paid £450,000 a year for his part-time position, partly paid in dollars and index-linked to salary increases in the United States.

On 31 May 1995 the shareholders of British Gas forced the issue at the annual general meeting of the company in the course of which a lobbyist group called Pension Investment Research Consultants (PIRC), aided by other groups of small shareholders, laid down a resolution that would have rescinded decisions on the payment of senior British Gas directors. seven thousand small shareholders attended the meeting in London and, in the course of a stormy debate, repeated speeches were made denouncing Messrs Brown and Giordano: not one voice being raised in their support. In the ballot at the end of the meeting, which Giordano made an issue of confidence, the shareholders' resolution was defeated by four votes to one. The 80 per cent who supported the Brown–Giordano team was made up almost entirely of the votes of corporate shareholders such as insurance companies or pension funds. This emphasised the point that shareholder democracy has little relevance in institutions where the majority of shares are held by corporate bodies who will always vote for a successful board without any consideration of other issues.[17]

PIRC, who spearheaded the challenge to the board of British Gas, are very concerned with the growing influence of institutional funds in the stock market and the implications this has had for shareholder democracy. In an article of October 1994 a director of PIRC outlined the revolution in share ownership represented by the growth of pension fund investment.[18] Over the past twenty years the amount of money invested by various pension funds and insurance schemes has increased more than tenfold to represent two thirds of the shares in British companies. In the mid-1990s the pension fund-holders have £500 billion invested through the City, with insurance companies having another £200 billion of investments. These investments represent eleven million contributors to pension schemes. Many of these are contributors to vocational pension schemes run by their employers but five million of them are the holders of personal pension plans. In addition there are something like thirty-five million people paying insurance premiums, including endowment mortgages.

These figures seem to bear out the contention that the ownership of industry is in the hands of the people but it is important to note that the ownership is not in the form of private share-holdings but indirectly through pensions and insurance institutional bodies. Moreover, as the British Gas dispute pointed out, ownership is not control. Voting shares are administered by the representatives of fund-holders who act impersonally and who, unwilling to act against the advice of the executive directors, usually vote for the *status quo*. If the concept of a shareholding democracy advocated by Margaret Thatcher is to become a reality the companies should be subjected to a new legal frame-work that will make them accountable to the real owners and there should be a procedure devised by which the fund-holders should respond to the preferred interests of the contributors to those funds. After the British Gas annual general meeting there was some talk among shareholders of withdrawing investments from those funds which own British Gas stock, but this is a pin-prick against the general lack of accountability on the part of major fund-holders.

Regulating the privatisations

One area where anxiety has been expressed over control and accountability is the management of those public utilities which have been privatised. The concern here is that these are industries which have a social aspect in that energy and water represent the necessities of life, and there is therefore a threat to the well-being of society if those services are provided by a monopoly supplier whose main concern is obtaining a good financial return for their investment rather than the ideal of public service. The perception is that the public is powerless and totally at the mercy of the utility companies both for the provision of services and for the size of the charges made for those services. When these businesses were in public ownership there was some degree of accountability through parliament and the relevant government department, but removal of government involvement also removed that measure of accountability. For the enthusiastic supporter of privatisation the model response to this objection is to state that a privatised enterprise is more democratic in that accountability to parliament is effectively replaced by accountability to the consumer through competition and market forces. The privatised British Telecom is held up as an example of increased efficiency and reduced costs as a result of competition in the marketplace.

The situation of utilities such as gas, electricity and, above all, the water industry, is very different because privatisation has not meant the introduction of market forces but rather the transition from a public monopoly to a private monopoly. There can be no curb on the utilities' activities through market forces because in these industries there is no competition. The answer produced by the government is to write a regulatory body into each act of privatisation, 'mimicking what private competition would have achieved had the industries not been monopolies'.[19] There have been instances where the regulators have worked in the public interest, largely in instructing the relevant concern either that they could not increase prices or that they should seek to lower prices to the consumer. In two areas, however, the regulators have proved both ineffective and out of touch with public opinion:

1 The regulators have failed to prevent the payment of highly inflated salaries and bonuses to the industries' chief executives, even when those executives have plainly failed to improve the efficiency of the industries.
2 The regulators have failed to regulate the takeover of privatised utilities by foreign or domestic competitors, without referral to the Monopolies and Mergers Commission, and without protection from asset-strippers or manipulation for tax purposes.

Of the privatised utilities British Telecom has been the most open to competition and, largely thanks to the efforts of the industry regulator, Oftel, has improved performance and reduced costs to the consumer by about 30 per cent, although these improvements are largely as a result of technological progress and, it can be argued, would have happened anyway, no matter who owned the telephone system. There have, on the other hand, been heavy job losses, massive pay increases for the directors and a huge rise in profits despite repeated calls by the regulator for these profits to be passed on to the consumer.

Electricity supply is supposedly regulated by Offer, but most of the beneficial effects of price reductions requested by Offer have been cancelled out by the Chancellor's imposition of VAT on fuel bills. In February 1995 the private company Trafalgar House made a bid for control of Northern Electric which Offer wished to refer to the Monopolies and Merger Commission for scrutiny. This was over-ruled by Michael Heseltine as President of the Board of Trade, who, as a result of this ruling, effectively declared open season on takeovers and mergers in the electricity supply industry. Among the anomalies produced by this is the fact that, having privatised the electricity companies to get them out of state control, the government is now permitting bids for control from energy companies that are state-owned by other countries such as France. There is also the point that, although the government may have imposed a regulatory authority on all privatised industries, the government will simply ignore the recommendations of those regulators when it suits them.

British Gas originally appeared to be one of the success stories of privatisation. In the first five years as a privatised concern British Gas managed to reduce the cost to the consumer by 20 per cent in real terms. But much of this gain was offset by the VAT on gas bills imposed by the Chancellor. Over the year 1994–95 much of the good will earned by the initial improvements were squandered by the failure of British Gas to justify the huge increases being paid to Cedric Brown and his management team when there were job reductions and squeezes on salaries at the lower levels. By October 1995 complaints against British Gas had reached such a level that the industry's regulator Ofgas, was threatening to remove the Charter Mark awarded to British Gas under the government's Citizen's Charter scheme, unless British Gas made a far greater effort to regain its lost efficiency.[20]

Of all the privatised utilities, the one which causes most concern to the public is water.

(1) There is a general feeling that a commodity so necessary to human life should not be subjected to market forces and the profit motive. Access to water should be the natural right of a citizen.

(2) Charges for water have risen more, and more quickly, than in any other privatised industry. The average annual charges for water supply and sewage were £118.91 in 1989 before privatisation: these had risen to £184.85 by 1994. In some areas the rise was even greater, as in the case of South West Water where those charges have risen from £146 to £322. According to the Centre for the Study of Regulated Industries water bills rose at double the rate of inflation every year since privatisation.

(3) There are serious doubts about the quality of the water being provided. Action has been taken through the courts against a number of water companies over polluted water and the companies have been the target of a number of complaints from Europe. For example, in the South West, which charges more for its water than any other authority, there have been periods of days in every month when the water has been undrinkable unless boiled beforehand. In the year 1993–94 complaints over the quality and cost of water rose to the astonishing total of 15 million.

(4) There seems to be a lack of investment in the distribution of the water supply, with a Victorian system of pipes failing to cope with demand. In the very dry summer of 1995 there were water shortages in many areas, most notably in Yorkshire. Yorkshire Water accused its customers of waste, only to have the accusation turned against them with the revelation that Yorkshire Water loses more than 103 million gallons of water a day through leaking pipes. Yet, out of annual profits of £142 million, the company was spending only £11 million a year on

action to stop these leaks. Over the country as a whole, something like 20 per cent of all water is lost through leakage. Yet Ofwat has refused to do anything to force the water companies into spending money on repairs.

(5) The water companies seem to be more open than most to accusations of unfair profiteering at the expense of the public. At the same time as customers are paying far more for an apparently worse service, annual profits for the water companies range from £90.4 million for Northumbrian Water to £303.7 million for Thames Water, while the chairman of North West Water is paid £315,000 a year, representing a 571 per cent increase since privatisation.[21]

Conclusion

It is clear that the whole field of finance and industry in which the government could be said to have an interest, from the Bank of England to the privatised utilities, pay only lip service to accountability and is only very lightly regulated if at all. Despite claims by the Thatcher governments to have turned Britain into a shareholding democracy, the trend has been in the opposite direction and everything has been done to de-regulate both financial institutions and privatised industry.

Notes

1 Will Hutton, *The State We're In*, Jonathan Cape, London, 1995, page 289.

2 *Ibid.*, page 289.

3 Both the Treasury official and Roy Jenkins are quoted in Peter Hennessy, *Whitehall*, Secker and Warburg, London, 1989, page 397.

4 Will Hutton, 'Why the Treasury needs a lesson in counting', the *Guardian*, 1 May 1995.

5 Larry Elliott, Ruth Kelly and Will Hutton, 'Treasury seeks changed image', the *Guardian*, 20 October 1994.

6 Will Hutton, 'The Treasury rules no more', the *Guardian*, 20 October 1994, page 24.

7 Gordon Brown in a speech to the Manchester Business School, reported 6 April 1996.

8 Hutton, *The State We're In*, pages 145–6.

9 John Kingdom, *Government and Politics in Britain*, Polity Press, Cambridge, 1991, page 401.

10 Lord Justice Bingham, *The Bingham Report*, 22 October 1992.

11 'The Bank can't have it both ways', the *Observer*, editorial, 5 March 1995, page 28.

12 The report on the Barings collapse was widely reported in the press of 19 July 1995. The quotations in this paragraph come from an editorial in the *Guardian* of that date.

13 David Kynaston, co-editor of *The Bank of England – Money, Power and Influence 1694 to 1994*, Oxford University Press, Oxford, 1994. Quoted by William Keegan, the *Observer*, 21 May 1995, page 24.

14 Speech by Gordon Brown to the Labour Finance and Industry Group, London, 17 May 1995.

15 Interview by Eddie George with the Spanish newspaper, *El Mundo*, 21 May 1995.

16 Figures quoted in a *Guardian* editorial, 15 December 1994.

17 Alex Brummer, 'City notebook', the *Guardian*, 1 June 1995.

18 Anne Simpson, director of Pension and Investment Research Consultants Limited, in the *Guardian*, 17 October 1994, page 11.

19 Hutton, *The State We're In*, page 291.

20 Much of this information was contained in a survey of the public utilities by Nicholas Bannister, the *Guardian*, 18 February 1995, page 23.

21 Information on water comes partly from the Bannister article referred to in note 20 and partly from 'Focus on water' in the *Observer*, 13 August 1995, pages 14–15.

III

Representation

5

Electoral systems

Voting is merely a handy device, it is not to be identified with democracy.

G. D. H. Cole

If voting changed anything, they'd make it illegal.

Written on a wall in London

It's not the voting that's democracy, it's the counting.

Tom Stoppard, *Jumpers* (1972)

There is a lot said and written about electoral reform and the argument can become very heated over the relative merits of majority and proportional electoral systems because, as has been said, 'electoral systems are not mere details but key causal factors in determining outcomes'.[1] Any argument over systems, however, is very seldom resolved, because the protagonists in the debate seldom argue from the same position. The fact is that elections meet a variety of different purposes and no one electoral system is effective in fulfilling all of them. An individual may choose to emphasise one purpose of an election rather than another and, by that prioritisation, the individual will also have indicated a preference for the type of electoral system to be used. If individuals are most concerned with clear-cut results and strong government they will opt for a majority system; if, however, fairness and equity are their main concerns, then a proportional system will be favoured.

The purposes of electoral systems

Basically, there are five criteria by which different electoral
systems can be judged:
1 accountability;
2 comprehensibility;
3 effectiveness;
4 proportionality;
5 value.

(1) *Accountability*. This book is about 'representative democracy' and we have already said that, since direct democracy is an
impossibility in any society larger than the classical Greek city-
state, the only way that a large-scale modern society can be said
to be democratic is through the citizens of that society electing
people to represent their interests in the legislature. However, for
a society to be regarded as a true representative democracy, there
has to be a clear link between the electors and their elected representative. As Edmund Burke, one of the foremost advocates of
representative democracy, put it, 'it ought to be the happiness
and glory of a representative to live in the strictest union, the
closest correspondence and the most unreserved communication with his constituents'.[2] In Britain this link has always been
maintained through the constituency, ward or division – a geographical area which has a seat on the parliament or council and
the inhabitants of which are represented by a specific MP or
councillor. Historically, representation in Britain has always
been more concerned with ensuring that all the geographical
regions and areas of the country are represented than it has
been with representing the people; other than as the inhabitants
of those regions and areas. Through linking MP with constituency, and councillor with ward, the electors ensure that
they have someone specific to look after their interests when
decisions are made, someone to whom they can take their problems for solution and someone whom they can blame and vote
out of office if that member fails in his or her duties. In Britain
the average parliamentary constituency contains about 65,000
electors, which is felt to be as small as it is possible to go without

swamping the House of Commons with an excess number of MPs, and the Boundary Commission conducts a review every ten years to ensure that movements in population do not upset this demographic distribution. What happens to the constituency link in the large constituencies common to proportional representation, can be seen in the arrangements made for holding elections for the European Parliament (EP). An insistence on retaining the link between member and constituency for a parliament with only eighty-seven British members has resulted in constituencies eight times the size of those for Westminster elections. With populations of between 500,000 and 600,000, it is little wonder that very few people feel able to identify with their Member of the European Parliament (MEP).

(2) *Comprehensibility.* Electors should find it easy to vote and easy to understand the outcome when the votes have been counted. The great benefit of the British system as it exists is that the voter has simply to put a cross against one name and then to understand that, in the result, the candidate with the most votes is the winner. A vote which requires placing a number of candidates in order of preference, or a count which requires quotas to be met, and votes to be transferred to second preferences, can appear far too complex to the average elector. Any complexity in elections should lie in the issues and arguments rather than in the mechanics of the voting system.

(3) *Effectiveness.* An effective electoral system ensures, as far as possible, that a general election results in a clear-cut victory for one of the parties contesting the election; that party having a clearly defined programme for government which has been declared and explained to the public during the course of the election campaign. Much the same can be said about local elections but not, of course, for European elections. In theory, it has to be said, the British system was not developed for this purpose. According to constitutional law a general election chooses a parliament representative of regional and sectional interests whose main task is to scrutinise the workings of government. Again, in theory that government need have nothing to do with the make-up of the House of Commons: under the theory of

Separation of Powers that Montesquieu believed he could see in the British parliaments of the eighteenth century and which was enthusiastically adopted by the founding fathers of the United States, the legislature is kept strictly separate from the executive. 'Constitutionally, in the British system there . . . are just separate contests in different constituencies to elect free-thinking and independent individuals to Parliament.'[3] It is only since political parties were formed in the nineteenth century that governments have felt they needed a guaranteed majority in the Commons in order to pass controversial legislation, and the constitutional convention has evolved that the party which wins the largest number of seats in an election forms the government or controls the council. There are many people who argue very strongly that a coalition government – which would almost inevitably arise from a proportional system – would be undemocratic in that its policy as a government would have to be negotiated with and between parties, producing a compromise policy that had never been presented to the people for their approval, and giving an undue influence over events to minor parties. Despite an increasing experience of shared power in local government there are still many people who fear coalitions and demand that an electoral system must produce a clear and outright winner.

(4) *Proportionality.* The outcome of an election should produce a parliament or council that accurately represents all shades of public opinion within the electorate. It is a natural consequence of the theory of liberal democracy we discussed in Chapter 1, in that 'an electoral system based on proportional representation would be fairer – ensuring a close correlation between the proportion of votes cast and seats won – and would be more likely to ensure policy continuity'.[4] The final justification of a government over its policy decisions is that it is carrying out the wishes of the public as expressed in the election. Yet, can any parliament truly claim to be representative of the public if the interests represented in parliament are not proportionate to the interests of society as a whole?

(5) *Value.* All votes should have an equal value in electing a

representative and any vote that does not affect the result of an election can be said to be wasted. In a safe parliamentary seat where the candidate for Party A has a majority of 20,000, there is a case for saying that not only are any votes for Parties B and C wasted, because they are unable to affect the result, but so also are all the votes for Party A that are surplus to the required majority of one. By that criterion in the present British system the vote of someone living in a safe parliamentary seat has a completely different value to that of someone living in a marginal constituency. There is also a different value placed on the votes of supporters of the two main parties, compared with supporters of third parties. A third party can build up a great deal of support in a majority system of voting, consistently coming a good second without ever quite winning. The effect of this can be very clearly seen if the total number of votes cast for a party is divided by the number of seats won, showing the number of votes required to elect one MP. In the 1992 general election, for example, the average number of votes taken to elect MPs of the three main British parties were:

Conservative	41,942
Labour	42,646
Liberal Democrat	299,922

Equally as revealing is the difference in value between votes of party supporters who are concentrated in a small geographical area as against those who are scattered widely throughout the community as a whole. This is very clearly seen in terms of the two nationalist parties in the 1992 election. The Scottish National Party (SNP), who won three seats, had four times the number of votes given to Plaid Cymru (PC), who nevertheless managed to get four MPs elected. It must be noted that votes for the SNP were spread thinly across the whole of Scotland, whereas votes for PC were concentrated in the predominantly Welsh-speaking north-west corner of Wales. The average number of votes required to elect a single MP from the two nationalist parties was:

Plaid Cymru	38,609
Scottish National Party	209,850

Criteria adopted by the Plant Committee

When assessing the merits of rival electoral systems in terms of reforming the British system it is important that the various systems proposed are measured in relation to how they can satisfy criteria such as those above and priorities have to be placed on those criteria. In 1990, when Neil Kinnock embarked on Labour's policy review, he instituted a committee of enquiry under the guidance of Professor Raymond Plant, with the brief of looking into electoral systems that might be used for the proposed Scottish Assembly but which might also be favoured by a future Labour government for local, European and Westminster elections. As part of the guidelines for this enquiry the criteria that such systems would have to satisfy were very clearly defined.

- Proportionality was an important criterion, but there were others.
- There ought to be fair representation for women, ethnic minorities and the regions.
- The power to create a government should lie in the hands of the people voting in the election, and not in the hands of party 'fixers' making deals to create a coalition after the election, often in secret.
- Elections should produce effective governments.
- Any proposal for electoral reform must have the support of a majority of MPs.[5]

First-past-the-post

The electoral system used in Great Britain for all elections is sometimes known as a *simple majority* system, although it is more properly known as a *plurality* system, in that a candidate merely needs one more vote than any other candidate to win: hence the alternative name of 'first-past-the-post' (FPTP). For parliamentary elections the country is divided into constituencies of between 60,000 and 70,000 electors each, and each constituency elects one MP. This is true also for Northern Ireland in Westminster elections, although different rules apply to local and European elections where the delicate politico-religious differences require a degree of proportionality. Peculiarities used to exist in the British system, such as extra votes for university graduates and owners of businesses, but the university seats and the business vote were abolished in 1949, as were the surviving twelve multi-member constituencies.

If the British system is measured against the criteria listed earlier, it can be seen that the system scores very highly on accountability and comprehensibility, quite well on effectiveness, but very badly as far as proportionality and value are concerned. As regards the public, the British system is remarkably easy to understand: the voter places a cross against one name on the ballot paper and, a little later, a straightforward count results in a clear winner for the constituency or ward. There is therefore, also a clear link between the constituency or ward and the elected member. In most general elections the results also provide a party with a good governing majority in the House of Commons.

The factor which affects the proportionality, value and, to some degree, the effectiveness of the FPTP system is that it only really works within a two-party system. As soon as a third candidate or party intervenes the chances are that the winner in an election will have gained the most votes but not a majority of the votes. Within the constituency this can mean that an MP can be elected on 30–40 per cent of the vote. Take, for example, the constituency of Brecon and Radnor in the 1992 election, which the Conservatives won on 36.1 per cent of the vote, as against the 35.8 per cent gained by the Liberal Democrats, 26.3 per cent by Labour and 0.9 per cent by the Nationalists. The implications for representative democracy in this is that Brecon is represented by an MP *rejected* by 64 per cent of those voting. At national level this same factor has meant that no government since 1935 has been elected on a majority of the popular vote. Even the Thatcher government's greatest victory in 1983 was won on a 42.4 per cent share of the vote. Prior to that, in the February 1974 election, there was an even more striking anomaly when Labour became the largest party in the Commons despite having only

37.2 per cent of the vote, as against the 38.2 per cent of the Conservatives.

In recent years this lack of proportionality, combined with the strength of third parties, has made the argument of effectiveness less easy to sustain. An ever-increasing number of councils, particularly in England, have come under no overall control and many counties and districts have administrations run by cooperation between either Conservative or Labour councillors and the Liberal Democrats, in exactly the type of coalition that was once thought of as peculiar to a system of proportional representation and which the FPTP system was supposed to make unlikely if not impossible.

The arguments against the current system put forward by those in favour of electoral reform are largely based on the criteria of fairness and value.

(1) The system produces too many wasted votes, particularly in the safe party seats which form something like three-quarters of the total. In safe seats large numbers of the votes cast for unsuccessful candidates are wasted, as are equally large numbers of superfluous votes for the winning candidates.

(2) Third parties are adversely affected, especially those with support spread thinly and widely. The most obviously unfair manifestation of this was in 1983 when Labour won 209 seats with 27.6 per cent of the vote, while the Liberal/SDP Alliance won only 23 seats with 25.4 per cent of the vote.

(3) Voters are disenfranchised because their views are never taken into consideration. It is significant that the Thatcher governments between 1979 and 1990 were able to introduce the most radical legislation despite being opposed by more than 55 per cent of those voting, and more than 65 per cent of the electorate.[6] Much of the alienation from politicians felt at the moment might well be as a result of the many people who felt that their lives had been adversely affected by the Conservative governments of the 1980s and yet found the Conservatives returned in election after election, despite their rejection by a majority of the people.

(4) The system leads to confrontational politics and the adop-

tion by parties of extreme positions, largely because there is no need for the consensus view required in the formation of coalition administrations.

The European dimension

The greatest anomaly over the FPTP system exists in the elections for the EP. According to the Treaty of Rome there should be a uniform system of election common to all member States of the EU, but, since direct elections to the EP were introduced in 1979 Britain has resisted any change in the electoral system for the Euro-constituencies of Great Britain, despite the fact that Britain is the only member State not to use a form of proportional representation and despite the fact that proportional representation is used for European elections in Northern Ireland, because of the sectarian nature of Northern Irish politics. And yet, two of the main arguments in favour of first-past-the-post do not apply in European elections. 'European elections do not exist to choose a government, but to send a body of members to the EP that is representative of the member state's people and, by the criterion of fair representation, the FPTP system clearly fails.'[7] Nor does the constituency link argument apply when it refers to constituencies that are often entire counties in area, with an electorate of 600,000 or so.

The 'third party effect' is even more noticeable in the European elections. From the time of the first direct elections in 1979, it was 1994 before the Liberal Democrats won their first two seats in the European Parliament, despite the Alliance having achieved 19.5 per cent of the vote in 1984, 3 per cent more than the Liberal Democrats achieved in 1994. In the 1989 elections the British Green Party gained 15 per cent of the vote, but had no MEPs elected, despite receiving more votes than many European Green parties which did gain representation in the EP. Even the major parties suffer from a lack of proportionality in European elections. In 1994 Labour received 44.24 per cent of the vote but won 62 seats (71.26 per cent). Yet, when challenged as to why Britain clung to the FPTP system for

European elections when the EU was aiming for a common proportional system, the government could only say that it would
confuse the electorate if they had to vote in a different way in
European elections to that with which they are familiar from
national elections.[8]

It is presumably some quirk of the Anglo-Saxon mind, since
only a handful of countries in the world use a FPTP system, and
all those countries have British roots, either historically, as with
the United States, or through membership of the Commonwealth, as with Canada.

The case for reform

The argument that the FPTP system should be replaced with a
more proportional system is quite old. Early in the present century
there was agitation that the fledgling Labour Party would never
get off the ground while the electoral system was so weighted
against small third parties. In 1917 legislation was drawn up to
introduce a fairer system of voting but failed as a result of disagreements as to the best system to be used, the Commons favouring the alternative vote while the Lords wanted the single
transferable vote (STV). Since then, and until quite recently, the
degree of support for proportional representation has fluctuated
dependent upon the popularity of the third party in British politics. After Labour had overtaken the Liberals as the alternative to
the Conservatives it was the turn of the Liberals to advocate electoral reform and MacDonald's Labour government of 1929 introduced the question once more, in return for Liberal support for the
minority Labour administration but this move in turn failed. It
can be said, however, that small parties have been the ones who
would benefit most from proportional representation and the two
larger parties who benefit most from the existing system.

During the peak years of the two-party system, between 1945
and 1964, while the third party share of the vote remained
below 10 per cent, as it did for the Liberals until 1974, the public
was not greatly concerned. However, when the Liberal vote grew
from 7.5 per cent in 1970 to 19.3 per cent in 1974, but the

number of seats gained by the Liberals only increased from six (1 per cent) to fourteen (2 per cent) it became rather too great a discrepancy to be overlooked. Nine years later, in 1983, the Liberal/SDP share of the vote grew to 25.4 per cent, but that only represented twenty-three parliamentary seats. The distortion created by the system was now too glaringly unfair to be overlooked and an increasing proportion of the population became disturbed. In 1988 the pressure group Charter 88 was formed, with proportional representation as one of the reforms for which it would campaign.

The Labour Party also began to take an interest in the topic again because, in 1987, they had lost their third successive election to the Conservatives and it was beginning to look as though Labour would never be able to unseat the Conservatives unaided, given the inequities of the electoral system. In 1990 the Plant Committee was set the task of examining a variety of electoral systems, originally for use in the regional assemblies that Labour intended to set up and for elections to a reformed second chamber to replace the House of Lords. In 1991 the scope of the committee was extended to include other elections, including Westminster elections. In 1992 Neil Kinnock actually introduced the topic of electoral reform into the election campaign as a sort of sweetener for the Liberal Democrats in case the parliament resulting from the 1992 election should be hung.

The Plant Committee reported in 1993 and it seemed as though the Labour Party became committed to some reform of the electoral system in the Scottish, Welsh or any regional assemblies that were set up, for European elections and for an elected second chamber. On Westminster elections the furthest the party will go is to hint at a possible referendum on the matter. The fact is that under Tony Blair Labour once more believed themselves capable of winning an election unaided and therefore the inequities of the system could well work in their interests. Whatever the commitment of Labour to reform it does look likely that the reform they would favour would fall short of full proportionality and would be some variant of an *absolute majority* system.

Although the Conservative Party appears to remain totally hostile to any talk of electoral reform, the Conservatives as much as anyone can suffer from the distortions of FPTP if they find themselves in a third party situation. In the 1995 elections for the metropolitan district councils the Conservatives polled 20 per cent of the votes cast, for a mere six per cent of councillors elected. Labour on the other hand gained 81 per cent of the seats for 57 per cent of the vote.[9]

Majority systems

Absolute or overall majority systems are designed to modify the 'winner-takes-all' aspect of the FPTP system so as to give a greater degree of proportionality and reduce the number of wasted votes by some device which results in the eventual winner being able to claim more than 50 per cent of the vote.

Second ballot

In a first ballot any number of candidates might stand and are voted for as in Britain, with a cross placed against the selected candidate's name. If any one candidate secures more than 50 per cent of the votes they are elected outright. If, as is more usually the case, no one candidate achieves the necessary target then the candidates gaining fewer votes retire and a second ballot is held, representing a straight fight between the two highest-scoring candidates from the first ballot. The intervening period between the two ballots is used in attempting to persuade supporters of the losing candidates to transfer their votes to one of the surviving candidates. Defeated candidates from the first round can also endorse one of the two remaining. This is the system used in France for presidential and other elections, where the two ballots are on successive Sundays.

Alternative vote

The principle is similar to that of the second ballot but without the need to have a second round of voting. The voter does not place a cross against the name of one candidate but lists all the candidates in order of preference – 1, 2, 3, etc. If no one candidate gains 50 per cent of the vote when first preferences are counted, the candidate with the fewest first preferences is eliminated and their second preference votes are distributed. If there is still no candidate with 50 per cent of the vote, the next lowest candidate is eliminated and their second preferences distributed. And this continues until such time as one candidate does emerge with over 50 per cent of the votes. This is the system regularly used in Australia.

Supplementary vote

This is a sort of amalgamation of the above two systems in that the voting requires listing the candidates in order of preference as in the alternative vote but, if no one candidate gains more than 50 per cent, the second preferences of all but the two leading candidates are redistributed between those two, the counting therefore being like the second ballot but without the second round of voting. Sometimes called the French system without the time-lag, this system was devised by the Labour Party's Plant Committee and is the system that Labour would recommend for future Westminster elections.

These overall majority systems satisfy the same criteria as FPTP in that they maintain close constituency links, produce clear-cut results and are relatively easy to understand. The system does eliminate the wasted vote factor in that, even if a voter's first preference has no effect on the result, their second preference might be crucial. Second ballot voting or the re-distribution of second preferences is also marginally more proportional in that it would tend to favour third parties which regularly take second place in FPTP contests. Take, for example, the constituency of Portsmouth South in the 1992 election, which the Conservatives won with 42.5 per cent of the vote against the Liberal Democrats' 42.0 per cent, with Labour trailing in third place with 14.6 per cent. If the Labour votes were redistributed it would seem likely that more of their second preferences would go to the LibDems than to the Conservatives.

Proportional and semi-proportional systems

List systems

Common to many countries in Europe, list systems are the only truly proportional systems. Each party contesting an election prepares a list that can be as long as there are seats to fill in the body to be elected. The elector then votes for the party list rather than a candidate and seats in the elected body are assigned to the parties in proportion to the percentage of votes cast for each party. For example, an assembly with 100 seats would mean that a party which received 30 per cent of the votes would declare that the first thirty names on its list were elected. In a very few countries such as Luxembourg or Holland the entire country acts as one constituency, with each party producing just one list. But most countries such as Italy or Spain are divided into regions for electoral purposes.

The division of a country into regions is one attempt to modify one of the failings of the list system, which is the lack of accountability. Without the existence of a local constituency the elector is without a specific person to represent them; any complaint or point to be raised cannot be taken to an individual representative but must be forwarded by way of the political party. The party usurps another democratic function as well. Unlike Britain, where candidates for election are selected by the local party members and candidates can influence their election by their skill in campaigning, under the list system candidates are chosen by the party headquarters and successful candidates are not elected as a result of their political expertise but through party patronage.

The main charge levelled against proportional systems in general, and list systems in particular, is that the proliferation of parties that they promote fails to grant a clear-cut result to elections in the form of single-party governments, but leads inevitably to coalition governments formed from two or more parties. The critics of proportional representation tend to concentrate their criticisms on the shortcomings and undemocratic nature of coalitions.

(1) Coalition governments are inherently unstable. The list system has notoriously produced so many ineffectual governments in Italy that moves have been made to introduce some elements of majority voting.

(2) Small parties who should be the junior partners in a coalition have a disproportionate share of power, both in the formulation of policy and in the making of decisions, through their ability to bring down a government by withdrawing support. In Germany the Liberal Free Democrat Party has always been a poor third in terms of popular support but they have always been able to dictate their own terms for entry into a coalition with either the Social Democrats or the Christian Democrats.

(3) It is hard to assess the performance of a party when it is not known which party in a government is responsible for which policy. A coalition government can therefore never be truly accountable to the electorate.

(4) The party policies for which a party received the votes of the public may have to be amended in the negotiations to create a coalition. Therefore the electorate can never know exactly what it is voting for.

(5) A small party which is the junior partner in a coalition can change their allegiance to a different larger party, thus changing the government without reference to the electorate. Chancellor Kohl originally came to power in Germany because the Free Democrats withdrew from a coalition with the Social Democrats to enter an agreement with the Christian Democrats.

Another argument that is often quoted against proportional representation is that it encourages the growth of small extremist parties. Those who argue from this standpoint will point out that fascist and communist parties have never achieved any success in Britain where the electoral system militates against them. Most European countries have imposed a threshold to guard against this, in that parties cannot win seats in the legislatures until they achieve a certain percentage of the votes cast: which might be anything from 1 to 17 per cent. Nevertheless, in some countries extremist parties can get past the threshold to win seats. In the 1992 election campaign, when both Labour and the Liberal Democrats were talking about electoral reform, the Conservatives argued against it by referring to elections in Germany and Italy which took place during the British campaign and where both countries saw a significant rise of support for far-right, neo-fascist parties.

Single transferable vote (STV)
As a system of voting this was developed by the British Electoral Reform Society as long ago as 1910 and was suggested to the Speaker's Conference on Electoral Reform in 1917 for possible adoption in British elections. That bid failed but STV was the electoral system used for the four university seats which existed between 1918 and 1949. The Electoral Reform Society kept the system in existence and it is regularly used in elections for public bodies, professional associations and trades unions, as well as being the system favoured by the Liberal Democrats and that recommended by the Kilbrandon Commission in 1976 for the Scottish and Welsh assemblies proposed by the Callaghan government. It is used in the Republic of Ireland and Bermuda, and it was introduced into all non-Westminster elections in Northern Ireland after 1972.

At the heart of STV is a multi-member constituency, electing three, four or five members to the parliament or elected body. For example, in European elections the whole of Northern Ireland is just one constituency, electing three MEPs. As in the alternative vote, electors vote by placing the candidates in order of preference, with the aim of reaching a quota of votes which is calculated by dividing the total number of votes cast by one more than the number of seats available, and then adding one. Any candidate reaching the quota with first preference votes is elected but then there is a complex procedure for achieving the full number of members. As a first step any votes surplus to the required quota that have been received by candidates elected by first preference have their second preferences distributed to the other candidates. If no other candidate reaches the quota and is elected, the candidate receiving fewest votes is eliminated and second preferences redistributed as under the alternative vote system. This process of redistributing both the votes of defeated candidates and the surplus of successful candidates serves to remove the wasted vote factor. If necessary this process of eliminating the lowest candidate and redistributing second preferences votes goes on until the necessary number of members for the constituency is elected.

For example, in the 1994 European elections the total vote in Northern Ireland was 559,867. Since there were three MEPs to be elected, the quota was 559,867 divided by four, plus one: which is 139,968. In the election, Ian Paisley for the Democratic Unionists, with 163,246 first preferences, and John Hume of the SDLP, with 161,992 first preferences, both exceeded the quota and were elected outright. The candidate who came third in the first preference vote, James Nicholson of the Ulster Unionists, gained 133,459 votes, only 6,508 votes behind the quota, a deficit soon made up in the distribution of preference votes if precedent was anything to go by. In 1989, when much the same result was achieved, Ian Paisley had received 26,407 votes more than the quota needed to be elected. At the second stage, when those surplus votes were distributed, 22,798 of Paisley's second preferences went to Nicholson, safely carrying him past the quota and not even requiring the distribution of Hume's surplus to attain the required three MEPs.

That example serves to illustrate the chief failing of STV as an electoral system. The case of Northern Ireland, where the three elected members nearly all made it on first preference, is complicated enough but very straightforward when compared to many STV contests, particularly when four or five seats are involved. The response from advocates of STV is that the system is not complex for the voter who has a simple choice to make on the ballot paper, the complication comes in the counting and arriving at a result. But that can be very complicated indeed in large contests, when the redistribution of second or even third preferences can drag on into the seventh, eighth or ninth stage, with the count extending over twenty-four hours or more and with complex mathematical calculations involved. If the public is unable to understand the results procedure there might well be alienation and also a feeling of distrust, because the suspicion will always be there that complexity can conceal malpractice.

STV is not particularly effective in choosing a one-party government and the likelihood is that elections will end in coalitions, with disproportionate influence for a proliferation of small parties. In the Republic of Ireland this was countered by reducing the number of seats for each constituency because, the smaller the number of seats, the larger the quota needed to get elected. With a large number of small constituencies the smaller parties are squeezed out of contention and for many years Fianna Fáil and Fine Gael, as the two main parties, retained as many three-member constituencies as possible. That, however, was seen as political manipulation of the electoral process and there were calls for reform. Since 1977 a boundary commission has altered the structure of Irish constituencies, considerably increasing the numbers of four- or five-member constituencies at the expense of those that are three-member. As a result recent governments in the Republic of Ireland have increasingly been coalitions formed by Fianna Fáil, originally with the Progressive Democrats but more recently with Dick Spring's Labour Party.

Because surplus first preference votes are used as well as second preferences of defeated candidates, it can be said that STV gives near equal value to all votes cast. The system is not strictly proportional but it is considerably more so than any majoritarian system such as FPTP. And it is a much fairer system in respects other than proportionality. Since parties can have more than one candidate in the constituency they are more likely to include candidates such as women or members of an ethnic minority, which the constituency party might hesitate to select as a candidate in a single-member constituency. In the same way a voter can split their vote between parties and give credit to one candidate for some personal reason other than their party label.

Obviously the constituency link is weaker when constituencies might be up to five times the size of present seats but they are nothing like as large as EP constituencies. In addition, at least in a multi-member constituency the constituent has a choice of representatives and would find it easier to seek help from a member for whom they had voted. At the moment, for example, a staunch Labour supporter living in a safe Tory seat has to seek help from a Conservative MP. Under STV there is every possibility that, among the several members for the seat, there would be at least one Labour member whom the Labour supporter could approach.[10]

Additional member system (AMS)

This system is an attempt to marry the best features of simple majority voting with the proportionality of regional lists. It was developed by the British occupying powers for use in the restitution of democracy to Western Germany as part of the de-nazification process. Introduced for Bundestag elections in 1949 it remains the voting system used in reunited Germany today. Although it has invariably produced coalition governments they have been exceptionally stable, and the economic success of Germany would seem to indicate that they could justifiably claim to have a successful government.

In Germany, with AMS, constituencies are double the size of FPTP constituencies and the elector votes twice, once for a constituency MP on strict simple majority terms, and secondly for a political party on a proportional list system. Half the seats in the parliament are filled by constituency MPs, exactly as is presently the case in Britain. The party votes are also counted and seats in parliament are allocated proportionately according to the percentage received by the party. This is done by 'topping up' the constituency representatives from regional lists compiled by each party. This makes it possible, not only that parties are represented proportionately, but that parties can win parliamentary seats without actually winning one constituency contest. For example, in the 1987 German elections the Christian Democrats came out on top with 47.7 per cent of the list vote, representing 223 seats. They had gained 169 constituencies and therefore only needed fifty-four seats from the list to achieve the number of seats to which they were entitled. The second party, the Social Democrats, had gained seventy-nine constituency seats and

39.2 per cent on the list, which entitled them to a total of 186 seats and this was achieved by the award of 107 seats to the SDP list. Neither of the other two parties with a place in the parliament won any constituencies but the Free Democrats with 9.1 per cent received forty-six list seats and the Greens, with 8.3 per cent, got forty-two seats from their list. To prevent the rise of extremist parties the German system operates a quota system whereby a party has to gain 5 per cent of the list vote before they are granted any list seats.[11]

The AMS would seem to satisfy many of the requirements of an electoral system. It is highly proportional but manages to retain a clear constituency link. It has the disadvantage of nearly always producing a coalition government and of giving disproportionate power to the third party (in Germany usually the Free Democratic Party) which forms a coalition partner with either of the two main parties. It does also tend to keep the parties very centrist in their policies, fighting shy of adventurous ideas for fear of alienating coalition partners. And, of course, it shares with the list systems the somewhat undemocratic aspect that half the MPs are chosen by the party machines rather than the electorate. Quite apart from this there is the somewhat negative implication that there are two classes of MP, with a member directly elected for a constituency being regarded as superior perhaps to a member nominated from the party list.

Nevertheless, the AMS proved sufficiently attractive to the Plant Committee for them to recommend it as the preferred system of proportional representation for a future Labour administration, rather than the STV favoured by the Liberal Democrats, although in Britain Plant suggests that there should be more constituency seats, with the list contribution limited to 25 per cent or thereabouts. In October 1995 the Scottish Constitutional Convention, formed largely by an alliance between Labour and the Liberal Democrats, announced their agreement on the form to be taken by a future Scottish Assembly. Among the points on which they agreed was that elections to the Assembly would be by AMS. The Assembly would have seventy-three members elected by simple majority under the FPTP system. These numbers would then be topped up proportionately with fifty-six party representatives, chosen from regional lists based on Scotland's eight European constituencies.

Conclusion

In public debate the argument over electoral systems and the possibility of electoral reform for Britain has all too often been reduced to arguments over fairness on the one side and an effective choice of government on the other, with, perhaps, a little discussion over choosing a constituency representative thrown in. Yet, as we have seen, the question involves more than that and in a way the argument is not capable of resolution while those involved in the argument disagree over what they see as their priorities regarding the various purposes for holding an election. Nor is there likely to be any change when the two major parties both feel secure in their ability to win an election on their own and unaided; with the desire for reform restricted to the minor parties who lack the power to do anything about it.

However, electoral reform is basic to the discussion of democracy because a change in the electoral system does more than merely change the way an election is conducted. Electoral systems are more than mere technicalities because, as David Butler has said, they 'lie at the heart of a nation's arrangements'.[12] And, as repeated by Cowley and Dowding: 'Any change in the electoral system will change the system of representation. Our prior decision really needs to be: what sort of representation do we want? We should then create our electoral system in terms of the answer to that question.'[13]

Notes

1 A. Reeve and A. Ware, *Electoral Systems – A Comparative and Theoretical Introduction*, Routledge, London, 1992.

2 Speech by Burke to his Bristol constituents, quoted by Philip Cowley and Keith Dowding, 'Electoral systems and parliamentary representation', *Politics Review*, September 1994, pages 19–21.

3 Cowley and Dowding, pages 19–21.

4 Philip Norton, 'The Constitution in question', *Politics Review*, April 1994, page 10.

5 The criteria imposed on the Plant Commission are reported in Bill Coxall and Lynton Robins, *Contemporary British Politics* (2nd edition), Macmillan, Basingstoke, 1994, page 274.

6 It must be remembered that when percentages of voting figures are quoted one factor that must be taken into consideration is that only 70 to 80 per cent of the electorate actually turn out to vote in general elections. Fifty per cent of those voting can mean no more than 40 per cent of those able to vote.

7 Colin Pilkington, *Britain in the European Union Today*, Manchester University Press, Manchester, 1995, pages 185–6.

8 Foreign and Commonwealth Office, *The European Elections – Why They Matter to You*, the COI for HMSO, London, 1994.

9 Peter Kellner in the *Observer*, 21 April 1996.

10 For much of the information on STV in this section I am indebted to Bill Jones, 'Reforming the electoral system', in *Political Issues in Britain Today* (3rd edition), Manchester University Press, Manchester, 1989 printing, pages 81–3. The figures for the 1994 European election in Northern Ireland come from the figures produced by the Central Press Division of the EP as document PE 177.791/fin. Details of the redistribution of votes in the 1989 election come from *The Times Guide to the European Parliament, 1989*.

11 The figures for the German elections of 1987 are taken from Bill Jones, 'Reforming the electoral system', pages 78–9.

12 David Butler, 'Electoral reform', in J. Jowell and D. Oliver (eds) *The Changing Constitution*, Clarendon Press, Oxford, 1985.

13 Cowley and Dowding, 'Electoral systems', page 21.

6

Mandates, delegates and representatives

What the hell's the point of electing MPs to represent us if the Government cheats and changes the rules? To tell MPs that their votes in parliament are worthless reduces democracy to a farce.

Editorial in the *Sun*, 18 February 1993

Now majority rule is a precious, sacred thing worth dying for. But – like other precious, sacred things . . . it's not only worth dying for; it can make you wish you were dead. Imagine if all life were determined by majority rule. Every meal would be a pizza.

P. J. O'Rourke, *Parliament of Whores*, 1991

Any reform of the electoral system that led to a proportional system would raise important questions about the nature of representation in Britain, since all forms of proportional representation are based on the principle of voting for a party. Yet, according to constitutional theory, political parties have no part in a British electoral system which is supposedly concerned with the election of an individual representative of constituents, not a party delegate. This view of representative democracy is sometimes known as 'Burkean', after the eighteenth-century parliamentarian, Edmund Burke (1729–97), who first elucidated the principle in a speech to his Bristol constituents in 1774. As he said, 'It is his duty . . . to prefer [his constituents'] interests to his own. But his unbiased opinion, his mature judgment, his enlightened conscience, he ought not to sacrifice to any man, or to any set of men living. . . . Your representative owes you . . . his judgment; and he betrays . . . you, if he sacrifices it to your opinion. Parliament is not a congress of ambassadors from different and hostile interests . . . but . . . a deliberative assembly of one nation, with one interest, that of the whole.'[1]

The view of Burke was therefore that an MP, once elected, was free of any restrictions – 'free to vote as they like, free to speak as they like, and free to join whatever party they like'.[2] In October 1995, the MP for Stratford-on-Avon, Alan Howarth, holder of one of the safest Conservative seats in the country, deserted the Conservative Party to join Labour, making it clear that he had every intention of remaining in parliament as an MP even if he now represented a different party. There was, of course, an outcry in Stratford and elsewhere that this was a betrayal of Howarth's constituents who had voted for a Conservative and thus had every right to be represented by a Conservative, having no wish to be represented by a member of the Labour Party.

Howarth's action could not have taken place in India, even though the Indian political system is based on the Westminster model. Under Indian constitutional law MPs are elected as party representatives and the legitimacy of their presence in parliament rests on their remaining loyal to their party. If they should vote in parliament against their party's wishes, let alone cross the floor of the House to join the Opposition, they would be disowned by their former party and would automatically lose their seat in parliament. This principle of having been elected as a party representative is one that in theory has no constitutional place in Britain, but is nevertheless a view that has tacitly prevailed since the growth of the party system after 1867.

The contrary view to that of Burke, a view which says that MPs should be bound by the wishes of their constituents and the policies of their party, was originally put forward by Robert Peel in the run-up to the election of January 1835. In the aftermath of the Reform Act the Tories had to appeal to the new middle class voters and, to that end, Peel spoke to his constituents in Tamworth, although with an eye to a wider audience. In his speech the Prime Minister made certain promises of further cautious reform as well as action to consolidate the reforms that had already taken effect, describing the Reform Act as 'final and irrevocable'. Known as the Tamworth Manifesto, this was the first time a politician had put forward a cohesive programme of government for the approval of the electorate. It was a seminal step in the creation of political parties and introduced into British politics the concept of the *mandate*, as an obligation to carry out in parliament the promises made before election.

The mandate

If a dictionary is consulted it can be seen that, in the political sense, the word 'mandate' has two subtly different meanings. The first and oldest, dating from the sixteenth century and derived from the Latin word *mandare*, means 'a command from a superior to a subordinate ordering him how to act'. The second meaning, originating in the late eighteenth century, and derived from the French word *mandat*, means 'permission to govern according to declared policies, regarded as officially granted by an electorate to a particular party or leader upon the decisive outcome of an election'.[3] This second meaning has little to do with representation but is more a legitimising device which gives governments the right to carry out actions because the electorate has given its approval to those actions by granting the government party a working majority. The most striking example of a government specifically seeking a mandate was in the general election of December 1910, in which Asquith's Liberal government sought the approval of the electorate for their plans to reform the House of Lords, in the Parliament Act of 1911.

This view of the mandate is certainly that taken by the Conservative Party, as has been shown by the use made of it by Tory governments in justifying their forcing of unpopular legislation through parliament by means of a whipped majority. After the 1987 Tory victory, the House of Lords on several occasions voted down government legislation that had been passed by the Commons. Margaret Thatcher used the threat of the

Parliament Act to over-rule these reversals, saying that an unelected second chamber had no right to overturn legislation approved by an elected chamber that was mandated to carry out those policies that had been included in the election manifesto.

There are defects in this use of the mandate to justify the actions of even a majority government:

- Can a party elected on a minority of the popular vote, as all post-war governments have been, truly be said to have the mandate of the electorate?
- Can the electorate be said to have granted the mandate to a government when the majority of the electorate, even the government's own supporters, are unaware of much of the content of the party manifesto? Research in recent years has seemed to suggest that electors are often unaware of party policy on a wide range of issues.
- Someone may be a strongly partisan supporter of a party, for whom they will vote regardless, but they do not necessarily have to support every party policy. Can an elector be said to grant a mandate for the implementation of policies in which the elector does not believe?
- It is well known that many measures, although they may have been in the manifesto, are unpopular with the electorate: the poll tax being a prime example. Are these unpopular policies included in the mandate?
- Many controversial policies are omitted from the election manifesto completely, as were any mention of reforms to the National Health Service (NHS) in 1987, but the elected government will still claim they are mandated to carry out these policies since they form an indivisible part of the total government package.

The mandate – the Labour perspective

In contrast to this view of the mandate, the Labour Party, for historical reasons, takes a very different line, believing that the mandate does not merely grant permission to carry out manifesto promises but in fact places an obligation on the government to carry out what it has promised. And that obligation extends to MPs and councillors who, having been elected on a Labour ticket, are expected to support party policy in all matters.

The Labour Party has this very specific attitude towards the mandate because of the history of the party. In its origins the party was a device to promote trade union representation in parliament: the party being the political wing of the working class movement which was largely funded by the unions. It is only natural that the paymasters of the party would be interested in ensuring that the party remained true to the interests of those providing the funds. Clause V of the party constitution, written in 1918, states that 'the work of the party shall be under the direction and control of the party conference'. Moreover, to extend the concept of the mandate, those party members who attend the conference and pass resolutions that are supposedly binding on the party, are delegates who are mandated to vote on conference resolutions in a way that is dictated to them beforehand by the union or constituency party which sent them there. Until John Smith introduced the principle of 'one-member-one-vote', delegates to conference used block votes, voting the declared strength of party members in either union or constituency party according to the wishes of the union or constituency. Since the parliamentary party is easily outnumbered by the extra-parliamentary membership, especially when the union block votes are taken into consideration, it is possible in theory to say that Labour MPs sit in parliament not as representatives of their constituents but as delegates of the Labour Party Conference.

Not that the parliamentary party was ever totally subservient to the extra-parliamentary party. As far back as 1907 Keir Hardie continued to support votes for women, despite the scepticism of male-dominated trade unions who controlled conference. Party leaders ever since, together with their parliamentary colleagues, have defied conference decisions and, indeed, have virtually ignored conference when Labour has been in power. There are reasons for this:

• It would be unrealistic for conference to exercise control over a Labour government; if only because of the time factor involved if the party were to be consulted over every government decision. The most that can be allowed the extra-parliamentary party is the ability to comment on government actions *after the event*.

- Most Labour leaders, with the possible exception of Michael Foot, have been able to 'manage' (cynics would say 'manipulate') the party and have thus avoided outright confrontation.
- Except for a spell in the 1980s the unions have supported the parliamentary leadership. Traditional union leaders have largely been on the right of the party, pragmatic rather than ideological in their approach to socialism, and ready to recognise that the unions need Labour every bit as much as Labour needs the unions.[4]

During the Wilson administrations, however, complaints increased in the party as to the extent to which the leadership ignored conference decisions when in power. Left wing politicians such as Tony Benn protested hard and long over the failure, as they saw it, of socialist governments to carry out socialist policies. These protests grew even louder during the Callaghan government of 1975–79 when Denis Healey, as Chancellor, had to introduce monetarist measures at the behest of the IMF, and the Labour government was seen tamely to submit to capitalist dictation and to endorse measures such as wage control and the use of unemployment to curb inflation. The cause of the Left was aided by the leftward move of many major unions, such as the National Union of Mineworkers (NUM) under Arthur Scargill, and the control exercised by the extreme Left over constituency parties; as was the case with the Militant Tendency on Merseyside. After their 1979 defeat at the hands of Margaret Thatcher, this confederacy of the Left claimed that Labour had failed not through any fear of extreme socialism on the part of the electorate but because the party was not being sufficiently socialist in its attitudes and policy statements.

The Left wished to re-assert the sovereignty of conference in order to keep the leadership and the parliamentary party true to socialist doctrine. They therefore campaigned for three reforms:

1 The party leader to be elected by the Conference and not by the Parliamentary Labour Party (PLP).
2 Conference through the National Executive Committee (NEC), rather than the leader, to dictate the writing of the party manifesto.
3 Labour MPs to be subject to mandatory re-selection by their constituency party.

As far as representation is concerned, the last of the three was the most important point. The objection raised by the Left was that MPs elected to a safe Labour seat were virtually given a job for life, since they would be almost automatically re-elected, no matter what their record. Some MPs, once selected, could constantly ignore the policies and wishes of their constituents and yet remain in position. What the Left wanted was the ability to remove an MP who did not follow constituency instructions: or, at least, to refuse that recalcitrant MP any future candidacy with the party. In other words, they wished to change the status of a Labour MP from representative to delegate. Critics of the Left claimed that the direction taken by the Labour Party in the late 1970s and early 1980s was rejecting the basis of *liberal democracy* and turning to the Soviet system of *democratic centralism*, in which the party rather than parliament or people is sovereign.

In the turmoil within the party after the 1979 election the Campaign for Labour Party Democracy which had existed since 1973, gained many influential members, including Tony Benn, and joined with other left wing groups like Militant to form the Rank and File Mobilising Committee, working as they saw it to democratise the party. Helped by a more leftward-leaning trade union movement and an increasingly left wing NEC, the reformers swept the board at the 1980 conference, adopting an electoral college for choosing the party leader and accepting the mandatory re-selection of MPs as party policy, only being very narrowly defeated on the manifesto issue.

The supremacy of the Left was ended by the disastrous defeat of 1983 and successive leaders have worked to return the Labour Party to social democratic ideas. In the process the election of the party leader has moved away from the electoral college with its union block votes and, under John Smith, settled on the principle of one-member-one-vote (OMOV). On the question of selection of MPs the mandatory aspect was largely disregarded. In 1990 it was agreed that instead of MPs having to submit themselves for re-selection at least once during the life of a parliament, the MP could remain in place unless the re-selection process were specifically requested by a majority of the constituency party.

Delegate or representative?

This argument within the Labour Party illustrates a major anomaly in the debate about representative democracy:

- If representatives disregard the wishes and interests of their constituents and merely follow their own beliefs according to Burkean principles, can this not be claimed to be undemocratic behaviour?
- If, on the other hand, representatives are bound as delegates to follow the wishes of their constituents and those wishes are most obviously expressed through the policies of a political party, then the representatives are being placed in a subordinate position in respect of their party. This is not necessarily more democratic and, indeed, may be described as undemocratic by those of the representative's constituents who do not support the representative's party.

As is so often the case in British politics, the anomaly arises because of the long, historic development of the British constitution, in which nothing is discarded, even when it has become totally irrelevant to current needs. Earlier in this book I mentioned that I had dealt at length with the historical development of the British constitution because 'patterns of government tend to be amended rather than reformed'. This is particularly true of representation which, according to constitutional theory, follows Burkean principles of *virtual representation*, evolved in the late eighteenth century long before the Reform Act extended the franchise, and even longer before the growth of the two-party system of adversarial politics. Churchill said that MPs had three loyalties: to their constituents, to their country and to their party – in that order of priority. And, constitutionally, that is still true, but practice and the power of the whipping structure of the political parties have probably reversed the order of priority.

The difference is between radicalism and conservatism, what Coxall and Robins call, 'minimalist and maximalist versions of representative democracy. For the radical, the representative is an agent of the people, a mere instructed delegate; to the conservative, while the representative must at all times listen carefully to what his constituents say, his ultimate responsibility is to his own judgement.'[5]

For much of the time there is no serious conflict over representation, despite the inherent anomaly. The problem is, however, highlighted under two conditions:

1 Where official party policy conflicts with what is believed to be majority public opinion. This is true of Europe, for example, where all parties, despite varying levels of commitment, are agreed on the necessity for Britain to remain part of the EU. The critics and Euro-sceptics on the other hand are convinced that the majority of the people are opposed to European membership.

2 On matters of conscience, over which MPs are granted a free vote and can vote exactly as they wish without pressure from the whips. Issues here are on matters like the re-introduction of capital punishment, the Sunday opening of shops, abortion, legalisation of homosexuality. On all these matters there are those who believe that MPs are out of touch with public opinion. For example, in every free vote in the House of Commons MPs have voted against capital punishment by roughly three to two, despite having a Prime Minister like Margaret Thatcher who was in favour of hanging. Yet research shows that something in the region of 60 per cent of the electorate is in favour of re-introducing hanging. This is another case, so they say, of MPs ignoring the democratic wishes of the people.

The Burkean system of representation is supported as the *status quo* by conservative democrats of all parties. Radical democrats, however, wish to move at least partially towards direct democracy, typified by:

- delegated representation;
- the mandate theory of elections;
- frequent reference to public opinion on contentious issues through referendums.

Representation as a cross-section

Philip Norton has identified four different forms of representation. Two are those we have already discussed as Burkean and delegate representation. A third, which is often overlooked, is 'a person or persons typical of a particular class or group of persons . . . as . . . when opinion pollsters identify a representative sample . . . in which members reflected proportionately the socio-economic and other characteristics of the population as a whole'.[6] Underlying this view is the belief that a problem has to be understood to be solved and therefore that representatives need to share the problems of their constituents before they can do anything about them. By inference then, the membership of an assembly should reflect in its make-up the demographic profile of the society which it serves as council or parliament. This form of representation is sometimes known as *microcosmic representation* because a parliament so formed acts as a microcosm of the nation.

Any consideration of the make-up of the House of Commons will show that on a national rather than local level, our electoral system produces an assembly that is very far from being a microcosm of British society. In the 1992 election only three MPs fell outside the age range of thirty to seventy, and two-thirds of all MPs were aged between forty and sixty. Nearly half were privately educated, with 62 per cent of Conservative MPs having been to public schools, while a good two-thirds of all MPs are university graduates, half of those graduates of Oxford or Cambridge. Among MPs of both main parties there is a heavy preponderance of lawyers (13 per cent), teachers and lecturers (16 per cent), while 20 per cent are businessmen, the vast majority of whom are Conservatives. Despite the fact that something like 5.5 per cent of the British population belong to ethnic minorities, they are represented by no more than six MPs from ethnic communities, less than 1 per cent of the whole. Although, as a rule, local and county councils are slightly more representative of their constituent populations, the profile of the average MP reveals someone who is overwhelmingly a white, middle-aged, middle-class university graduate. He is also, almost certainly, male.[7]

There is no doubt that women form the most seriously underrepresented group in British politics, only 171 women having been elected to the Commons since women were first admitted in 1918. Women form 52 per cent of the population but, of the MPs elected in the 1992 general election, only 9.2 per cent were women, representing 60 of the 651 members: even the five women added later, as a result of by-elections, did not quite take the figures to 10 per cent, although the 1992 statistics did show the highest proportion of women ever elected to Westminster at one general election; and a great improvement on the performance of women in recent years, even during – perhaps especially during – the Thatcher governments. It is ironic that the 1979 general election, which saw the first woman prime minister take office, also saw a mere nineteen women MPs elected, the lowest female representation since 1951.

When it comes to the representation of women in government the male dominance of national politics is even more apparent since only forty-five women have become ministers in any government since women first entered the Commons in 1919. A report of the European Commission on 7 September 1993 showed that the United Kingdom had one of the worst records for the representation of women in the whole of the EU. Britain's 9 per cent compared very unfavourably with 33 per cent in Denmark, or 22 per cent in the Netherlands.[8]

Many reasons have been advanced to explain the failure of women to gain adequate representation in parliament:
- Women are socialised not to be assertive. While the characteristics of politicians are thought to be aggression, ambition and

self-confidence, these are seen as masculine rather than feminine characteristics.

- There is an in-built male chauvinism which suggests that women are not really up to the job. Women occupy a different sphere to men; they are mothers and carers, not decision-makers or administrators, and are too emotional for rational political thought. The running joke on the television programme, *Spitting Image*, suggesting that Margaret Thatcher was a man in drag, only reflected a deeply-held belief that a 'proper' woman would not be capable of doing the job.

- Centuries of social conditioning means that even a successful career woman is still expected to devote herself to the children and running the home. The dual needs of family commitments and a career leave little time for political involvement as well. Most women in politics tend to become involved rather later in their lives than do the men.

- The House of Commons is like a man's club; with working hours and practices that are not suited to a woman's life-style, as well as not providing toilet and other facilities in a building where the expectation seems to be that the only women present will be secretaries and clerks.

- The most decisive factor, however, lies in the constituency committees which are called to select parliamentary candidates and these are notoriously reluctant to select women candidates for winnable seats (they are a little less reluctant in seats the party is not expected to win). This is not necessarily because of any prejudice or discrimination on the part of committee members but because they assume that the electors will not vote for a woman and therefore see no point in choosing one in the first place. On the whole, statistical evidence seems to suggest that this view is correct. For example, 'this was clearly the case in 1987 when only 14% of candidates were women, and their success rate was less than half that of men – one in eight women candidates was elected, compared to one in three men'.[9]

As Coxall and Robins say, 'If a potential woman candidate expects there to be a slim chance of being selected by the party in the first place to fight an election, and then sees her sex as an electoral liability if the candidates put forward by rival parties are men, we cannot be surprised that there are so few women in Parliament and on local councils.'[10]

It must be said that, suitably modified, the reasons why women do not get elected are equally applicable to all minority groupings whether that minority involves class, age, occupation or ethnic origin. Candidates are said to be ruled out because the need to earn a living does not leave them sufficient time to cultivate potential support in their constituencies; they are said to be insufficiently educated or to lack experience; or it is claimed that their cultural background distances them from the majority of their potential constituents. Above all, the selection committees of whatever party do not think that people in a particular constituency will vote for a working class, non-graduate or black candidate any more than they would for a woman. There was the famous instance in the 1992 election of the black lawyer, John Taylor, who was selected to fight Cheltenham for the Conservatives against the protests of many within the constituency Conservative party. The main criticism made of Taylor was that he came from an alien culture outside the constituency and while, overtly, this was said to be because he came from Birmingham and similar criticisms would have been made against a white candidate originating from that city, there is little doubt that in fact protests against his selection were racially inspired.

In considering what may be done to correct these democratic shortcomings it has to be said that the solution is often as capable of being designated undemocratic as the problem it is intended to overcome.

Positive discrimination

The question as to what to do about the under-representation of women began in 1980 with the formation outside parliament of the all-party 300 Group under the leadership of Lesley Abdela. The group had as its aim the election of a minimum 300 women

MPs to the Commons before the year 2000. Throughout the 1980s the group pursued this aim but the only apparent result was that the number of women MPs actually went down and it is now agreed that the group's original aim is no longer realisable. Many women lost faith in all-party ventures like the 300 Group and turned to attempting to influence the individual parties, as was the case of Emily's List, a group formed within the Labour Party to raise funds to support women candidates.

The Conservative Party has always been slow at addressing the issue but, finally, Emma Nicholson was made vice-chairman of the party with a special responsibility for women members and, since the 1992 election the proportion of women on the party's list of approved candidates has almost doubled. Nevertheless, when the National Conservative Women's Conference debated this matter in November 1995 it had to be stated that the Conservative parliamentary party contained only eighteen women, two of whom would be standing down at the next election, and, of the first 146 Tory candidates selected for the next general election, only fifteen are women, all but four in seats held by Labour or Liberal Democrats which the Tories seemed unlikely to win. The Liberal Democrats on the other hand have always been more favourably inclined towards women. In 1992 the party had the highest number of female candidates – 143 compared to Labour's 138 and the Conservatives' 62. Although not going as far as all-women shortlists the Liberal Democrats did introduce the requirement that each shortlist of candidates' names must contain those of at least two women.[11]

In the Labour Party, however, opinion has slowly changed in favour of the belief that, if the change was not going to take place naturally, then it would have to be forced through the compulsion of positive discrimination. This already worked in some European social democratic parties such as that of Sweden, where the Social Democrats were committed to fielding equal numbers of male and female candidates in the 1994 elections.

Under the process of reform that began under Neil Kinnock and continued under John Smith and Tony Blair, the Labour Party moved slowly towards adopting positive discrimination in favour of women. Kinnock began the process in 1989 with a quota system requiring Labour MPs to cast at least three votes for women candidates in elections to the Shadow Cabinet. The quota was raised from three to four in 1993 but this resulted in a male backlash that cost Harriet Harman her Shadow position.

However, the main aim became to increase the number of women candidates and, hopefully, MPs in parliamentary elections. Identifying the main opposition to change as being the attitude of selection committees that would not select a female candidate if they could help it, the proposal arrived at was that of imposing all-women shortlists on certain constituencies. The 1993 conference at Brighton, at which all attention was focused on the OMOV debate, also passed a resolution by which only women would be included on selection shortlists in 50 per cent of winnable constituencies and 50 per cent of seats where Labour MPs were retiring. The decision as to what constituted a 'winnable' seat and which seats would be chosen to be subject to this rule, was supposedly left to 'regional consensus meetings'. Very quickly it became apparent that accepting the policy was very far from putting it into practice. It proved very difficult to arrive at the consensus and, while agreeing to the policy in principle, very few constituencies proved willing to accept the policy as applying to them. Finally, in January 1996, a tribunal in Leeds, faced by an appeal from unsuccessful male candidates, found that the policy of all-woman lists was unlawful and the process was quietly dropped, with fourteen candidates left to select.

Those opposed to all-women shortlists argue that it is undemocratic.

- The essence of democracy is to allow the people to choose for themselves. How democratic is it if you are invited to choose anyone just as long as they are on the list presented to you by the party leadership?
- The essence of representative democracy is to choose the person who will best represent your interests; in other words you select on merit. Is it right therefore if you are told you cannot have the most meritorious candidate because he is a

man and your constituency has been designated by the party
as one to have a woman candidate?

During the 1980s the arguments over positive discrimination
were also used in the Labour Party to deal with the growing
problem of black representation. As the only part of Labour's
traditional vote to remain loyal at a time when large sections of
the working class were deserting them, the black vote became
very important to the party and a committee was formed to
examine the best way to gain and retain black partisanship for
Labour. This committee recommended the setting up of black
sections in the party; similar to the women's sections that had
existed for some time. Despite overwhelming support from the
unofficial black groups that already existed in some constituencies, the idea was rejected by the NEC and conference because
the Labour Party claims to be an integrationist society and the
setting up of black groups would suggest that there is something
'different' about people of disparate racial groups and such a
suggestion would mean an acceptance of segregation.

Another form of positive discrimination in electoral reform
was rejected outright. This was the suggestion that minorities, of
whatever kind, could be formed into separate electorates each of
which would vote for their own MPs. Those who argue for this
solution point to the example of New Zealand where the Maoris
have elected their own representatives for many years. But that
is being phased out in New Zealand and the system has too many
overtones of the South African 'separate development' known as
apartheid.

Minority representation through proportionality

Many people believe that the recipe for fairer treatment, whether
for women or for under-represented minorities, lies in some form
of proportional representation (PR). With any form of list
system, or a semi-list system like AMS, the problem of under-represented groups is easily solved by the parties making up their
quota of elected members by the requisite numbers in the category of candidate they felt to be entitled to PR. If STV were used,

the existence of multi-member constituencies would remove one of the main barriers to minority groups being represented. At the moment constituency parties are reluctant to select women or ethnic candidates when there is only one member to be elected: if you have only one chance of getting your candidate into parliament you are not going to choose any candidate whose electability is in doubt. When a party can enter two, three, four or five candidates for the same constituency they are all the more willing to take a risk on one or more of those candidates, because they have hedged their bets, as it were, with other, safer candidates.

In the previous chapter, in discussing fairness and proportionality, it was said that most proportional systems are every bit as much undemocratic as majority systems, because the power to dictate who should become MPs or councillors is taken out of the hands of the electorate and passed to the political parties. This is even more true of any form of microcosmic representation, especially if that involves the imposition of quota numbers for designated categories. What can be done to correct imbalance and unfairness, if the remedy is itself unbalanced and unfair?

Proportional power

The arguments over proportional representation, laid out in the previous chapter and this, have concentrated on the fairness of proportionality in representing the opinions and nature of the electorate. What has not been considered is the impact proportional representation would have upon proportional power, when power is defined as the ability to influence a government's legislative programme. In the previous chapter the third purpose of an electoral system was said to be effectiveness in choosing a government with a working majority. For this purpose the simple majority system of FPTP is seen as effective in that it usually produces a clear-cut winning party who can form the government. Any proportional system is less likely to produce a clear winner in that the most usual outcome is a hung parliament or council and the formation of a joint or coalition administration. In which case PR has produced an assembly that is fair and proportional in terms of the representation of interest but one that is not necessarily fair and proportional in the distribution of power.

In a recent article,[12] Ron Johnston, the Vice-Chancellor of the University of Essex, pointed out that, whenever a coalition government is formed, the small party, with which a large party must negotiate in order to construct a majority, always has the whip-hand in negotiations. In order for the small party to agree to sustain the larger party in office, the small party can demand a disproportionate number of government posts for its members and can virtually dictate the terms on which they would agree a legislative programme. As Johnston says, 'A party may get 10% of the votes cast and so be allocated 10 per cent of the seats in the House, but does it also get 10% of the political power?' The power of a political party in this situation is related to its ability to break up a coalition government by withdrawal. If party A, with 40 per cent of the seats, combines with party B, with 20 per cent of the seats, party A is twice as large as party B in terms of representation but, in the power to make or break the coalition through the inability of the other party to create a majority alone, the two are equally matched in terms of power.

Of course, as Johnston points out, this is only true where there is no separation of powers and where the executive is drawn from the legislature. In his report on electoral systems for the Labour Party, Professor Plant made it very clear that there are two different kinds of assembly:[13]

1 A *deliberative* assembly, which considers and passes legislation in pursuance of government policy, with the government as executive forming part of the legislature.
2 A *consultative* assembly, where issues are discussed and scrutinised but without their having any power over the formulation and promotion of government policy which is in the separate hands of the executive powers.

It is because of this perceived difference that the Plant Report recommended a form of proportional representation for the EP or the proposed regional assemblies which are, or would be, consultative bodies; but recommended the retention of majority voting for the Westminster parliament which is a deliberative assembly. It reinforces the point that electoral reform cannot be considered on its own but only as part of a much wider and more general constitutional reform programme involving the dispersal, devolution or redistribution of power as it is presently distributed. As has already been said, to correct a democratic deficit in one area is merely to create one in another.

Direct democracy

There has been much talk in recent years about the resurgence of direct democracy. The obvious failures of representative democracy to reflect the public's attitudes have led to an alienation from party politics and politicians on the part of the electorate, particularly the young electorate. There are two major factors in this:

1 The successive elections of 1983, 1987 and 1992 have shown that the composition of parliament, and therefore the composition of government, bears little relation to the wishes of the public. Britain has had what has been one of the most unpopular governments ever for a large section of the population. And yet that government was elected with the support of little more than a third of the electorate and there was nothing the remaining two thirds could legitimately do about it. As a result many of the electorate feel frustrated and powerless in the face of traditional party politics.

2 The behaviour of politicians, with corruption, scandal, self-interest and broken promises evident in many countries of the world, not only in Britain, has led the electorate to distrust them as true representatives of the people's interests.

In the autumn of 1993, Martin Jacques, former editor of *Marxism Today*, compiled a programme for BBC2 television in which he concluded that there is currently a crisis of political leadership and that organised politics as we have known them are in terminal decline. This is not to say that individuals do not care about political issues but simply that they now choose other ways to express their political ideas, other than through politicians and parliamentary means. Jacques pointed in particular at the Live Aid campaign headed by Bob Geldof, where a major political movement achieved considerable success because it was expressed by pop musicians rather than politicians. Increasingly, people wishing to become involved in politics choose to do so through interest groups. Whether it is protesting about the building of a new motorway or the export of veal calves, it is direct action, cutting out the intervention of an unreliable representative who ultimately will fail to represent the wishes of their constituents.

For those wishing to become involved in the political debate without having to join a political party, the growth of the computer Internet has opened up vast areas of information and discussion at both a national and international level. 'There's green activism and notices about demonstrations, on-line issues of the American radical magazine *Mother Jones*, updates on political prisoners and debates about women-only shortlists in the Labour Party.'[14] In the United States there are those who believe that future elections will largely be conducted on the Internet. And, since the Internet is inter-active, the possibility exists of the electorate sitting at home in front of their computers, receiving information and propaganda, asking questions and becoming involved in debate like a giant multi-media phone-in and, finally, by way of pressing the computer keyboard, instantly voting on legislative or policy matters. Direct democracy died out after the great days of Athens because society became too large, complex and dispersed. Modern communications and computer technology have once more shrunk society to what is known in the jargon of the age as the 'global village'. This means that literally millions of people can take part in political debates and have their votes on the matter registered almost simultaneously.

Until such time as the entire population is wired into the Internet the focus of those advocating direct democracy rests on the referendum. Only one referendum has been held throughout the whole of the United Kingdom, which was the 1975 vote on

Britain remaining within the European Community (EC), although it should be noted that this referendum was advisory only and would not have been binding on the government had it gone against them. There have been referendums in Scotland, Wales and Northern Ireland on questions of devolution or membership of the Union, while there are regular referendums in Wales on the Sunday opening of public houses; but successive governments have resisted calls for further referendums on matters as diverse as a single currency for Europe or the re-introduction of capital punishment. On these matters the politicians have argued that, since everyone has a representative in parliament and those representatives can be mandated on policy matters through election, there is no need to undermine the sovereignty of parliament by approaching the electorate direct.

There are basically three factors which are used to justify the advocacy of referendums:

1 It is argued that any major constitutional change should be put to the people. This was the argument for the 1975 referendum on Europe and for the 1979 referendums on Welsh and Scottish devolution. It is also the reason given by the Labour Party for pledges to hold referendums on possible proportional representation after the next general election. It was also the argument used by the Eurosceptics who wanted the government to hold a referendum before signing the Maastricht Treaty, just as there had been in France, Ireland and Denmark. This was ignored because the government argued that there was no constitutional change involved with Maastricht: the constitutional question had been settled when parliament passed the Act of Accession in 1973.

2 It is argued that a referendum is needed when there is cross-party policy agreement on a matter between government and Opposition, so that the issue is not in dispute at election time and therefore the electorate are not permitted the choice by which they might be said to have had their say, so as to grant or withhold their mandate for the policy.

3 The demand for a referendum is always made by advocates of a policy which is rejected by MPs in a free vote, despite what

is seen as widespread support for that policy in the public at large. The classic instance is capital punishment where successive opinion polls seem to indicate that 60 per cent of the population are in favour of hanging and yet the measure is always defeated by a free vote in the Commons. Those who argue against a referendum in this instance almost always use Burke's argument for the independence of the representative, 'Your representative owes you . . . his judgment; and he betrays . . . you, if he sacrifices it to your opinion'.[15]

In some countries such as Switzerland, and in some states within the United States, the use of referendums is institutionalised. If sufficient electors petition for a measure to be put before the public then a referendum must be held. In Switzerland any measure passed by the federal legislature, that is not classified as 'urgent' by that legislature, can be challenged by being made the subject of a referendum, if this is demanded either by a petition of 50,000 citizens or at the joint demand of eight cantonal administrations. In the United States, where they are known as 'initiatives', contentious matters can be put to the electorate in several states, the normal procedure being to put the question at issue on the ballot paper when some other state or city election is being held. The device is used quite often in California on matters as diverse as nuclear power and taxation.

There are those who would like to see a similar system introduced into Britain, reform in the direction of direct democracy being seen as preferable and more democratic than simple reform of the electoral system. It is, however, questionable as to how practical such a solution might be. The safeguards there would have to be to prevent the legislative process from grinding to a halt through frivolous challenges, would in themselves make the referendum process so complex that it would hardly be used. 'Perhaps two million signatures would be required to put the offending legislation into question on the ballot paper. That number of signatures would be difficult to obtain . . .'[16] Yet, if such a system had been in place it is probable that such potentially disastrous legislation as the poll tax or VAT on domestic fuel would have been seriously challenged before they reached the statute book and before they forced the humiliating climb-downs by the governing party.

Summary

Almost all electoral systems are democratically flawed in respect of their representation, either proportionately or micro-cosmically. Yet almost every solution that is put forward presents as many problems as answers and any change in the electoral system will inevitably lead to widespread changes in the system of representation. Almost certainly the reformer needs to start by asking what sort of representation is really wanted. Only then can an electoral system be created that matches the answer to that question.

Notes

1 B. W. Hill (ed.), *Edmund Burke on Government, Politics and Society*, Harvester Wheatsheaf, Hemel Hempstead, 1975, pages 446–7.

2 Philip Cowley and Keith Dowding, 'Electoral systems and parliamentary representation', *Politics Review*, September 1994, page 20.

3 Definitions taken from Chambers Dictionary, 1993 edition.

4 Most of the discussion about Labour Party attitudes to the mandate can be found in chapter seven (pages 160–93), Robert Garner and Richard Kelly, *British Political Parties Today*, Manchester University Press, Manchester, 1993.

5 Bill Coxall and Lynton Robins, *Contemporary British Politics* (2nd edition), Macmillan, Basingstoke, 1994, page 14.

6 Philip Norton, *The Crown*, in Bill Jones (ed.), *Politics UK* (2nd edition), Harvester Wheatsheaf, Hemel Hempstead, 1994, page 296.

7 The figures are taken from Andrew Adonis, *Parliament Today*, Manchester University Press, Manchester, 1993, page 48 and that, in turn, was largely based on D. Butler and D. Kavanagh, *The British General Election of 1992*, Macmillan, Basingstoke, 1992.

8 Reported by David McKie, *The Guardian Political Almanac 1994/5*, Fourth Estate, London, 1994, page 132.

9 Adonis, *Parliament Today*, page 55.

10 Coxall and Robins, *Contemporary British Politics*, page 422.

11 Most of the figures on female representation come from Matt Cole and Julia Howe, 'Women and politics', *Politics Review*, November 1994, pages 17–18.

12 Ron Johnston, 'Proportional representation and proportional power', *Politics Review*, April 1995, pages 28–33.

13 R. Plant, *Democracy, Representation and Elections – A Working Party Report on Electoral Systems*, The Labour Party, 1991.

14 Linda Grant, 'Everybody wants to rule the world', in Connect, the *Guardian* guide to the Internet, August 1995.

15 Hill, *Edmund Burke*, pages 446–7.

16 Anthony Batchelor, *Talking Politics*, 3:1, 1990. Quoted in Coxall and Robins, *Contemporary British Politics*, page 277.

7

Sleaze, patronage and financial advantage

An honest politician is one who, when he is bought, will stay bought.
Simon Cameron (1860)

The conception of an 'honest' politician is not altogether a simple one. The most tolerant definition is: one whose political actions are not dictated by a desire to increase his own income.
Bertrand Russell (1923)

To many people the question mark which looms over the issue of representation is a suspicion that MPs and councillors are working, not in the interests of their constituents, but in the interests of various outside bodies who are paying those same representatives very well for the privilege. It is felt that, in the last resort, representatives are not working in the interests of constituency, country or party but largely for their own personal benefit, financial and otherwise.

There are three main areas where the probity of politicians is called into account:

1 The general issue of sleaze and scandal among individual councillors and MPs, which is itself sub-divided into:
   (a) personal scandals, usually sexual in nature, that lay representatives open to charges of hypocrisy or double-standards.
   (b) the acceptance of financial rewards for representing outside interests.

2 The rewarding of ministers, civil servants and other politicians with important and lucrative offices after retirement
   from politics, always with the possible connotation that it is
   payment for services rendered.
3 The acceptance of money by political parties which also suggests a *quid pro quo* of payment for favours received.

Personal scandals

The media, particularly the tabloid press, make the most of scandals involving the personal behaviour of MPs or ministers,
which usually means their sexual peccadilloes. Ironically, it is
very seldom that MPs or ministers feel driven to take any action
as a result of their sexual practices being revealed. The number
of adulterous love affairs indulged in by David Lloyd George,
including keeping a mistress in 10 Downing Street while he was
Prime Minister, was an open secret in the 1920s, but it did not
lead to his resignation. 'His colleagues . . . protected him from
public criticism because of his value to the party in attracting
votes.'[1] Sexual misbehaviour in itself is not thought to be a
serious political issue such as would require resignation from
office: it is usually some other issue which forces that.

In 1963, a Conservative minister, John Profumo, was shown
to have had an affair with a teenage girl, Christine Keeler, and
been involved with a circle of high-class call girls. The significant
fact was that Profumo, as War Minister, had shared Keeler's bed
with a naval attaché at the Russian Embassy, Eugene Ivanov, and
fears arose that Profumo might in this way have passed on
government secrets to the Russians. Challenged in the House of
Commons, Profumo had denied his relationship with Keeler and
therefore the reason for Profumo being required to resign was
not his adultery but the fact of his having lied to Parliament as
to the extent to which he himself was a security risk.

In 1992, the Conservative minister, David Mellor, was exposed
as having had an extra-marital affair with an actress, Antonia de
Sancha. Details of the affair were plastered all over the tabloid
press, including such points as Mellor wearing the strip of

Chelsea FC while love-making. Yet it was not this which forced his resignation, but rather the suggestion that Mellor had received a number of favours, such as holidays at her villa in Spain, from Mona Bauwens, a prominent figure in the Palestinian movement.

During the first half of 1994 the government was rocked by a series of sex scandals in the tabloid press and these all helped to reinforce what was increasingly being called the 'sleaze factor' surrounding the government, and which led to the setting up of the Nolan Committee. Again, it was not the sex scandals as such which harmed the government as two other factors:

1 The rather sordid details of these affairs gave an air of decadent seediness to the Conservative government and produced the general impression that the government had grown careless and run-down through having gone on for too long. It is worth noting that the greatest incidence of sex scandals in recent history – in 1963 and 1994 – both took place at a similar point in long-serving Conservative administrations. The simple fact seems to be that a governing party that has gone on too long becomes jaded, careless and therefore accident prone, alienating the electorate as it does so. As even a good friend of the Conservatives said, 'We've had it all: sex romps with actresses, researchers, men friends and a satsuma. . . . At this rate even abolishing income tax and doubling pensions wouldn't persuade most people to vote for this lot again'.[2]

2 More importantly from the viewpoint of democratic accountability is the element of hypocrisy and double standards in governments which say one thing and do another. 'It is interesting to note that, although Labour ministers are not immune in this sphere, the Conservatives seem to make a speciality of the sex scandal . . . this can be ascribed to the Conservative Party's penchant for describing itself as the "party of the family". . . . Those who seek to seize the moral high ground are vulnerable when their own personal failings are exposed.'[3]

The Conservative government entered 1994 having announced

a 'Back to Basics' campaign in October 1993, which was to restore a sense of family values and establish the importance of public morality. Ministers made speeches preaching the virtues of family life, selecting as their target for particular blame unmarried mothers and single-parent families. Well to the fore in the campaign, making a number of speeches castigating the irresponsibility of children born outside wedlock, was a government environment minister, Tim Yeo. Yet, in January 1994, within a few months of making these speeches, Yeo was forced to admit to having recently fathered an illegitimate child on a Tory councillor from Hackney. At first Yeo resisted calls for his resignation but, a week later, further revelations in the press forced Yeo to confess that he had also fathered an illegitimate child while at university and at that point he did resign.

Over the next few weeks a junior minister, Lord Caithness, resigned because his wife had committed suicide, allegedly because of depression over his infidelities; the MP Stephen Milligan was found dead after indulging in the strange sexual practice of auto-eroticism; the Chief of the Defence Staff resigned over an affair with a Tory MP's wife; one Tory MP was accused of a homosexual affair; and at least three Tory MPs were revealed as having had heterosexual adulterous affairs. The hypocrisy of government ministers in criticising the immoralities of the British public while indulging in such practices themselves was too much for the public and the 'Back to Basics' campaign, while never officially abandoned, pretty well disappeared. Nor was it only over sexual matters that the hypocrisy of government ministers was revealed. In September 1990 the Department of the Environment launched a major campaign against drunken drivers. Leading the campaign was a junior minister, Patrick Nicholls, who, just a few hours after making a major speech on the subject, was arrested for driving while under the influence of drink. In the autumn of 1992, while the country was involved in the turmoil of 'Black Wednesday', the Chancellor of the Exchequer, Norman Lamont was involved in a rather messy dispute about some purchases from a Threshers off-licence and an invalid Access card. The implication was that the country's economy was in the hands of someone incapable of the straightforward purchase of a bottle of whisky and the handling of a credit card account.

There is a tendency to dismiss personal scandals as unimportant: matters which refer only to the politician's private life over which the public need not be concerned. Within the context of this book it could be argued that sexual and other personal misdemeanours pose no threat to democracy. On the other hand, the hypocrisy and duplicity involved in most of these affairs do have their importance: 'What causes a scandal, how it unfolds and how it is or is not resolved, reveals much about how the political world works, its set of values and its priorities'.[4] Most importantly, the aura of immorality and sleaze which surrounds cases such as those mentioned above tars all MPs with the same brush and helps contribute to the low esteem in which an alienated public is coming to regard all politicians.

Representing interests

It is accepted that MPs represent their constituents and their party but it is also legitimate that members should represent special interests. The only problem here is when the nature of the interest, or the nature of the influence brought to bear in that interest, is seen to be undemocratic or otherwise corrupt. Concern over corrupt behaviour by people involved in government, local or national, is almost as old as parliament itself. The first legislation against government misconduct was enacted in 1410 in order to prohibit government officers from receiving gifts. But that did not eradicate the problem nor did it reduce the possibilities for those in public life to abuse the system.

In the nineteenth century there was much concern over electoral corruption, as typified by Dickens' portrait of an early Victorian election through his account of Eatanswill in The Pickwick Papers – a caricature, but not unrepresentative of what went on at that time. This electoral corruption was virtually eliminated in the last years of the century, 'through three devices: the secret ballot; the transfer of jurisdiction over disputed elections from Parliament to the courts; and the Corrupt Practices Act of 1883'.[5] During the same period, the Gladstone reforms mentioned in Chapter 3 largely did away with the risk of financial corruption and the misappropriation of public funds. In much the same way, the Northcote–Trevelyan reforms of the civil service in 1854, also sponsored by Gladstone, helped to eliminate nepotism in the civil service by instituting recruitment through competitive examination rather than through aristocratic patronage.

Although these three areas of public life may have been cleansed, the question of undue influence by outside interests remains a problem as far as councillors, MPs and ministers are concerned. Since, as has been said, some, if not all, of those interests might be considered legitimate, we should look at the categories into which these interests fall.[6]

(1) *Sponsorship of an MP*. This is typified by the numerous Labour MPs who are sponsored by trade unions. Of the 271 Labour MPs elected in 1992, 143 were sponsored by unions (thirty-eight by the TGWU (Transport and General Workers' Union) alone). This practice of sponsorship began in the early years of this century when MPs were not paid and working-class Labour candidates could not have afforded to stand for parliament without the financial support of the unions. Even at the end of the century union sponsorship was still worth having for candidates, being worth between £2,000 and £3,000 in election expenses, as well as a grant of no more than £600 a year to the MP's constituency association.[7] There is no obligation on the part of a union-sponsored MP to act under union direction, that would be an offence against parliamentary privilege. But it can be assumed as only natural that any sponsored MPs would bear their union's interests in mind when speaking or voting on an issue which concerned that union.

In February 1996, as part of the process of modernising the Labour Party, and in the light of the Nolan Committee's strictures on the need to reduce the extent of paid external influences on MPs, Tony Blair announced changes in the nature of sponsorship. In a deal very carefully negotiated with the unions over six months, Blair announced that sponsorship would be transferred from the individual candidate or MP to the constituency party. This would help to eliminate the inbuilt advantage a sponsored candidate has in gaining selection by a constituency when the constituency knows that that candidate comes with guaranteed financial backing. The party leadership also hoped that the new rules might help to transfer union funds from the safe seats of party frontbenchers, as was often the case under the existing rules, and provide financial assistance for marginal seats where the extra money could probably be used to far more effect.

(2) *MPs as advisers or consultants.* Many MPs, particularly Conservatives, are given directorships or employed as advisers or consultants in a wide variety of organisations. Research for the Labour Party in 1993 showed that over half of all Conservative backbenchers were employed on a permanent basis as advisers or consultants, and most of those were advisers to more than one organisation. Organisations and firms which have a controversial public image are particularly interested in having people in parliament to advise them on possible government policy and legislation. Examples are firms dealing in tobacco, alcohol, pharmaceuticals or arms, or organisations supporting field sports, certain medical research projects or property development.

(3) *Help with research assistance.* Many commercial groups, particularly public relations companies, will offer to pay the cost of an MP's research assistant. The assistant will in fact be an employee of the public relations or lobbying organisation, who is repaid for the work done on behalf of the MP by the issue of a House of Commons pass, giving the lobbyist free access to the lobbies and bars of the Palace of Westminster. Figures quoted by Coxall and Robins suggest that over 200 MPs, from all parties, were giving House of Commons passes to research assistants who were really employed by outside organisations.[8] A typical example of the more legitimate use of this device was the Liberal Democrat MP, David Alton, an opponent of abortion who had the costs of a research assistant paid by the Society for the Protection of the Unborn Child.

(4) *Directorships and employment.* Many MPs will be offered directorships with private companies, on either an executive or non-executive level, or they will be employed in some directorial capacity on freelance terms. As is the case with sponsored MPs, those members with directorships will earn a useful supplement to their MPs' salaries in return for support in parliament when the organisation's interests are discussed or debated.

(5) *Professional lobbyists.* The growth of professional lobbying on the American model, by which a 'parliamentary consultant' will offer clients the benefits of high-level political contacts in return for a substantial fee, is a fairly recent phenomenon. The lobbying organisation will offer their clients the services of MPs willing to do various things such as host public relations dinners in exclusive parliamentary surroundings; give advice on the correct avenues through which to bring influence to bear; open up contacts with ministers and senior civil servants; or even, as we have seen, to ask questions in parliament on the client's behalf. Virtually unknown before 1980, commercial lobbying has expanded with great rapidity. There are now over sixty such organisations in Britain with a joint turnover of tens of millions of pounds. One of the largest, and most famous (or infamous), is Ian Greer Associates, with an annual turnover of £3 million, and of whom the *Guardian* said, 'The company's clients include Coca Cola, Taylor Woodrow, British Airways and Cadbury Schweppes. Mr Greer relies on parliamentary and civil service contacts he has built up over 30 years. His friendship with John Major, for example, goes back a quarter of a century. When his leadership bid was announced, Mr Greer put himself instantly at the putative PM's disposal, offering a Jaguar to ferry Mr Major around.'[9]

As has already been said, much of this work done by MPs on behalf of some special interest is quite legitimate, as long as the interest is declared openly by them beforehand. Traditionally, the attitude of the Commons towards a declaration of interests has not gone very far beyond the vague indication in Erskine May that an MP with a personal interest in a matter under debate should declare that interest before speaking in the debate.

However, Erskine May was written before the introduction of professional lobbying made activities other than the debating chamber important in the eyes of outsiders. As Professor Butler says, 'Every good cause, every business, every citizen has the right to make its voice heard in government. Often guidance is needed on where to shout in Westminster, and it is not wrong to pay for help. But lobbying must be controlled lest it distort decision-making.'[10]

Declining standards

In the early 1970s the media unearthed a web of corruption centred on the architect John Poulson. Poulson's activities were based in the north-east and involved the acquisition of property development deals through national and local government contracts. The most guilty individual, who went to prison with Poulson, was T. Dan Smith, a prominent figure in the local government circles of Newcastle, but a network of corruption involved an ever-widening circle of councillors, local government officials, civil servants and MPs. Among those forced to resign because of their association with Poulson was Reginald Maudling, Home Secretary at the time but a former Chancellor and Ted Heath's opponent in the Conservative leadership election of 1965. The scale of the corruption was so great and politicians of such seniority were involved, that the affair sent shock waves through local and national government, with considerable ramifications. The fall out from the Poulson affair included the Redcliffe–Maud report on local government rules of conduct, which was issued in 1974 and helped influence the local government reforms of that year. There was also a Royal Commission on standards in public life, led by Lord Justice Salmon, which produced new rules in parliament for the declaration of MPs' interests and the introduction of a Register of Members' Interests. The Salmon Report was largely ignored by government and was not even debated in the House of Commons. The Register, moreover, proved to be a toothless watchdog. One prominent parliamentarian, Enoch Powell, would not acknowledge the legitimacy of the Register and refused to register his interests. Since he was such an honourable man, whom no one could suspect of dubious practice, the committee on members' interests was reluctant to enforce its demands for disclosure in his case. But, unfortunately, if one MP was seen to get away with lack of disclosure without sanction, then others did not feel inclined to conform to the committee's requirements. Most MPs did register their interests, but there were always those who did not and many of those who did were very selective in what they did or did not disclose.

The 1980s, with the Thatcherite ideal of the entrepreneurial, professional politician, and with the growth of professional lobbying, led to renewed worries about the extent to which MPs might abuse their position on behalf of outside interests. Concern here culminated with the case of Michael Mates who was a member of the Defence Select Committee but who failed to inform his colleagues on that committee that he had interests in certain companies whose business was discussed in the committee: Mates was reprimanded and the *ad hoc* Select Committee on Members' Interests investigated ways in which rules governing the declaration of interest might be tightened up. Reports from the Committee in 1991 made a number of specific requirements:

- There should be a register of recognised professional lobbyists with the right to work in parliament. These companies would need to reveal the names of their clients and to identify the MPs working for them. There should also be a code of conduct preventing the payment of money to MPs and civil servants for influencing legislation.
- Members of parliamentary select committees should be forbidden to have any financial interest in companies in receipt of government contracts. Chairs of these committees would not be allowed either directorships or consultancies in these companies and, although ordinary members would be allowed to remain as consultants, they would not be allowed to be directors.

Despite these new measures it was evident that the self-regulation of MPs was not really working. A number of allegations were made against ministers and backbenchers alike, and there were a number of resignations in 1992 and 1993, although not necessarily over members' interests. Then, in July 1994, came the first in a number of damaging revelations.

(1) The *Sunday Times* printed a report that one of its reporters, posing as a businessman, had approached a number of MPs to ask if they would ask certain questions in the Commons on behalf of the 'businessman'. Most MPs had rejected the suggestion, some only after long consideration, but two Conservatives, David Tredinnick, MP for Bosworth, and Graham Riddick, MP for Colne Valley, had agreed to ask questions in return for £1,000 per question. The two MPs were found guilty of a breach of parliamentary privilege, reprimanded by the Privileges Committee and suspended from the House, Tredinnick for twenty days and Riddick for ten.[11]

(2) Three months later, the *Guardian* newspaper was given a great deal of information by Mohammed Al Fayed, owner of Harrods, who was disgruntled by the treatment he had received from the Conservative Party. Al Fayed revealed that he had made cash and other gifts to two junior ministers, Tim Smith and Neil Hamilton. Smith accepted that he was guilty at once and resigned from his position. Hamilton on the other hand tried to ride out the storm by denying everything; deriding the triviality of declaring interests by announcing on television that he wished to declare having received the gift of a biscuit and a cup of coffee from a school he was visiting in his constituency. Al Fayed then made further revelations of some thousands of pounds worth of hospitality given to Hamilton at the Paris Ritz, and the minister was forced to resign.

(3) Similar allegations about the Treasury Secretary, Jonathan Aitken, were investigated by the Cabinet Secretary, Sir Robin Butler, but were declared to be unfounded. Aitken did resign later, to prepare for a libel suit he is bringing against the *Guardian*.

The significance of this flood of allegations was that it came on top of the revelations of personal misconduct discussed earlier in this chapter. During the course of 1994 the Conservative Party was hit by no fewer than eighteen different scandals, sexual, personal, financial and concerned with abuse of members' influence. The total effect was to make the word 'sleaze' the most over-used cliché of the year in the press and contributed to a continued decline in public respect for politicians. The government response was to set up a Standing Committee on Standards in Public Life under the chairmanship of Lord Nolan.

The Nolan Committee

At the time that the Committee was set up in 1994, it was supposed that it would be a short parliamentary enquiry into the current wave of sleaze which seemed to be swamping MPs. However the committee, as it was constituted, had a wider remit, a wider membership and a considerably longer projected life than had been anticipated.[12]

The committee's frame of reference was to 'examine current concerns about standards of conduct of all holders of public office, including arrangements relating to financial and commercial activities, and make recommendations as to any changes in present arrangements which might be required to ensure the highest standards of propriety in public life'.

Those at whose activities they would be looking included: ministers, MPs, MEPs for the United Kingdom, civil servants, policy advisers, local government councillors and officials, senior officers of public bodies (including NHS bodies) and all officers of publicly-funded bodies.

The committee of ten members included five with parliamentary connections: two were serving MPs and former ministers, Tom King and Peter Shore; there was a former minister who is now a member of the House of Lords, Lord Thomson of Monifieth; Sir Clifford Boulting, a former Clerk of the Commons, could be said to be an experienced parliamentarian; and the chair was Lord Nolan, a Law Lord. The other five members were recruited from outside parliament: Sir Martin Jacomb, Chairman of the British Council; Tony King, Professor of Government at Essex University; Sir William Utting, Chair of the National

Institute for Social Work; Dame Ann Warburton, a former ambassador; and Diana Warwick, Chief Executive of the Westminster Foundation for Democracy. The composition of the committee angered many MPs who claimed that it represented a form of external policing of parliament which would be better done by self-regulation.

The Committee was appointed for an initial three years but it was made clear that it could have an indefinite future: this would not be a one-report committee as the Salmon Commission had been. Once the matters which led to its institution had been investigated and reported upon, the Committee would turn to other matters in a rolling programme of enquiry that could become a permanent feature of parliamentary life.

Among the subjects given priority by Nolan was the question of MPs' interests and the receipt by MPs of payments from outside bodies. When the committee began its work it was an open secret that members of the committee were:

> startled to discover how unwilling some MPs were to recognise any accountability in their private business lives, or to obey the resolutions of the Commons. They have been reluctant to disclose interests at all, studiously misleading about the interests they have disclosed, infantile in disclosing the pettiest benefactions to ridicule the system, and delinquent in not regarding resolutions of the House as having the same impact as laws, even though they are the law of Parliament.[13]

In Nolan's first report, published on 11 May 1995, the severest judgements were those made concerning MPs' behaviour:

- The Committee agreed that MPs should only be free to undertake any outside employment if it did not have a direct relation to their parliamentary role.
- MPs should be prohibited from working for professional lobbying companies.
- MPs should not be prohibited from working as political consultants but each consultancy should be considered individually on its merits and the size of payments made to MPs for consultancy work should be disclosed.

- It was felt that the interests listed in the Register of Members' Interests are given in too vague a fashion, and that a much clearer description of the nature of those interests must be given in future. The Register must be constantly updated and the updated version must be widely available, including access through computer networks.
- An independent Parliamentary Commissioner for Standards should be appointed, who would administer a code of conduct for MPs, handle complaints against MPs and clarify the legal position as regards the bribery of MPs.

The government accepted most of Nolan's recommendations for the executive, civil service and quangos. But, when the recommendations on parliament were discussed, on 18 May 1995, feelings ran very high. In one infamous incident, a Conservative MP, Alan Duncan, blocked Lord Nolan's way into the Commons, verbally abusing the judge, claiming that he was attempting the financial ruin of many MPs in the current parliament and stating that no able individual would even consider standing for parliament in the future if the Nolan proposals were accepted. Duncan was an extreme example but there were enough of a like mind on the Tory backbenches to make the government wary of implementing the measures as they stood. The contender for the party leadership, John Redwood, even claimed that Nolan was subverting the idea of parliamentary sovereignty. 'Those who seek to marginalise Parliament, or ignore it, or set it under external control, are out to undermine the very foundations of our settled and unwritten constitution.'[14] A committee of senior MPs was asked to look again at what Nolan was proposing for the regulation of MPs and implementation of this part of his report was delayed until the new parliamentary session.

When the issue returned to parliament at the start of the 1995/96 session, the advice from the government's advisory committee was that the Nolan proposals should be accepted in the main. But the government, under pressure from Tory backbenchers, were unwilling to make the disclosure of earnings compulsory. Despite widespread condemnation of the practice it seemed that backbench MPs, almost all of them Conservatives, were ready to make the non-disclosure of their earnings into a major matter of principle. As Hugo Young had said in July, 'A Tory MP demands the right to earn any amount of money from politics, as long as nobody knows what it is'. Rather than face them, the government backed down and omitted any such requirement to disclose from the legislation endorsing the Nolan proposals. The Labour Party, however, put down an Opposition amendment to reinstate the measure. Despite impassioned pleading from Tory MPs, including the now-hackneyed claim that such a measure could well destroy parliamentary sovereignty, the amendment was passed and accepted by the government. The disclosure of MPs' earnings is now statutory.

Jobs for the boys

It has always been easy for former ministers to acquire lucrative directorships after their retirement; since companies believe that they gain prestige from the addition of a famous name to their letterhead. 'When James Prior was sacked from the Thatcher cabinet he soon re-emerged in public view as chairman of GEC, and when Cecil Parkinson departed in disgrace in 1983 he joined the boards of no fewer than nine companies.'[15] In 1995 Douglas Hurd retired as Foreign Secretary and immediately stepped into an important directorship with the National Westminster Bank.

There is nothing constitutionally wrong about former ministers benefiting in this way; the doubts only arise when the possibility exists that the directorship is a payment for past favours received. It would be a little obvious if a Defence Secretary, with the awarding of many defence contracts in his gift, were to be offered a directorship with an arms manufacturer after his retirement. Less obvious connections are still present, and become most noted when an industry is privatised and the minister wholly or partly responsible for that privatisation is later offered a directorship with the privatised company. The minister concerned does not have to be directly responsible of course: the ministerial connection is enough. During the privatisation of the prison service considerable doubt was expressed as to the number of contracts that were being given to the private security firm, Group 4. It was noted that Norman Fowler, former government minister and currently chairman of the Conservative Party, was a director of Group 4, and the Home Affairs Select Committee, reporting in April 1994, actually said, 'Who can say that Sir Norman Fowler's presence on the board of Group 4 has no way influenced government policy on the privatisation of the prison service?'[16]

It is not only past favours that a private company can gain from a former minister. It is very useful for the company's future planning if they have knowledge of the government's recent thinking and the thrust of the government's future policy direction, both for trade and industry in general and for the company in question in particular. This has been recognised for some time insofar as it concerned the civil service. It was noted that the civil service team which handled the privatisation of British Telecom was totally dispersed very shortly afterwards; they had all been 'lured by private sector employers impressed with the relevant knowhow of the privatisation process.'[17] A code of conduct was introduced for senior civil servants by which there has to be a waiting period between the civil servant's actual retirement and his or her taking up employment within the private sector. This code of conduct was suggested as a model by the Nolan Committee when recommending rules governing ministerial conduct both while in office and after leaving government. Concerning cabinet ministers in particular, Nolan recommended a minimum of three months waiting time after leaving office before a former minister could take up an appointment. In certain, more delicate cases, the waiting time could be further extended, up to a maximum of two years.

Paying for the Party

Considerable controversy surrounds the sources from which the main political parties gain their financial support. Whether it is

Labour arguing over the sums paid to the Conservatives by big business and the commercial world, or the Conservatives responding with accusations concerning Labour's trade union links, the implication is that the parties are 'in hock' to their paymasters and must repay the donations in the form of favours granted once the party is in government.

The Conservative Party is by far the richest of the parties, spending more on the 1992 election (£10.1 million) than the Labour and Liberal Democrat Parties combined (£7.1 million and £2.1 million respectively).[18] Revenue for all the parties has been falling in recent years, partly because membership of the parties has been going down, but also because of a reluctance or inability to pay quite so much on the part of the traditional donors.

In this respect the Labour Party is worst hit because their funding has been affected by government action. Since 1913 the trade unions have each had a political fund based on contributions made by a levy on members' subscription dues, this fund being largely paid over to the Labour Party and worth around three-quarters of all Labour's election costs. In 1984, part of the anti-union legislation brought in by the Thatcher government demanded that union members would have to opt-in to pay the political levy (before this members had the levy deducted automatically unless they 'opted-out') and there had to be a ballot on political donations. The result, as was intended, was a fall in the political levy and therefore a drop in the amount which the trade unions could contribute to party funds. One cannot but wonder what the reactions would have been in the Conservative Party if big business had been obliged to ballot its shareholders before contributing to Tory funds: on the one occasion this was done (with the National Freight Corporation in 1991) 85 per cent of shareholders voted not to make a contribution. As an editorial in the *Observer* of 14 April 1996 said, 'The great insurance companies and pension funds invest the savings of millions and these savers' political opinions are bound to mirror that of the country at large – indeed they will number among the millions of voters who plan to vote against the Government. It is perverse that their own money is being used to counteract their democratic verdict.'

The contributions made by industry to the Conservatives are also falling. Contributions of £4.5 million in 1988 had fallen to £2.8 million even in the election year of 1992.[19] The drop was caused by the recession, either directly, because industry could not afford the donations in recession, or indirectly, because industry blamed the Conservative government for causing the recession in the first place. By mid-1993, with many bills outstanding from the 1992 election, the deficit in Conservative spending had increased and the party was said to have an overdraft of £19 million!

In 1993, just as concern was being expressed as to the financial difficulties of the Conservative Party, new worries were put forward on two aspects of Conservative funding:

1 The amounts contributed by foreign donors, often with rather dubious backgrounds.
2 The extent to which firms and individuals were willing to make contributions in return for recognition in the honours list.

In May 1993, the former owner of Polly Peck, Azil Nadir, jumped bail while being held on charges alleging fraud of £30 million. Nadir fled to Turkish Cyprus, refusing to return to Britain to face trial. After his flight it was revealed that Nadir was a major contributor to Tory Party funds and that in return (it was suggested) senior members of the Tory Party, such as Michael Mates, had lobbied on his behalf. On 15 September the Conservative Party was threatened with a summons that would have forced a disclosure in court of funds contributed to the party by Azil Nadir. In fact it was shown that Nadir had contributed around £440,000 to the 1992 election campaign. It was not clear as to the exact source of the money but the party promised to repay it if it were shown to be criminally or fraudulently acquired. It is almost certain that the Conservative Party had committed an offence in keeping the knowledge of this payment from creditors of Polly Peck. What other doubtful donations there might have been is not known but in the party accounts, the sources of £19 million were not identified, and, although some of this could be traced, the origin of about £14 million remained a mystery.

The aftermath of the Azil Nadir affair lifted the lid on a can of worms as it was revealed how much money was contributed to Conservative Party funds by other foreigners, not always of the highest reputation.

- Before the 1992 election foreign backers provided more than £7 million towards the Tories' election fund. Among those contributing up to £2 million were Li Ka-Shing and Rong Yiren, members of the Chinese Communist parliament.
- The Sultan of Brunei contributed heavily in return for military aid from Britain, as did the ruling families of Kuwait and Saudi Arabia.
- The former head of Nissan UK, Octav Botnar, was charged with defrauding the government of £97 million, but he paid more than £1 million towards Conservative Party funds between 1976 and 1983.
- More than £2 million was contributed by John Latsis, a Greek shipping millionaire who was a Nazi collaborator in the Second World War and who supported the Greek military junta.[20]

At the same time as there was this evidence of foreign involvement, there were further revelations that industrialists and businessmen were contributing to party funds from their business assets in return for personal honours. This was originally revealed by Azil Nadir's attempting to buy a knighthood, but research showed that, between 1979 and 1992 a total of eighteen life peerages and eighty-two knighthoods went to industrialists in seventy-six companies which, between them, contributed £17,000,000 to Tory Party funds.

The outcome of these disclosures was a decision, in 1993, that the Commons Home Affairs Select Committee should investigate the funding of political parties, with special emphasis on secret donations. When the committee reported on April 1994 the members were too deeply divided to produce a single report and there was both a majority report supported by the Conservative members and a minority report signed by Labour.

The Conservative majority saw no reason to change the situation as it exists, and in particular saw no justification for disclosure as to the source of funds. 'In a free society which cherishes the secret ballot we believe that it would be wrong to oblige the disclosure of commitment to a political party by a requirement to identify financial benefactors.'[21] As a result, the committee proposed that there should be no statutory guidelines on party funding but proposed the continuation of self-regulation through a voluntary code of practice which would make it clear that:

- Money does not buy influence or honours.
- Money obtained illegally (as with Azil Nadir's Polly Peck contributions, or Robert Maxwell's contributions to the Labour Party) would not be acceptable and, if shown to be so, would be returned.
- Very large donations given anonymously would be refused.
- Donations from foreign governments or heads of state would be refused.

The Labour minority report took a very contrary view, saying that, 'the funding of the Conservative Party is one of the great mysteries of British politics. No one, least of all most Conservatives, know where the party's money comes from'.[22] Practices identified as dubious by the minority report, and which it said should be regulated, included:

- The giving of donations should not be rewarded by access to ministers, particularly on behalf of those involved in the privatisation process. Singled out for mention were donations made to the Conservatives by Michael Green of Carlton TV, at a time when ITV franchises were up for allocation.
- No honour should be given to an industrialist whose company had donated funds to a political party within the previous five years.
- Official overseas visits by politicians, paid for by tax-payers, should not be used for fund-raising activities. During 1991, visits to Hong Kong by the Prime Minister and Foreign Secretary were used to raise money for Conservative Party funds running ultimately to some millions of pounds.
- The official residence of the Prime Minister in Downing Street should not be used as the location of fund-raising parties and

receptions. It was estimated that guests at a Number 10 goodwill dinner were persuaded to contribute £20,000 a head to party funds.

The fact that these criticisms were included in a minority report, while the majority saw no reason for change, ensured that no reforms would be made in the regulation of party funding in the foreseeable future. The damage to the democratic process is twofold:

1 There will always be a suspicion that parties receiving large sums of money from certain interest groups will be susceptible to undue influence from those interests.
2 Parties, such as the Liberal Democrats, without large scale backing, will always be disadvantaged by being comparatively under-funded, which cannot be good for a pluralist liberal democracy.

Gerrymandering

Perhaps the most extreme case of corrupt malpractice in politics is that manipulation of electoral districts and populations for party advantage which is known as 'gerrymandering'. This gets its name from Governor E. Gerry of Massachusetts who, in 1812, re-arranged the boundaries of congressional districts in his state so as to ensure the victory of his party. When someone asked whether the redrawn districts did not look as tortuously involved as a basket of snakes or salamanders, he received the reply, 'Gerrymanders more like', and the name stuck.

In the United Kingdom the most common incidence of gerrymandering was in Northern Ireland during the Stormont years, when wards and constituencies were carefully constructed so as to ensure a Unionist majority and a Catholic minority, whatever the distribution of the two communities in the country as a whole. In Great Britian there is little scope for gerrymandering in national politics, although it is far from being unknown in local government, particularly in those authorities where one party has a monopoly of power. There have been many accusations of electoral malpractice levelled against powerful Labour authorities: such as the Poulson scandals affecting Newcastle in the 1960s, the mismanagement of Liverpool under Derek Hatton in the 1980s and suspect council activities in the late John Smith's constituency of Monklands during the 1990s. These scandals, however, fail to match the excesses committed by the Conservative flagship borough of Westminster under Dame Shirley Porter in the 1980s; activities described by Labour spokesman Frank Dobson as 'the biggest financial scandal in the history of local government.'[23]

In the local elections of 1986 the Conservative majority on Westminster council was cut from twenty-six to four and the Tory head of the council, Shirley Porter, was conscious of the very real possibility that the next elections in 1990 could well result in a Labour victory. In the summer of 1986 she began to lay plans to counteract the Labour threat. Eight marginal wards were identified as being at risk and measures were put into place that would shift the balance of power in those wards in favour of the Conservatives. These measures included the sale of council properties to upwardly mobile residents who would be certain to vote Tory in gratitude; together with council grants to suitable tenants to enable them to buy their homes. At the same time, the homeless and others likely to vote Labour were encouraged or manoeuvred into moving out of Westminster into other boroughs.

In 1988 the target for sale of designated properties in Westminster was set at 500 a year, to a total of 9,660 homes so designated. As council properties fell vacant, steel shutters were put up to prevent re-occupation and it was made clear that these properties were for sale and not for re-letting, despite the length of the council's housing list. This fact was reported to John Magill, whom the Audit Commission had appointed as district auditor for Westminster, by a local doctor. Magill was already involved with Westminster after the council had sold three cemeteries in 1987 for a total of fifteen pence.

In 1989 the situation was becoming rather too obvious to be concealed. The cost of selling council homes was escalating through lost rent and rates on barred empty properties, subsidies given to incoming purchasers of property and money paid to encourage tenants to move out. Homeless people were being concentrated in two tower blocks which were later shown to be riddled with poisonous asbestos. Nearly sixty local authorities had been approached to take the homeless uprooted from Westminster. Labour revelations over the policy led to BBC's *Panorama* doing a programme about the scandal and thirteen residents submitted a formal complaint to the district auditor.

Despite the enquiry that had been instituted the local elections of 1990 proved the efficacy of the programme the councillors had insituted. The Conservative majority increased from four to thirty. An added bonus, thanks to very generous grants from the Conservative government, was that Westminster had the second lowest poll tax in the country, at £195 per head.

In 1994 a provisional report from Magill labelled the costs of the home sales policy as being 'disgraceful and unlawful'. Six councillors, including Dame Shirley, and four council officials were accused of corrupt practices and threatened with a £21.25 million surcharge. One of the accused, Michael Dutt, committed suicide but Dame Shirley herself, despite having resigned from the council, led a counter-attack against Magill, challenging his competence. To no avail. In May 1996, six years after he began his enquiry, Magill produced his final report, clearing three councillors and one official of the accusations but finding that the purpose of the six remaining individuals had been 'to manipulate the composition of the electorate so as to gain an unfair advantage for the Conservative Party'. As such the three councillors and three officials had been guilty of wilful misconduct and would be surcharged for the losses created by the sales programme, a sum likely to approach £32 million.

Summary

There is still evidence that self-interest and financial considerations can obtain influence with MPs, ministers and political parties. However, there is now a watchdog in place which has already shown that it has teeth. The Nolan Committee did not end its task with its first report but will continue its task into the indefinite future, with the result that all the abuses mentioned in this chapter may receive further and repeated attention.

Notes

1 Alan Doig, 'Scandal, politics and the media', *Politics Review*, November 1994, pages 2–6.
2 Editorial in the *Sun*, October 1994.
3 Robert Pyper, 'Individual ministerial responsibility: dissecting the doctrine', *Politics Review*, September 1994, pages 12–16.
4 Doig, 'Scandal, politics'.
5 David Butler, 'No, Minister, 109 times no', the *Guardian*, 22 October 1995, page 25.
6 The classification of MPs' interests is based on the summary produced by Bill Coxall and Lynton Robins, *Contemporary British Politics* (2nd edition), Macmillan, Basingstoke, 1995, pages 204–5.
7 Robert Garner and Richard Kelly, *British Political Parties Today*, Manchester University Press, Manchester, 1993, page 165.
8 Coxall and Robins, *Contemporary British Politics*, page 205.
9 Special feature on Ian Greer Associates, the *Guardian*, 6 October 1993.
10 Butler, in the *Guardian*, 22 October 1995.
11 Tredinnick was more harshly treated than Riddick because he actually asked the question for which he was paid £1,000. Dreamed up by the *Sunday Times* Insight team, the question involved a fictional drug called Sigthin (which is of course an anagram of Insight). As recorded in the *Guardian* on 14 July 1994, here is the actual Hansard entry: 'David Tredinnick: "To ask the Secretary of State for Health how many times the drug Sigthin has been prescribed on the National Health Service over the past three years." Dr Brian Mawhinney (health minister): "We are unaware of any drug by the name Sigthin."'
12 Details of the Nolan Committee are taken from Rob Baggott, 'Putting the squeeze on sleaze?' *Talking Politics*, Autumn 1995, pages 33–8.
13 Hugo Young, 'Time to tamper with the great untouchable', the *Guardian*, 18 July 1995.
14 The words of John Redwood, reported by Hugo Young in the *Guardian*, 18 July 1995.

15 John Kingdom, *Government and Politics in Britain*, Polity Press, Cambridge, 1991, page 272.

16 The *Guardian*, 14 April 1994, page 2.

17 Bill Jones, 'The policy making process', in Bill Jones (ed.) *Politics UK* (2nd edition), Harvester Wheatsheaf, Hemel Hempstead, 1994, page 249.

18 Figures quoted in this passage are based on Coxall and Robins, *Contemporary British Politics*, page 243.

19 Figures given in the *Guardian*, 13 March 1993.

20 David McKie, *the Guardian Political Almanac 1993/4*, Fourth Estate, London, 1993, page 29.

21 The findings of the Commons Home Affairs Select Committee reported in the *Guardian*, 14 April 1994, page 2.

22 *Ibid.*

23 Details of the Westminster affair are taken from press reports, particularly from articles by James Meikle and Dave Hill in the *Guardian* of 10 and 11 May 1996.

IV

Accountability

8

Ministerial responsibility

Look Sir Humphrey. Whatever we ask the Minister, he says it is an administrative question for you. And whatever we ask you, you say is a policy question for the Minister. How do you suggest we find out what is going on?

Jay and Lynn, *Yes, Minister* (1982)

Falsehood and delusion are allowed in no case whatsoever. But, as in the exercise of all the virtues, there is an economy of truth.

Edmond Burke (1796)

Accountability in the administration of government is based upon a delicate balance of relationships between ministers who are responsible for the formulation of policy on the one hand, and the civil servants who must execute those policies in operational terms on the other. According to the tenets of liberal pluralist democracy, the British civil service was believed traditionally to have three particular strengths:

1 *Permanence and continuity.* Governments might change with an election but the civil service would continue, ensuring stability of administration. Ministers could be appointed, knowing nothing of the department they had to run, but senior civil servants would have years of experience as professional administrators, ensuring the smooth continuity of the department's work.

2 *Political neutrality.* Civil servants do not make policy, they merely carry out decisions made by the politicians. Their

duty is to serve the government of the day, regardless of the party that is in power. As a result civil servants were not expected to play any role in party politics, nor to take any actions which could be interpreted as serving the partisan interests of either government or opposition.

3 *Anonymity.* Civil servants were never named or their identity made known to the public. This had two main objectives:

    (a) Civil servants could not be 'got at' by either bribery or threats and thereby could maintain their neutrality.

    (b) Civil servants need not fear to take decisive action nor to give frank advice to their ministers since, if civil servants are not named, they cannot be blamed if anything goes wrong.

These three characteristics were backed up by the doctrine of ministerial responsibility which stated that a minister was personally responsible for the workings of his or her department and therefore for all the actions of civil servants under his or her control. This convention whereby the minister would take the blame for any wrong actions by unnamed civil servants has been described by Kingdom as 'the very heart of democratic theory' – 'Civil servants are not themselves supposed to speak concerning their work; they must remain anonymous; and when praise or blame is apportioned, it must fall on the minister who should, in cases of serious error, resign like an officer and gentleman.'[1]

The politicisation of the civil service

Loss of neutrality

Over recent years this division between civil servants and the politicians has been eroded by a process whereby the civil service has become embroiled in political matters. For example, it has been increasingly common since the election of 1992 for Treasury civil servants to be asked to cost out possible Labour policy decisions so as to be used in Conservative Party literature as proof of Labour profligacy.

One example of a growing political involvement has been the presence of temporary and nominated civil servants as part of a prime minister's entourage. Increasingly it has been the case that new prime ministers bring with them their own advisers and press officers who are then employed as civil servants and paid by the State, even though they are carrying out a function where the dividing line between government and party interest is very blurred. Harold Wilson was the first to make much of this with his so-called 'kitchen cabinet' of Marcia Williams (now Lady Falkender) and the Mirror journalist, Joe Haines. But Margaret Thatcher went even further, with her own policy research unit under Brian Griffiths functioning as civil servants, working alongside her own influential advisers such as Sir Alfred Sherman, Alan Walters and Sir Anthony Parsons. 'Mrs Thatcher had the most extensive retinue of personal advisers of any prime minister in our history.'[2] By April 1996 the number of special advisers employed by the government had risen to thirty-eight, compared with thirteen in 1979.

More important for the politicisation and declining neutrality of the civil service than these advisers, even when masquerading as civil servants, were those genuine civil servants like Bernard Ingham and Charles Powell who were appointed to Margaret Thatcher's private office. They were personally selected by her for what she recognised as qualities sympathetic to her own beliefs and attitudes and who therefore rapidly became so closely associated with her as to appear political and ideological allies. 'He [Ingham] was seen at home and abroad to know her mind, speak for her, even on occasions exceed her in the zeal of his commitment to the cause . . . [Powell] was a man of great ability and great understanding and also, more exceptionally, had developed a close personal rapport with the leader'.[3]

In another area which affected neutrality, civil servants became increasingly reluctant to carry out instructions unquestioningly, if those instructions offended their consciences. Ever since the last war there had been public criticism of German public servants who carried out Nazi atrocities and then pleaded innocence on the grounds that they were 'only obeying orders'. Civil servants in Britain who were asked to perform tasks which offended their consciences were aware that 'only obeying orders' was no longer an acceptable excuse and therefore became less willing to participate in strategies designed to keep from the public what might be interpreted as unacceptable government behaviour. The most famous example of this was Clive Ponting, a senior civil servant, who deliberately leaked secret government papers concerning the Falklands War to Tam Dalyell, an Opposition MP, because Ponting disapproved of government policy and felt the public had the right to know about it. Ponting was prosecuted and taken to court under the accusation that his breach of secrecy was against the national interest. But Ponting argued – apparently with the agreement of the jury because he was acquitted – that his actions were not against national interests but merely against the interests of the Conservative Party. In a climate that quite regularly used the argument of national interest and the weapon of the Official Secrets Act to cover up certain government actions, the judicial ruling that a civil servant could not be considered guilty of a misdemeanour, if his or her action had merely been against a political decision that was not within the remit of the civil service, was very important.

Ponting was an exception, however, and comparatively few civil servants have proved willing to thwart the political will of their ministers. As Will Hutton says, 'if ministers are minded ruthlessly to bend the state to serve hegemonic party ambitions the Civil Service must go along with them'.[4] Hutton goes on to list the ways in which civil servants have been used to serve political ends in recent years:

- The Treasury paid part of Norman Lamont's legal costs in his dispute with a sex therapist who rented rooms in his house.
- Treasury officials costed Labour proposed spending plans, for use in Conservative literature during the 1987 and 1992 general elections.
- Senior civil servants in the Department of Health publicly campaigned for the establishment of hospital trusts.
- Officials of the Department of Employment have made more than thirty changes to the definition of unemployment, in a bid to massage government unemployment statistics.

Loss of anonymity

For some time it has ceased to be the practice of ministers to resign because of the mistakes of their civil servants but the Westland Affair, in 1985, was probably the first time that it became almost routine for ministers actually to name particular civil servants as being the ones to blame. When Leon Brittan, as Trade and Industry Secretary, deliberately leaked a letter from the Solicitor-General designed to harm the cause of Michael Heseltine, the convention would normally have required the resignation of Brittan as the minister responsible. Instead of which Brittan named the civil servant responsible for the leak, Colette Bowe. She in turn made it clear that she had only released the letter with the consent of Number 10, and named Bernard Ingham and Charles Powell as the persons giving that consent. The convention regarding the civil service was therefore repeatedly broken: not only were civil servants publicly named and blamed, but politicians who had ordered that action – and that included the Prime Minister herself – avoided resignation by claiming that the civil servants had acted on their own initiative.

The most senior civil servant has always been the Cabinet Secretary, but convention always stated that he was merely the servant of the Cabinet and, as such, did the bidding of the Prime Minister. Yet, on a number of occasions, Margaret Thatcher required her Cabinet Secretary, Sir Robert Armstrong, to face the public and reveal his involvement in government policy. The first occasion was after the Westland Affair when Armstrong was summoned to give evidence to the Defence Select Committee – the first time that a Cabinet Secretary was summoned before parliament to answer questions that, theoretically, were the responsibility of the Prime Minister. In 1988 Armstrong was made to do something else that no civil servant had been asked to do. Margaret Thatcher was obsessively trying to prevent the publication of a book, *Spycatcher*, by the former MI5 officer, Peter Wright. Wright now lived in Australia and the case for an injunction against the book was brought in the New South Wales courts. The person sent to give evidence as to why the government wished the book to be suppressed was not a government minister but the Cabinet Secretary. By forcing Armstrong to face a court of law, to defend a policy that was a political decision and to admit, as he did, paraphrasing Burke, that he had been 'economical with the truth', Margaret Thatcher destroyed even the appearance of 'anonymity' and 'neutrality' in the civil service with one action.

Changes in the civil service under Margaret Thatcher

According to Peter Hennessey in a review of the period from 1979 to 1987, 'Mrs Thatcher has already had more impact on the management of the civil service than any previous prime minister'.[5] When Margaret Thatcher came to power in 1979 she pledged to reduce the role of government, and that primarily meant cutting back on the civil service, reducing the service in both numbers and powers and bringing it far more under political control.

(1) Between 1979 and 1995, under a series of programmes initiated by the Thatcher administration, the number of civil servants was cut, from 732,000 to 524,000.[6]

(2) The appointment of senior civil servants was closely supervised by Margaret Thatcher and the Cabinet Secretary, Sir Robert Armstrong. Appointees were considered as to whether they were 'one of us'. They did not have to be Conservatives but they had to share the Prime Minister's confrontational, conviction view of policy. There was a large turnover of senior civil servants during the first two Thatcher administrations, eleven permanent secretaries being replaced between 1981 and 1983. It was noted that the new appointments were all given to men liked and admired by the Prime Minister: such as Peter Middleton, the man who drew up Margaret Thatcher's 'money back' campaign in Europe. 'The permanent secretaries of most major departments are now known as Margaret Thatcher's personal appointments, often promoted over the heads of more senior candidates.'[7]

(3) Any input into policy formulation was taken away from the civil service, the Central Review Body (the Think Tank) being abolished in 1983, and the role that was previously seen as being

the prerogative of senior civil servants was given to special policy advisers such as Sir Alan Walters, Margaret Thatcher's economic adviser, or to right wing groups like the Adam Smith Institute.

(4) In response to cases such as those of Sarah Tisdall or Clive Ponting, where civil servants had expressed doubts about carrying out policies they did not agree with, Robert Armstrong issued guidelines which stated that civil servants are responsible to their ministers and senior officials, not to Parliament or to the people. Under that ruling there was official recognition that civil servants are obliged to follow the instructions of politicians, even when those instructions are in the interest of a political party rather than in the national interest.

(5) The Civil Service Department was disbanded in 1981 and control of the civil service passed jointly to the Treasury and the Cabinet Office.

The first two terms of Thatcher government were dominated by the *Financial Management Initiative (FMI)* drawn up in 1982 by Lord Rayner of Marks and Spencer. This was essentially an exercise in streamlining the bureaucracy and the application of business efficiency methods to civil service practice. The measures introduced resulted in the saving of £1 billion in civil service spending over the five years to 1987. However, Rayner himself believed that the civil service would not be able to proceed much beyond this level of saving because administrators steeped in civil service values would fail to feel any urgency in doing so since, as public servants, they were not subject to the profit and loss constraints suffered by those working in the private sector. Opinion therefore moved from merely reforming the traditional ways of working and turned to the means by which the civil service might be introduced to market forces. This task was given to a committee headed by Sir Robin Ibbs, formerly of ICI.

The Ibbs Report into the structure and workings of the Civil Service – *Improving Management in Government: The Next Steps* – was finished in 1987 but was judged to be so sensitive that its findings were kept secret until after the 1987 general election.

The Next Steps programme was published in February 1988. The principal aim was to split up the monolithic structure of the national civil service into a number of discrete operational areas of activity, each of which would have its own management structure free of the civil service hierarchy, within which there would be a clear divorce between the policy and operational areas of competence.

The new civil service structure would consist of a small central core of government departments, comprising, with their ministers and senior civil servants, no more than 20,000 staff, but with most of the staff and work transferred to executive agencies over which ministers would have no operational control. Departments would decide on policy, fix the size of an agency's budget and monitor the agency's work but, beyond that the agencies would have considerable autonomy. Where it appeared to be required, some agencies could go beyond even this level of autonomy to become completely independent of government, or alternatively their functions or activities could be contracted out to a private supplier. Civil service activity would be measured against three possible criteria to produce three possible outcomes:

1 *The activity needs to stay with the government department* – there should be no change in the organisational structure.
2 *The activity can be best managed outside the control of either government or civil service* – the activity should be either contracted out to a private supplier (privatised) or passed to a non-governmental organisation (quango).
3 *The activity should be controlled by government but managed outside the civil service* – the activity should be passed to a government agency.

Ibbs had recommended that the chief executives of agencies should be directly accountable to parliament but Margaret Thatcher over-ruled this, although agency staff could be questioned and required to give evidence to departmental select committees, in the same way as civil servants were required to do. However, such appearances would not make agency staff accountable themselves: their function is to assist the minister who is accountable to the committee. As regards an agency dependent on a government department, ministers would be responsible for policy but would no longer be accountable for operational matters. Chief executives of the agencies are therefore answerable to the government, through the agencies themselves, but are accountable to parliament only in the most indirect fashion. According to a leader in the *Guardian*, the aim was to create a state where 'a simple majority in the House of Commons will run a federation of executive agencies and semi-autonomous departments . . . complete with an increasingly casualised workforce, as the old Civil Service disappears'.

Next Steps[8]

Although the decision to reform the civil service had been made by the Thatcher government, the Next Steps process got off to a very slow start under her leadership and it was only under John Major that any real progress was made. In the first year a mere eight agencies had been created, and these were mostly existing agencies of peripheral importance, like the Stationery Office (HMSO). But, despite criticism, the agencies were giving indications of success and the publication of a report, *Making the Most of the Next Steps*, in 1991, increased the tempo considerably.[9] By April 1996, after little more than seven years, a total of 125 Next Steps agencies had been set up, including eleven within Northern Ireland. Even parts of the civil service that were not hived off into agencies, like the Inland Revenue, were reorganised internally on the agency model. By mid-1996 68 per cent of all civil servants, nearly 400,000 in all, were working in Next Steps agencies, or were working under Next Steps conditions. The government had also announced their intended creation of a further fifty agencies, employing a total of 84,000 civil servants, which would bring the numbers of civil servants employed within the agency structure to over 450,000, more than 80 per cent of the whole.

There is no uniform standard pattern for the government

agencies created as a result of the Next Steps programme. They come in all sizes, from the very large, such as the Benefits Agency, with 65,405 staff, to the very smallest, which is the Wilton Park Conference Centre, with a mere twenty-five employees. These various agencies cover an enormous range of central government services but generally they fall very roughly into two main categories.

(1) *Mainstream agencies* which exist either to carry out the specialised functions of their respective government departments or to execute the regulatory or statutory functions of those departments. This group includes some of the largest and most important agencies such as the Benefits Agency for the Department of Social Security, the Employment Service Agency for the Department of Education and Employment, and the Prison Service for the Home Office. The three agencies mentioned above are the three largest in the Next Steps programme and, as such, have not only assumed massive operational functions that were once the direct responsibility of the civil service but, in the drive for efficiency and savings, have made quite considerable changes in the numbers of staff directly employed in the ranks of the civil service, since the three agencies between them are responsible for a staff of nearly 150,000.

(2) *Specialist service agencies* which supply services either to other departments or to the public. Such agencies include bodies like the Central Office of Information, which acts as the advertising agency or press office for all government services, or the Meteorological Office. A number of these agencies are operated as what are called *trading funds*, which means:

    (a) They can operate as commercial concerns and introduce market-orientated profitable enterprises as a subsidiary to their main purpose – as in the case of the Royal Mint which not only produces notes and coins for general circulation but also produces special commemorative mint coins and medals in presentation sets for sale to numismatists and other collectors.

    (b) They are funded from income, freeing them from government control on managing their funds and capital investment, and allowing them to increase their income through marketing their services.

Whereas the civil service used to have a single hierarchical structure for all departments, with uniform national pay scales and central recruitment, the various agencies have considerable autonomy in these areas. As from April 1994, any agency with more than 2,000 staff (twenty-one different agencies) has been able to fix its own pay scales and conditions of service, and to negotiate independently with the unions; special emphasis being laid upon performance-related pay. From the start the agencies possessed the ability to recruit their own staff below the administrative level of principal, without reference to the Civil Service Establishment, and to alter their staffs' terms of service without reference to the centre.

Those at the head of the agencies, the chief executives, were originally all career civil servants, internally appointed. However, under pressure from the Treasury and Civil Service Select Committee of the House of Commons, the procedure was changed so that nearly all chief executive positions are openly advertised, both inside and outside the civil service. Over half the appointments of chief executives under open recruitment have gone to applicants from outside the civil service: quite frequently from the private sector. For example, one prominent chief executive, Derek Lewis, the controversial head of the Prison Service who was dismissed by Michael Howard, had previously held a senior position with Granada, the leisure group. Without exception, the chief executives of the agencies are paid much more than their civil service counterparts and predecessors. An example of this was again Derek Lewis, who was paid a salary of £133,280 for running the Prison Service, whereas the comparable grade in the civil service proper was worth a maximum salary of £73,000. It used to be the case that senior civil servants were criticised for being 'generalist' administrators without the skilled expertise that might be needed to run their departments: critics have pointed out that it is not necessarily progress to replace administrators who are not specialists in a particular service with industrialists or businessmen who are no more specialists in that particular service than were the bureaucrats.

The most significant aspect of the Next Steps programme is the key factor that the agencies and their chief executives are not accountable to parliament or the electorate, as government ministers and their departments used to be. This is of no particular importance when the agency is peripheral to public concerns as with the Weights and Measures Laboratory. It is, however, of major importance when public welfare is in question, as with the agencies supporting the Department of Social Security. When the Child Support Agency was proved to be so ineffective and maladroit that it was in a virtual state of collapse, questions in the House of Commons produced the response from the then Secretary of State, Peter Lilley, that 'it has nothing to do with me'. As will be seen later, much the same response was made by Michael Howard over errors and inefficiencies in the Prison Service. Members of the public who have a complaint against the administration used to be able to challenge the government minister concerned through their MP. This is no longer the case because there is no one specifically accountable for the actions of these agencies.

After Next Steps

The Citizen's Charter

The concept of a citizen's charter that would ensure the public's satisfaction with public services was the brainchild of John Major in 1990, although it was rethought and relaunched twice more, both before and after the 1992 election. Public services were encouraged to set targets of consumer satisfaction, with penalties for failure and with success rewarded by the 'charter mark of excellence'. The scheme is intended for all public services and is of particular relevance to the privatised utilities but it is well suited to the Next Steps agencies, nine of which have issued their own charters. It is, of course, a form of accountability; although a form of accountability to the consumer rather than the citizen and, as has been stated, 'the charters can hardly be spoken of in constitutional terms because, although containing statements of *legal* rights, they do not generally increase them'.[10]

Market testing

This practice was developed as the result of *Competing for Quality*, a White Paper issued in 1991. Government thinking followed the competitive tendering initiatives introduced into local government and the NHS during the 1980s and involved government departments and agencies market testing their activities to see whether those activities could be more efficiently provided by outside organisations. There was a two-fold purpose in the exercise in that, if the service could be provided more efficiently and economically by an outside contractor then that was a gain. But, even if it were decided to keep the activity in-house, the act of considering it for tender would involve a re-evaluation of the activity which might well in itself lead to that activity's more effective execution. The stated aim in 1992 was the transfer of 25 per cent of departmental work to outside bodies. In the first two rounds of market testing which ended in October 1994 some £2.1 billion worth of activities were considered; many of those activities were contracted out as a result, at the cost of 27,000 civil service positions. Critics of the market testing programme have mostly concentrated on the dramatic contraction in the civil service and the loss of jobs. Nevertheless, other fears have been expressed, including doubt about the implications for accountability. 'It is clear that so long as any firm carries out the requirements of a contract no minister will be able to interfere with the work of that firm either . . . in operating methods, or in terms of policy.'[11]

Prior options

Market testing is only one way in which the civil service is being asked to contemplate contracting-out or privatisation as part of the government's search for greater efficiency. In 1993 it was announced that Next Steps agencies would review their activ-

ities every five years and this review would require one of four
options:

1 The activity is no longer required and should be abolished.
2 There is a continuing need for the activity to be provided by
  the government agency.
3 There is a continuing need for the activity, which should be
  market tested for contracting out.
4 There is a need for the activity, but it would be more effectively delivered if it were privatised.

The government made it clear that reviews of Next Steps agencies would be announced to the public in advance, obviously
inviting the private sector to put in bids to acquire agencies,
either in part or in total.

The Office of Public Service and Science

During the formation of a new government after the 1992 election
John Major announced that there was to be a new office, the Office
of Public Services and Science (OPSS), that would not only take
over the overview of science from the old DES, but would take
charge of the Next Steps programme and such spin-offs as the
Citizen's Charter, prior options and market testing. This office was
to be the prime responsibility of the Chancellor of the Duchy of
Lancaster, thereby taking a place in the Cabinet and making reform
of the civil service part of the government's central planning.

Research in 1996,[12] however, showed that changes in the civil
service have led to a significant decline in the standards and
morale of the service:

• 92 per cent of civil servants believed that morale was much
  lower in 1996 than it had been in 1992.
• 91 per cent believed the government had gone too far in its
  privatisation of civil service functions.
• 77 per cent said they would welcome a change of government.
• 73 per cent claimed that they would not recommend the civil
  service as a career to young people today.
• Only 28 per cent of respondents believed that their jobs were
  secure.

Decline in ministerial responsibility

The public perception of the government is of the Cabinet, and most people think in terms of the government having about twenty-five members. But of course the government is much larger, with a whole layer of junior ministers beneath the more visible Secretaries of State. In all, the Major government has something like sixty-five junior ministers spread across the various departments. It was not always like this: in the Attlee government of 1945–51 there were only thirty-three junior ministers. Yet, as Hugo Young pointed out in an interesting pair of articles, a minister today is far less busy than one of fifty years ago.[13]

There is one obvious reason for an increase in the size of government: someone who is a member of the government cannot criticise it nor make trouble from the backbenches. At a time when the threat of backbench revolt is an ever-present danger, a prime minister finds it useful to have something like one third of government MPs constrained by being inside the government, while yet another third behave themselves because they are hopeful of promotion. Therefore, at a time when private industry and commerce is cutting the number of jobs in the name of efficiency ('slimming down in order to be leaner and fitter' as they used to say in the days of the Thatcher administration), the size of government itself is steadily rising. And yet, asks Young, what do ministers do these days?

The answer as to what ministers do, used to be that they ran their departments. But, after fifteen years of deliberately diminishing the role of government, there seem to be less and less departmental operations that need running, since government has withdrawn from whole areas of activity, as far as administration is concerned. Typical of this hiving off process is the opting out of schools into grant-maintained status; or NHS Trusts with self-governing hospitals and budget-holding doctors. Such changes in the bureaucracy of operation mean that ministers at the departments of Education and Health have very little left to say concerning the day-to-day running of the education and health services. Elsewhere, whole areas of public provision are in the hands of private firms and the Next Steps initiative has led to the autonomy of many civil service agencies. In early 1994 it was estimated that over 30 per cent of all public expenditure was now in the hands of autonomous agencies or quangos over whom the relevant ministers have very little control. As a former Labour minister said, 'We have the biggest government ever, the least accountable government ever, the most expensive government ever, and the most under-occupied government ever.'[14]

With operational power out of their hands there is little left for ministers to do, apart from make policy. And it becomes questionable as to whether a Social Security Secretary needs six junior ministers to help him make policy decisions. And if ministers only make policy and leave operational matters to other agencies, the question of who is accountable throws considerable doubt on the convention of ministerial responsibility. In the past, during the Attlee administration for example, convention stated that civil servants were anonymous and that a minister, being personally accountable for any act of maladministration, was expected to resign over the matter, even if the error was committed by an official, without ministerial approval. Today, with named agencies in charge of operational matters, ministers are far more likely to apportion blame rather than accept it. As Vernon Bogdanor has said, the convention of ministerial responsibility has been stood on its head and 'instead of the minister taking the blame for the misjudgment of his or her officials, his or her officials must now take the blame for the misjudgments of their minister'.[15]

Following the introduction of the Next Steps programme, important changes were made to one strand of the doctrine of ministerial responsibility. Under the old system ministers were called upon to answer questions from MPs about the workings of their departments. Whether the answers to these questions were given in writing, or verbally in the debating chamber during Question Time, both question and answer were recorded in Hansard and were therefore available for public scrutiny. Under the new system, however, chief executives of Next Steps agencies are required to answer operational questions in letters sent direct to the MP asking the question, thus by-passing the issue of ministerial responsibility and leaving no public record of the exchange. After prolonged protest the situation was amended and it is now standard procedure for the letters between chief executives and MPs to be published in a supplement to Hansard.[16]

Ministerial responsibility and resignation

It is a major convention of the unwritten British constitution that a government minister is responsible for the conduct of his or her department and indeed for the actions or inactions of the civil servants in that department. The minister is accountable for this responsibility to parliament and, in the past, it was always understood that parliament could require the resignation of a minister for failure to meet that responsibility, even if the fault was that of civil servants rather than that of the minister personally. The classical instance of this was the Crichel Down affair in the 1950s, when a Conservative minister resigned because of mistakes made by his civil servants under the previous Labour incumbent. The most recent example of a traditional resignation on a point of principle was the resignation of Lord Carrington as Foreign Secretary after the invasion of the Falkland Islands in 1982.

In fact, despite a few honourable and even anachronistic exceptions like Carrington, the willingness of ministers to resign has all but disappeared in recent years, even in the face of gross errors and manifest incompetence. Andrew Rawnsley has referred to the current attitude among politicians as 'the spirit of this political age, the guiding principle of which is that nobody resigns'.[17] On the other hand Pyper has pointed out that the willingness of ministers to resign can easily be over-stated, and has never been particularly noticeable. In 1956, S. E. Finer made the point that he could only find evidence for twenty ministerial resignations in the century since 1855.[18] It has always been the case that erring ministers have attempted to sit tight and brazen it out: what has changed is the increased seriousness of the transgressions which ministers feel can be overlooked.

- In 1992 the entire economic policy of the government collapsed on Black Wednesday, when billions of pounds were lost in an attempt to prop up a discredited system. Afterwards the Prime Minister actually wrote a note to his Chancellor affirming that he did not intend to resign and saying that he hoped the Chancellor would not do so either.
- In 1994, thanks to an admission by Alan Clarke during the Matrix Churchill trial, it emerged that four ministers were prepared to see three innocent men go to prison rather than admit to ministerial errors over the arms-for-Iraq affair. Despite the facts becoming known and widely published in the press, three of the four men continued to hold high government office while they awaited the findings of the long drawn-out Scott Enquiry.
- In the 1994 Budget the Chancellor lost a major plank of his financial legislation with the defeat of his measure to impose the higher rate of VAT on fuel bills. At one time defeat in a Budget Debate was as much an issue of confidence as a defeat in the Debate on the Queen's Speech, but on this occasion resignation was not even mentioned.
- A succession of government ministers have been exposed as indulging in conduct incompatible with high office but none of them, from David Mellor onwards, resigned of their own free will but had in effect to be squeezed out after prolonged pressure and a great deal of damaging publicity.
- Douglas Hurd admitted that he thought about resignation when found guilty of wrong-doing in the Pergau Dam Affair. But he also admitted that he did no more than think about it.

One major innovation in the 1980s was the growth of the select committee system in parliament. Departmental Select Committees have the right to summon anyone to appear before them, including ministers, and have become, as we shall see, one of the main instruments of parliamentary accountability. In any inquiry into departmental affairs not only the minister is expected to appear before the select committee, but also civil servants. The constitutional position is that these civil servants are appearing before the committee simply as a means of 'helping their ministers account to Parliament' but 'it is possible to argue that, de facto if not de jure, direct civil service accountability to Parliament is developing through these committees'.[19]

The case of the Home Secretary

Perhaps the most blatant example in recent times of a minister who would once have been expected to resign but who did not do so was Michael Howard, the Home Secretary, despite a whole series of errors and misjudgements. After a disastrous 1994 during which he had suffered an adverse judgment in the High Court and when guns and Semtex had been smuggled into a prison, Howard suffered a week in January 1995 when, on three successive days, an alleged mass murderer committed suicide in one prison, there was rioting in another prison and three dangerous criminals escaped from a third. The response of the Home Secretary was to deny that there were any grounds for his resignation. He pointed out that the operation of the prison service was in the hands of the Prison Agency while he himself was solely responsible for policy and not operational matters. As many commentators pointed out, his response was like the criminal who tells the arresting officer, 'Nothing to do with me guv. It's all down to him.'

If 1994 had been bad for the Home Secretary, 1995 was as bad, if not worse. During the course of the year he was found guilty of malpractice by the High Court and acquired the worst legal record of any government minister; he had also offended and enraged the judiciary, the police, the probation service, the prison service and virtually every other service over which he supposedly had control.

When, back in November 1994, the Master of the Rolls threw out the Home Secretary's scheme to reduce the cost of compensation for victims of crime, a scheme which had been imposed without the knowledge of parliament, the Home Secretary was judged to have 'acted unlawfully and abused his prerogative'. This was just one in a series of judgments brought against Howard as Home Secretary. In a period of just two years he had had nine judgments made against him in the British High Court, with further adverse judgments made by the European Court of Justice and the European Court of Human Rights. During 1995 two new groups sought High Court rulings against him – the Probation Officers and the Magistrates' Courts Committees.

Also during 1995, there was widespread outrage at Howard's new proposals for restricting asylum and immigration. These seemed to suggest that many refugees are falsely claiming political asylum in this country by pretending to be threatened by a regime that is in fact no threat to their liberty. What offended protesters most was that Howard was using the provisions of his bill to return dissidents to Nigeria by claiming that there was nothing wrong with the Nigerian government; and this at a time just following the execution by Nigeria of the dissident Ken Saro Wiwa. The greatest irony, however, was that under his own rules, Michael Howard's own parents – Jewish refugees from Romania – would not have been allowed to settle in this country.

At the Conservative Party Conference, Howard made a speech in which he claimed that judges were too lenient and that he intended to impose mandatory harsh sentences for repeat burglars, and automatic life sentences for sex and violent offenders. The speech was immediately attacked by the Lord Chief Justice and later still by the former Master of the Rolls, Lord Donaldson. Other of the country's senior judges joined in the criticism until most of the Bench were ranged against a Home Secretary whom they accused of abusing the country's freedoms; Howard, they said, had so reduced public confidence in the judiciary as to destroy the rule of law. Again, there was a time when the combined hostility of the country's senior judges would have been a resignation matter for a Home Secretary, but one which was ignored by Howard.

In October Michael Howard sacked Derek Lewis as Director General of the Prison Service. At once Lewis attacked Howard for improper interference in the day-to-day running of the Prison Service. Some indication of the extent of Howard's involvement was given in the Learmont Report into lapses of security in the Prison Service. According to Learmont, Howard had demanded that Lewis provide him with 1,000 documents, including 137 'full submissions' in just four months. Lewis also offered to provide evidence that the Home Secretary had intervened in internal prison disciplinary matters; even attempting to determine to which prison certain offenders should be sent. All of which seemed to run counter to claims that the Home Secretary was accountable only for policy matters and had no interest in operational issues.

The most important charge against the Home Secretary was the accusation that Howard had over-ruled Lewis in dealing with the aftermath of the Parkhurst breakout. Lewis had wanted to transfer the governor, John Marriott, to non-operational duties, pending a disciplinary hearing, but Howard had over-ruled Lewis, saying that Marriott was to be dismissed immediately. There was evidence that part of the blame for the problems at Parkhurst lay at the door of the Home Office but that Howard avoided the blame by claiming that he, as minister, was responsible only for policy decisions while the Prison Service was responsible for operational matters. Lewis continued to claim that his dismissal was wrong and this seemed to be upheld by Judge Tumim, the chief inspector of prisons, who said that the Home Secretary's distinction between policy and operations was 'bogus'.

Christmas Eve 1995 saw the retirement of John Marriott, the former governor of Parkhurst Prison, who had been removed from his post by Michael Howard the previous January. Free to speak now that he was retired, John Marriott used Radio 4's *World at One* to launch a bitter attack on the Home Secretary, accusing him of incessant meddling in prison affairs, indecisiveness and incompetent leadership. Papers were also leaked by Lewis which proved conclusively that while a disciplinary hearing into Marriott's conduct was proceeding at Parkhurst a telephone intervention by Howard had insisted on Marriott's immediate suspension: a clear case of an operational rather than a policy decision being imposed by a minister on an agency chief executive.

The Labour Party called a debate on the issue; Tony Blair was accused by the Home Secretary of 'abusing his position' by using a Labour Party platform as 'a vehicle for the spleen of a bitter man'. The strength of the criticisms against the Home Secretary was such that it was widely expected that he would be forced to resign. But in the end a lack-lustre speech by Jack Straw for the Opposition let Howard off the hook and the minister remained in office. Within two months, however, the Home Office was forced to concede that Derek Lewis had been wrongfully dismissed and to award him £125,000 in compensation. Howard continued to claim that he had done nothing wrong, although many on the Conservative benches were forced to admit that, if this judgment had been made before the debate on the issue, the Home Secretary would have been forced to resign.

The whole picture of Howard's tenure of the Home Office is a reflection of the status granted to ministerial responsibility in the 1990s. Certainly the possibility of ministerial resignation over a matter of principle seems to have gone for ever. The true nature of the relationship between government minister and government agency, as it is now understood, was captured in a statement by Derek Lewis after his dismissal, '[it] gives the ministers authority without responsibility and the agency responsibility without authority'.[20]

Conclusion

The government have presented their reforms of the civil service, which helped to eliminate the anonymity of the service, as leading to a greater openness in government through making the operational process transparent to public accountability. However, the first impressions of initiatives, such as the Next Steps programme, seem to suggest that they have significantly blurred the lines of accountability, especially in as much as they affect ministerial responsibility, and to that extent can be said to contribute to a sense of democratic deficit.

Notes

1 John Kingdom, *Government and Politics in Britain*, Polity Press, Cambridge, 1994, page 369.

2 Robert Harris, the *Observer*, 27 November 1988.

3 Hugo Young, *One of Us*, Macmillan, London, 1989, page 445.

4 Will Hutton, *The State We're In*, Jonathan Cape, London, 1995, page 35.

5 Peter Hennessey, 'Mrs Thatcher's poodle', *Contemporary Record*, Vol. 2, No. 2, 1988, page 4.

6 Figures taken from Tony Butcher, 'The civil service in the 1990s: The revolution rolls on', *Talking Politics*, Autumn 1995, page 39.

7 *The Economist*, 10 March 1984.

8 Most of the factual information contained in this section is based on two articles by Tony Butcher, 'The changing civil service', *Politics Review*, September 1995, pages 18–21; and 'The civil service in the 1990s', pages 39–43.

9 Andrew Gray and Bill Jenkins, 'The management of central government services', in Bill Jones (ed.), *Politics UK* (2nd edition), Harvester Wheatsheaf, Hemel Hempstead, 1994, page 434.

10 Bill Coxall and Lynton Robins, *Contemporary British Politics* (2nd edition), Macmillan, Basingstoke, 1995, page 473.

11 B. O'Toole, 'The British civil service in the 1990s: Are business practices really best?', *Teaching Public Administration*, Vol. 14, No. 1, 1994, page 29.

12 Research conducted by ICM/*Observer* during March 1996. 10,000 questionnaires given to members of two civil service unions, IPMS and PTC. 1,911 completed questionnaires returned, despite warnings from Sir Robin Butler, head of the civil service.

13 Hugo Young, the *Guardian*, 11 and 13 January 1994.

14 Gerald Kaufman, the *Guardian*, 30 December 1994.

15 Vernon Bogdanor, the *Guardian*, 14 June 1993.

16 Robert Pyper, 'Individual ministerial responsibility', *Politics Review*, September 1994, pages 12–16.

17 Andrew Rawnsley, the *Observer*, 8 January 1995.

18 S. E. Finer, 'The individual responsibility of ministers', *Public Administration*, Vol. 34, No. 4, 1956.

19 Pyper, 'Individual ministerial responsibility'.

20 Most of the statements concerning the relationship between Michael Howard and Derek Lewis come from an editorial in the *Guardian* of 30 March 1996 – the morning after Lewis was awarded a quarter of a million pounds for wrongful dismissal.

9

Scrutiny, probity and secrecy

It is damaging to the public interest to have any decision-making
process exposed.
        Andrew Leithead, assistant Treasury solicitor (Scott inquiry)

Our first duty is to our Minister, not the general public interest. We
are trained to tell a half truth or quarter truth to MPs which often
gives an absolutely false impression. As long as we don't tell a
downright lie, that is perfectly acceptable, indeed desirable.
    Senior civil servant, commenting on the Scott Report, February
                                                                1996

If ministers are to be held accountable and responsible for their
actions then there have to be procedures in place which will
maintain scrutiny of those actions, with the mechanisms also
present by which an offending minister can be called to account.
As has already been outlined there are channels in parliament
through which MPs can question ministers but as a means of
controlling the executive it is flawed by the impotence of an individual MP when faced with an intransigent minister. If the minister is reluctant to face the situation there is very little the
individual member can do, either to extract an explanation or to
force the executive to make amends. And, if the individual MP
fails, the only course available for an individual or group is to
challenge the government through the courts or the constitutional device of the ombudsman. If those challenging the
government have more influence – if they have the support of

the Opposition, a major pressure group or the media, for example – then it may be that they can force an examination of the issue by a parliamentary select committee or a public enquiry.

The ombudsman

The term 'ombudsman' is Swedish and literally means 'a grievance man'. Originating in the Scandinavian countries, and Sweden and Denmark in particular, the ombudsman was instituted as a sort of 'tribune of the people' to whom individuals could take their complaints about bureaucratic mistakes or the errors of government. These complaints the ombudsman would then investigate in a judicial sense; seeking redress if the administration was found to be at fault.

Demand for the creation of such a post in Britain came in a report published in 1961 by the legal group Justice.[1] This called for the introduction of an independent judicial figure who could deal with errors and faults in government bureaucracy. The suggestion was much resented by senior civil servants and constitutional lawyers who saw the creation of such a post as subverting the twin planks which underpin the constitution – the supremacy of parliament and ministerial responsibility. The idea found no favour with the Conservative government and the report was shelved. It re-emerged, however, under Wilson's Labour government and, in 1967, the post of Parliamentary Commissioner for Administration (PCA) was created; the PCA, or ombudsman, being assisted by a staff of between sixty and ninety civil servants and supervised by a nine-member select committee. The ombudsman himself (there have not as yet been any women appointed to the position) is appointed by the Prime Minister with the advice of the Lord Chancellor and, since 1977, in consultation with the PCA Committee.

According to Richard Crossman, when introducing the bill to the Commons in 1967, the remit of the ombudsman would be to check on such bureaucratic abuses as 'bias, neglect, inattention, delay, incompetence, ineptitude, perversity, turpitude, arbitrariness, and so on'.[2] This sounded like a satisfactory remit for the ombudsman but the position, when finally defined, was considerably more restricted, both in access and jurisdiction.

The concept of an official recipient for complaints against maladministration was later extended beyond central government and ombudsmen were appointed to deal with Northern Ireland (1969), the National Health Service (1973), Local Government in England and Wales (1974) and Local Government in Scotland (1976). These later appointments have wider remits and greater powers than the PCA but they are all seen as servants of parliament rather than servants of the public. Despite many requests for such an individual there has been no mechanism put in place for appointing an ombudsman to investigate complaints against the police, nor one to scrutinise the armed services. Under the provisions of the Maastricht Treaty for European Union, an ombudsman answering to the EP was appointed as from 1994.

In 1977, Justice published the Widdicombe Report, an examination of the first ten years' operation of the PCA's office,[3] and found that the office of ombudsman as it had been established was rather less effective than had been envisaged originally, because of the restrictions that were placed on it in framing the institution.

(1) *There is limited access.* Members of the public are not allowed to approach the PCA directly themselves but must go through the medium of their constituency MP. This is not the case for the ombudsmen for either national health or local government, who can be approached directly: which presumably explains why the NHS ombudsman deals with almost double the number of complaints as the PCA, while the local government ombudsman receives something like fifteen times as many. Many people since the Widdicombe investigation have pleaded for there to be the right of direct access to the PCA, including requests for this from the PCA himself. But parliament, as represented by the controlling select committee, has resisted such a move. People do, however, continue to ignore correct procedure and write directly to the ombudsman, to the tune of around 1,000 complaints each year. The PCA gets around any

legal obstacle to dealing with these complaints by offering to find an MP willing to refer the matter on behalf of the direct complainants, if they so wish it.

(2) *There is no adequate definition of maladministration.* Despite Crossman's claims as to the wide range of complaints the PCA could deal with, there is a limited number of cases where he has jurisdiction. For example, he is not allowed to question the *nature* of decisions but only faults in *procedure*. Which means that decisions that are seen to be grossly unfair cannot be challenged if correct procedures have been followed. This in turn has meant that only about 10 per cent of complaints have been upheld, because so many complaints are judged not to come within the PCA's remit.

(3) *The ombudsman has limited jurisdiction.*

- The PCA must not deal with any matter which might more easily and effectively be dealt with by a law court or tribunal.
- No investigation of the police or armed services is allowed.
- The PCA is barred from any consideration of the government's commercial or contractual undertakings.
- Only 14 per cent of quangos and other extra-governmental bodies are open to scrutiny by the ombudsman.

(4) *There is only limited autonomy.* Many of the early PCAs were former civil servants, the majority of PCA staff are currently civil servants, the department is funded by the Treasury and legal advice comes from government lawyers. This means that investigations into civil service maladministration are largely carried out by representatives of the civil service, turning the work of the ombudsman into some form of self-regulation. When a former ombudsman, Sir Edmond Compton, gave evidence to the PCA select committee he paid tribute to former civil service colleagues by suggesting that the fact that he made so few adverse judgments was indicative of the general excellent standard of British administrative procedures.

(5) *Decisions are hard to enforce.* When the PCA has concluded his investigation he reports to the MP who originally referred the matter, with a copy to the department concerned, and there the matter may well rest. There is no mechanism by which the

ombudsman can ensure that any of his recommendations are carried out. This is not true of the Northern Ireland ombudsman because there the complainant can apply to a county court for redress, if the finding is in their favour. Other than in that one case, government departments can feel free to ignore the ombudsman's decisions, except in as much as too blatant a display of indifference would bring down considerable odium onto their heads, in the form of unwelcome media attention.

Most successful complaints taken before the PCA are very minor procedural details which do very little for the image of accountability or government acceptance of responsibility. The last significant judgment of the ombudsman was the Barlow–Clowes case in 1989 where the Department of Trade and Industry (DTI) was judged to have mishandled their rules and advice on investment and the government was forced to pay out large sums in compensation to aggrieved investors. On the whole, however, complainants over government actions would be better advised to look elsewhere.

Select committees

Select committees are yet another example of parliamentary institutions with a very ancient history; being a common feature of Tudor and Stuart parliaments. The investigative select committee of today, however, owes rather more to the example of Congressional Committees in the United States, whose investigatory role became prominent in a number of notorious, televised hearings, most recently the Watergate and Irangate affairs. From the 1960s onward there was a feeling that those faults of the British parliamentary system that can be ascribed to the secrecy with which government surrounds itself could be dispersed, if only Britain possessed investigative bodies of a similar type. It was particularly felt that opposition and backbench MPs were at a distinct disadvantage in countering the government, because they lacked that vital information which the government kept concealed from them. The need was felt for a system of committees which could examine government actions with the force and authority of a court of law and with the ability to demand the production of evidence and witnesses.

Yet there is sufficient difference between the British and American systems as to make it doubtful that the American committee system could be transferred to Britain without a wide-ranging reform of British constitutional conventions. 'Congress is set within a constitutional separation of powers backed by a written constitution, whereas in Britain the Cabinet and Prime Minister are the dominant members of the House from which the committees are drawn. All the formidable powers of government to control Parliament can be used to limit its committees.'[4]

Although committees such as the all-important PAC, discussed at length in Chapter 3, have survived from the nineteenth century, the modern departmental select committee system really only dates from the 1960s. As Leader of the House in Wilson's government of 1966, Richard Crossman used the establishment of departmental select committees as he had done the introduction of an ombudsman; to act as a weapon in his proposed reforms of parliamentary procedure. Under his guidance committees were set up to examine such subjects as agriculture, education and Scottish affairs and were given powers such as the right to 'send for persons, papers and records'. Crossman's ideas were not very popular with his Labour colleagues and very little progress was made before Labour was replaced by the Conservatives in 1970.

The Heath government continued to establish select committees, the most significant being the Expenditure Committee which replaced the Estimates Committee in 1971, and was followed by committees set up to scrutinise European legislation after British entry into the EC (now EU) in 1972. The structure of the system and the *ad hoc* way in which committees were being created was proving most unsatisfactory, not to mention the way in which committees that became too intrusive for the government's liking were being scrapped. The issue was passed for examination to a Procedure Select Committee in 1976 and it was this committee which recommended the establishment of a series of investigative select committees, each of which would examine the work of an individual government department, 'with wide terms of reference, and with power to appoint specialist advisers as the committees deemed appropriate'.[5]

The Leader of the House in 1977 was Michael Foot and he disliked intensely the concept of select committees, which he saw as devaluing the importance of the debating chamber in the Commons. Nevertheless, the idea found favour with a majority of backbenchers in all parties and the introduction of departmental select committees was one of the major reforms undertaken during the early days of the Thatcher government of 1979.[6] Credit for introducing the reforms belongs to Norman St John Stevas who, as Leader of the House, succeeded in putting into place a scrutinising machinery despite the Prime Minister's dislike for much of that scrutiny. 'For a government self-consciously bent on radical change, the Stevas reforms of the House of Commons should have been a badge of seriousness. . . . Commons select committees shadowed the Whitehall departments from the start of the Thatcher years: a major innovation which ensured that a government which showed great resistance to all forms of openness and accountability was sometimes invigilated quite uncomfortably. The leader had not really wanted this. Stevas pushed it through cabinet when her mind was on larger matters in 1979'.[7]

The Stevas reforms of the select committee system were in place by June 1979, little more than a month after the general election. There was a complete shake-up, with some existing committees being abolished, while others, such as the PAC, were strengthened. The important innovation, however, was the establishment of departmental committees which had the specific aim of closely scrutinising the departments which they shadowed. Immediately, twelve of these *investigative departmental select committees* were formed; these being Agriculture, Defence, Education, Employment, Energy, Environment, Foreign Affairs, Home Affairs, Social Services, Trade and Industry, Transport and Treasury and Civil Service.

Very shortly afterwards committees for Scotland and Wales

were formed, while the Energy committee was disbanded when that department was merged with the DTI in the mid-1980s. As of the 1992 election the number of select committees had returned to sixteen, due to the formation of committees dealing with Health, National Heritage and Science and Technology. In 1994, as part of negotiations over the peace process and as a gesture towards the Unionist lobby, a Northern Ireland committee was formed; although with a different composition and a slightly different remit compared with the others.

All committees, bar that for Northern Ireland, have 11 members. The 16 regular committees therefore have a total membership of 176, provided by the parties in proportion to their representation in the House of Commons. After 1992 the distribution was 96 Conservatives, 70 Labour, 5 Liberal Democrats and 5 from the minor parties, these then being distributed between the committees in roughly the same proportions, ensuring that the government party has a majority of at least one on each committee. (The Northern Ireland committee has 13 members, of whom 5 are members of Northern Ireland parties; membership of this committee not counting towards the proportional ratio mentioned above.) Membership of the committees is very popular and there is a less than a 15 per cent turnover of members between elections.[8] Marcus Fox, chairman of the Committee of Selection in 1992, reported that, after the election, over 200 Conservative MPs had applied for the 96 places available. An unusual aspect of the selection committee is that it operates strictly according to party membership, so that members are only responsible for choosing committee members for their own party – Conservatives choosing Conservatives and Labour choosing Labour. Members are chosen for the entire parliament, not just for the session, as is the case with standing committees. Members are always backbenchers and appointment to the government or Opposition front bench is the most common reason for resignation between elections.

The two main parties divide the chairs of committees between themselves; except for the Northern Ireland committee, the chairman of which is always from one of the Northern Irish parties. The division of committees between the parties is the result of agreement between party representatives but varies according to party representation in the House, so that the 1987 division into nine Conservative and four Labour chairs became ten Conservative and six Labour after 1992. Once the party allegiance of the chairs is decided, the committee members themselves choose the chairman[9] they want from the relevant party. Chairmen of the select committees are usually experienced backbenchers and very often are people like Frank Field, Greville Janner or Sir Ivan Lawrence, who have not held office but have many years experience of parliament.

Legally speaking, the party organisations, and particularly the party whips, should have no say in the nomination of either committee members or the chairs. But in 1992 there was a row over a previously unknown rule which states that Conservatives cannot serve on the same committee for more than three parliaments. This was in fact a blatant attempt by the Conservative whips to get rid of Nicholas Winterton, who had been a strong and independently-minded chairman of the Health Committee and had repeatedly embarrassed the government. Imposition of the rule meant that the Conservatives also lost the popular Sir John Wheeler from the Home Affairs committee and critics blamed the party whips for undue interference in the affairs of the committees. However, the 'three-term rule' does not apply in the Labour party.

The politician members of the committees are helped by officials, who are civil servants from the Clerk's Department of the House of Commons; between three and six being assigned to each committee. Most committees also have one or two full-time research assistants to help with their specialisation; the assistants often being young graduates on short-term contract. Because the committees are dealing with specialised issues and politicians cannot be guaranteed to have, or be able to acquire, the expertise required in this subject area, all the committees also have specialist advisers, usually academic experts from the universities or research establishments, either called in at need on a specific enquiry or sometimes holding a watching brief for the whole life of the parliament and committee.

Powers and effectiveness of select committees

The committees were given quite wide-ranging powers, although not as great as was envisaged in the Procedure Committee's report that led to their establishment, and certainly falling far short of the powers enjoyed by the American Congressional committees on which they were supposedly modelled. Nevertheless the investigative committees had a far greater remit than the select committees which preceded them.

(1) The appointment of committees for the life of a parliament guarantees their independence since a government angered by the findings of a committee is unable to dismiss it.

(2) The choice of topics for investigation is entirely in the hands of the committee members and will be examined even if the government would like to keep the matter concealed. In this way the existence of the committees act as a deterrent to over-hasty action on the part of the government, since a minister knows that he or she may be called before a committee to justify and defend publicly his or her actions.

(3) They are free to call anyone to give evidence before them, whether from within or without parliament, and to call for documentation from any source, having legal powers to compel attendance or submission. They are thus an important agency for open government since they have access to people and information that is not available to MPs' questions on the floor of the House. This is also a way to get information from civil servants and others onto the public record since, not only are committee meetings public hearings and open to radio and television, but all the data contained in the written and oral evidence submitted and heard is published for distribution to interested parties.

(4) Being members of the same specialised committee for several years, and having the services of specialist advisers, the committee members can acquire a substantial and specialised

expertise in the area of interest that will prevent ministers and civil servants being able to pull the wool over their eyes because of the ignorance of the interrogators. The work of the select committees ensure that MPs of all parties are better informed and thus better able to challenge ministers as to their behaviour.

(5) The select committees offer an avenue for interest groups to gain access to parliament. Groups with specific interests such as agriculture or the environment know that there are parliamentary committees concerned in the close scrutiny of their particular area of interest who are able and willing to receive evidence and documentation on that matter, thus raising the public profile of the interest group in parliament and outside it. In this way there is greater access for the effective lobbying of parliament than existed previously. For example, it is far easier for a group representing rail passengers to raise their concerns with the Transport Committee than it would be to raise the matter on the floor of the House of Commons through the offices of a friendly MP.

(6) The select committees sit around a horse-shoe shaped table rather than facing each other. Therefore, despite the party allegiances of the members, sessions of the committees are not confrontational. Indeed, it sometimes seems that the loyalty of committee members to each other is greater than their loyalty to their respective parties. The aim of the committees in their investigations is to produce consensual reports which, since they are spoken of as being from 'an all-party committee' or 'cross-party group', give the committees much greater authority and can help to influence the government's policy decisions.

There is little doubt that the system of investigative select committees is an important weapon in enforcing the accountability of government ministers. Since their introduction in 1979 the committees have produced hundreds of reports and have had a moderate success, perhaps not so much in influencing government policy but certainly in amending or forcing reconsideration of a whole range of legislative or administrative issues such as defence, energy conservation, health service provision and various privatisations. The greatest impact in the long term, however, is probably the deterrent effect represented by the mere existence of the committees. As two political commentators have stated, there is 'much evidence that ministers and civil servants are influenced in policy-making by the knowledge that what they propose may well come under the scrutiny of these committees and by the very process of committee inquiries'.[10]

Shortcomings of the select committees

There are four areas in which the investigative select committees can be criticised as not having fulfilled the hopes that had been resting on them.

(1) *Inadequate resources.* The committees work on a shoe-string since the total number of staff for the fourteen committees existing in 1988 was only fifty-nine, which is about the size of the support staff for *one* US Congressional standing committee. The Procedure Committee which examined the first ten years of the system's operation in 1990 received the suggestion that the committees should increase the numbers of research staff to about four for each committee. Although all committees have the right to employ research assistants not all of them do so and most committees only manage to produce one or two reports each year because they are too heavily dependent on outside experts. It is believed that large areas of government activity evade scrutiny as a result. One Labour MP who has studied the matter believes that the committees together should employ a pool of skilled researchers, particularly those with skills such as statistics, accountancy, computer management and economic forecasting which are common skills required by all the committees in varying degrees and at varying times.[11] Yet the Procedure Committee of 1990 decided that there was no significant demand for extra resources and left things as they were.[12] Indeed, there is evidence that spending on the select committees has been reduced in real terms since 1979.

(2) *Limited powers.* The select committees are not allowed to examine legislation, which is theoretically the preserve of the

standing committees, nor are they permitted to examine expenditure and financial management of the departments. Most select committees circumvent the prohibition on their examining legislation by setting up an enquiry into a subject, such as rail privatisation, just a few weeks before the government is due to introduce controversial legislation on that issue. However, some committees, most notably the Foreign Affairs Committee, are very reluctant to appear as if they are treading on the government's toes.

Having entered on an investigation the committees can still meet with difficulties. It is not so much the difficulty of getting some people, like senior civil servants and ministers, to appear before them, as the difficulty of getting them to answer questions once they are there. The most outstanding case was that of the Maxwell brothers who were called before the Social Services Committee after the death of their father, to answer questions about the Mirror Group pension fund. Despite sitting there for the best part of a day's session both brothers claimed the right to remain silent and refused to say a word. And there was nothing the committee members could do about it. As for civil servants the situation was made very clear during attempts by the Defence Committee to investigate the behaviour of civil servants during the Westland Affair in 1985. When the Permanent Secretary of the DTI, Sir Brian Hayes, was reminded by the committee that they could demand the attendance of the civil servants in question, Hayes replied that they could get the civil servants to attend the committee but their ministers could still forbid them to say a word. Later, Sir Robert Armstrong, Cabinet Secretary and head of the civil service, went before the committee himself to tell them in even stronger terms that the civil servants in question would not appear before them at any time.

(3) *Disregard of reports.* Select committees must produce reports on their work and the government is obliged to respond to their reports, but there is no obligation for there to be any action taken as a result of these reports. Only about 25 per cent are ever debated by the Commons and even these can be disregarded by the government. It would be easy to dismiss the action

of the committees as futile but investigation by a select committee does in fact draw the public's attention to an issue and it is a counter against excessive government secrecy.

(4) *The approach of committee members.* Although long-term members of the committees can become expert in their field, not all are re-appointed with a new parliament and new members tend to be amateurs who need time before they can make a proper contribution. Because of the 'three-parliament' rule introduced by the Conservatives in 1992 to curtail the influence of Nicholas Winterton, there was a substantial removal of long-serving Conservative members after the election of that year, to be replaced by a large number of new MPs who very often had no experience of the House of Commons, let alone experience of the purpose and procedures of the select committees.

Since the select committees attempt to produce consensual reports and ignore party divisions there are accusations that select committee reports are bland and unchallenging. As was said in looking back at the first two parliaments which supported the select committee structure, 'consensus was secured at the high price of excessive blandness and marginality as committees cast around for subjects that will not be too divisive'.[13] It has to be said that since that was written the committees have shown themselves more willing to tackle partisan issues such as the pit closures of 1992 or the future of the Health Service. Reports are less likely to be bland but when, as has happened, a committee's findings are divided into majority and minority reports it is hard to regard the work of the committees being as definitive as it should be.

The amateur standing of those MPs nominated to the committees sometimes affects the quality of the work done by them. Some MPs are members less for the sake of presenting a critical and objective view of a topic than to pursue a hobby horse, or the personal bees in their bonnets, considering the evidence on a purely subjective basis. Another effect of this amateurism is on the questioning of witnesses: the majority of committee members are not lawyers and they show themselves as inexpert in the arts of questioning, missing or overlooking important points, or letting witnesses off the hook by pursuing a new line of questioning at inopportune moments.

It seems to be the general view that, for all the faults inherent in the system, of which the shortage of resources is the most serious, the departmental select committees have proved the most effective means of democratic scrutiny to have emerged in recent years although, as two prominent commentators have said, 'scrutiny . . . has improved considerably in the last decade; what remains inadequate is parliament's own ability to deploy to maximum effect the information they provide'.[14]

Ministers and the Rule of Law

The establishment of the select committee system by the Thatcher government of 1979 was an isolated act of increased accountability by an administration that often seemed to be determined to remove any form of accountability whatsoever. As Will Hutton said, 'There has not been such a determined effort, since the advent of universal suffrage to use the machinery of the British state to prosecute a particular party programme as that undertaken by the modern Conservative Party . . . There is no constitutional protection of a public interest that transcends party concerns because no conception of the public interest exists independently of what the government defines it to be.'[15] One of the disturbing features of the period after 1979 has been the number of occasions when government ministers have seemed to regard themselves as above the law and when, despite judicial decisions made against them, those ministers have appeared to ignore the law.

In 1991, a teacher from Zaire, known simply as M, sought political asylum in Britain. The Home Office decided that he had no grounds for political asylum and refused to grant him permission to stay in the country. Despite a campaign to allow M to stay, on the grounds that he faced imprisonment or death if he returned to Zaire, the Home Office disagreed and the then Home Secretary, Kenneth Baker, signed a deportation order in July

1991. M's supporters went to the High Court to seek to reverse this decision and a judge, Justice Garland, issued an injunction to prevent the deportation. However, by the time the injunction was issued, M had been taken as far as Paris. Under the terms of the injunction M should have been returned to London but Home Office officials advised Kenneth Baker that the judge had no jurisdiction in this matter, the injunction was ignored and M put onto a flight from Paris to Zaire. Once in Zaire, M disappeared – presumably into the hands of the police, as his supporters had claimed would be the case.

M's supporters took the Home Office to the High Court, claiming in vain that by ignoring the judge's injunction the Home Office was guilty of a contempt of court. But, although the High Court originally found the Home Office not guilty, the Master of the Rolls, Lord Donaldson, reversed the decision on appeal in November and found Kenneth Baker guilty of contempt. The Home Office went to the House of Lords in an attempt to have the Appeal Court's judgment overset. But the Law Lords upheld Lord Donaldson, ruling that, while they did not find Kenneth Baker personally guilty of contempt of court – so that he himself may not be punished under the law – they did find him guilty of contempt in his capacity as Home Secretary. The Home Office was made liable for all costs in the case.

This was a judgment of considerable importance; the issue being considered as the most important constitutional test case of this century. The central issue was the age-old argument as to whether the executive should be bound by the law. The government case was that injunctions cannot be granted against the Crown, in the same argument that had been used by Charles I at the time of the English Civil War. Yet one of the features of the Act of Settlement at the end of the seventeenth century showed that the definition of 'constitutional monarchy' was that the Crown undertook to govern under the rule of law and that the Crown was as subject to the law as anyone else.

In his judgment, Lord Templeton said that if the government's argument was accepted it would mean that the executive would obey the law as a matter of grace and not as a matter of necessity (in other words the government only need obey the law when it suited them). This would overturn all the gains of the seventeenth-century settlement and reverse one of the basic principles of British government, which is the equality of all under the Rule of Law.

Ministers acting illegally

In November 1994, in the Appeal Court, the Master of the Rolls threw out a scheme devised by the Home Secretary to reduce the cost to government of compensation payments for victims of crime. This scheme had been imposed by ministerial decision without the knowledge of parliament. The Home Secretary was judged to have 'acted unlawfully and abused his prerogative'. This was the second time in little more than a year that a senior government minister had been found guilty of acting illegally by the High Court. Yet, within a day, another of the principal Officers of State was also awarded an adverse judgment.

This was the culmination of unease that had been expressed about aid payments that had been made to Malaysia by Britain for building a rather suspect dam at Pergau. There were suggestions that the aid was linked to securing arms contracts for British suppliers such as GEC, and was therefore public money used to gain commercial advantage for a private firm. The allegations were investigated by two parliamentary committees, the Public Accounts Committee and the Foreign Affairs Committee.

Sir Tim Lankester, former permanent secretary of the Overseas Development Administration, told the Public Accounts Committee that he had warned that the Pergau Dam project was not really eligible for overseas aid, calling it 'an abuse of the aid programme' and 'a very bad buy'. He had been supported in this view by Lady Chalker who was his minister, but they had been over-ruled by John Major and Douglas Hurd. The Public Accounts Committee reported on 30 March 1994 and accepted that the government had had good reasons for going ahead with the deal.

A report by the Foreign Affairs Committee, led by Labour's George Foulkes and Liberal Democrat Sir David Steel, was, however, far more scathing and accused George Younger, then Defence Secretary, of forcing the deal through without inform- ing the Foreign Office of what he was doing. Margaret Thatcher, then Prime Minister, and her overseas aid minister, Chris Patten, were also criticised in the report, though not as severely as Younger. To minimise the impact of the report, it was published on 20 July 1994, when all the attention of the media was given to John Major's Cabinet re-shuffle.

The matter was taken up by a charity pressure group, the World Development Movement, who took Douglas Hurd, as Foreign Secretary, to court over the Pergau Dam affair (and three other aid projects in Indonesia, Turkey and Botswana). On 10 November 1994, the High Court delivered its decision and found that the government, in the person of Douglas Hurd, had acted illegally. According to Lord Justice Rose, the Pergau Dam project did not promote the development of the country's economy and there was therefore nothing in law to justify the use of public money. 'The project was so economically unsound,' he said, 'that there was no economic argument in favour of it.' The govern- ment was refused leave to appeal and Ben Jackson for the World Development Movement said that this shows that 'the law expects the government to use aid for development purposes, not for commercial or political reasons'.

The day following the court's decision, Douglas Hurd admit- ted that his actions had been illegal and said that he would not appeal against the judgment. Payments still due under the Pergau deal would be made from contingency funds and that amount of overseas aid pledged to Pergau would be re-allocated to legitimate aid programmes, probably in Bosnia or Rwanda. There was, however, no suggestion that Douglas Hurd, or any other minister, would resign over the matter.

The Scott Report

The most severe test of government secrecy and ministerial accountability for many years was the report by Lord Justice Sir Richard Scott, setting out the findings of his three-year enquiry into the sale of arms to Iraq. The significance of the enquiry was set out by Hugo Young:

> Whatever else Scott achieves, he will supply a unique public guide to the private, secretive, double-dealing world of unaccountable power which Whitehall created for the purpose of selling weaponry to Iraq. He will show just what ministers and officials are prepared to get up to and then either conceal or justify. He will lead many people to doubt not only whether present ministers were honest but whether the system, behind the screen of executive power, is any longer capable of integrity.[16]

The origins of the Scott Enquiry go back to 4 November 1992 when a former minister at the DTI, Alan Clark, was giving evidence in the trial of three executives from the firm of Matrix Churchill who were accused of selling war materials to Iraq. Under examination, Clark admitted that the DTI had known all along that the equipment sold by Matrix Churchill was not for peaceful purposes. Asked about the paperwork which suggested otherwise, Clark said, 'Well, it's our old friend being economical, isn't it?' – 'With the truth?' – 'With the *actualité*'. The case against the Matrix Churchill directors collapsed on 9 November 1992 and on the following day an enquiry was set up into the question of supplying arms to Iraq.[17] The remit of the enquiry went beyond the Matrix Churchill case to take in the whole question of the government's policy on arms sales during the Iran–Iraq War, and the secrecy with which the government surrounded their policy. Among a variety of lesser issues, there were four main questions to be answered:

1 Did the government break, or turn a blind eye to, the guidelines laid down by the then foreign secretary, Sir Geoffrey Howe, in 1985?

2 Were those guidelines changed in 1988 without parliament being informed?

3 Why, if the guidelines had been changed, were the directors of Matrix Churchill prosecuted for breaking those guidelines; particularly when one of the accused was known to be working for British Intelligence?

4 Why did a number of government ministers sign Public Interest Immunity Certificates to suppress evidence that was vital to the defence of the Matrix Churchill accused? And why did the attorney-general tell those ministers that it was their duty to sign when this was not the case?

The enquiry was drawn out over 3 years, during which time there were 276 witnesses delivering 430 hours of evidence, 61 witnesses being heard in public hearings and 19, including John Major and Margaret Thatcher, being heard in private sessions, the remainder giving written evidence. The enquiry requested and received 200,000 pages of official documents. At the end of all that, the report itself stretched to 1,800 pages in 4 volumes, delivered to the government on Wednesday 7 February 1996, 8 days in advance of the general release of the report. The total cost of the enquiry and report was £3 million.

During those three years there were constant impediments put into Sir Richard's way. At the start Sir Geoffrey Howe accused the enquiry as acting as 'detective, inquisitor, advocate and judge' rolled into one and wanted lawyers to represent government witnesses who could cross-examine other witnesses. Such a time-wasting move was ruled out but, in the name of fairness, Scott allowed every witness to have a list of questions in advance and the right to correct transcripts of what was said. Although the work of the enquiry was finished by the summer of 1995 there was a further delay because ministers who were criticised in the enquiry were sent copies of what was said about them and allowed to prepare replies to those criticisms. Finally, the government was allowed eight days to study the report before publication and a statement in the Commons; Robin Cook for Labour and Menzies Campbell for the Liberal Democrats were allowed three hours in a closed room to study the report on the morning of the day it was published; the rest of the Commons were able to obtain copies a mere thirty minutes before publication.

The behaviour and attitude of the government concerning the report made it very clear that they saw their main mission as being to cover up and minimise the errors made by ministers and that, as the rebel Tory MP, Richard Shepherd, put it, 'the underlying problem that Scott identifies [is] that considerations of embarassment and administrative convenience are so routinely given precedence over the public's right to information'.[18]

The report was very long and Lord Justice Scott's language, with its superfluity of double negatives, was less than transparent. This, combined with the time granted to the government for a trawl through the pages of the report for favourable quotations with which to defend their position, enabled the government to survive the initial attacks of publication day.

The Scott Report found that:

- Ministers, including William Waldegrave, repeatedly misled Parliament in breach of ministerial accountability and this failure to inform Parliament properly was 'deliberate'.
- Sir Nicholas Lyell, the Attorney-General, mishandled the Matrix Churchill case, which should never have been brought. Sir Nicholas had assured Michael Heseltine that the limited application of the Public Interest Immunity certificated would be drawn to the attention of the judge but this was not done.
- Whitehall officials and lawyers did try to prevent crucial evidence about arms sales being revealed and, although it could not be called a conspiracy, ministers did collectively conceal government policy from parliament.
- The view held by ministers that the guidelines on arms sales to Iraq had not changed but merely interpreted more flexibly, was 'not remotely tenable'.[19]

The government was attacked on all these points by the combined opposition parties and even by some of their own backbenchers. Yet the government used the obscure wording of Sir Richard Scott's report to claim that:

- William Waldegrave may be guilty of 'consistently misleading Parliament' but he did not do so with the intention to mislead.
- Sir Nicholas Lyell may be 'constitutionally guilty' of mishandling the Matrix Churchill trial, but he was not 'personally guilty'.
- Because arms-making equipment rather than actual

weapons was exported to Iraq the guidelines were not really broken but merely interpreted liberally.

Conclusion

Through their selective acceptance of the Scott Report the government escaped the full consequences of its actions. They avoided a substantive vote of confidence on the matter and, indeed, won the Commons vote on a more anodyne motion. No one resigned, the government claimed it had been exonerated and the affair was virtually forgotten within a month. Yet the media and political commentators had claimed that the Scott Enquiry and Report represented a definitive examination of the principles of parliamentary sovereignty, democratic accountability and ministerial responsibility. What it did reveal was the way in which the executive's passion for secrecy negates all three principles. The conclusion of the Scott Report states: 'Without the provision of full information it is not possible for Parliament, or for that matter the public, to hold the executive fully to account'. As the *Observer* put it, 'the survival of Mr Waldegrave and Sir Nicholas has made a mockery of accountability and, indeed, parliamentary democracy'.[20]

Notes

1 J. Whyatt, *The Citizen and the Administration*, Justice, London, 1961.
2 Richard Crossman, quoted by John Kingdom, *Government and Politics in Britain*, Polity Press, Cambridge, 1994, page 534.
3 D. Widdicombe, *Our Fettered Ombudsman*, Justice, London, 1977.
4 Kingdom, *Government and Politics*, page 301.
5 Philip Norton, chapter seventeen of *Politics UK* (2nd edition), Harvester Wheatsheaf, Hemel Hempstead, 1994, page 337.
6 Much of the information on select committees comes from two articles by Professor Philip Norton 'Select committees in the House of Commons: watchdogs or poodles?', *Politics Review*, November 1994, pages 29–33; and 'Resourcing select committees', *Talking Politics*, Autumn 1995, pages 27–32.
7 Hugo Young, *One of Us*, Macmillan, London, 1989, page 209.

8 Andrew Adonis, *Parliament Today*, Manchester University Press, Manchester, 1993, page 161.

9 There is no sexist agenda underlying my use of the term 'chairman'. As Norton points out, the chairs of all committees in parliament are referred to as 'chairmen' regardless of gender and this is how they are labelled in all official documentation.

10 J. A. G. Griffith and M. Ryle, *Parliament*, Sweet and Maxwell, London, 1989, page 520.

11 J. Garrett, *Westminster, Does Parliament Work?* Victor Gollancz, London, 1992.

12 *The Working of the Select Committee System, Second Report from the Select Committee on Procedure, Session 1989–90*, HMSO, London, 1990.

13 Gavin Drewry, *The New Select Committees* (revised edition), Clarendon, Oxford, 1989.

14 Bill Coxall and Lynton Robins, *Contemporary British Politics* (2nd edition), Macmillan, Basingstoke, 1995, page 219.

15 Will Hutton, *The State We're In*, Jonathan Cape, London, 1995, pages 31–5.

16 Hugo Young, 'Look forward in anger', the *Guardian*, 8 February 1996, page 17.

17 The sequence of events leading up to the Scott Enquiry is set out in *The Guardian Political Almanac 1993/4*, Fourth Estate, London, 1993, pages 232–4.

18 Richard Shepherd, 'The secret guardians', the *Guardian*, 28 February 1996.

19 The findings of the Scott Report are taken from Richard Norton-Taylor who has written a book and a play about the Scott Enquiry and was here writing in the *Guardian*, 26 February 1996.

20 Anthony Bevins and Polly Ghazi, 'Duplicity', the *Observer*, 18 February 1996, page 19.

10

Unelected and unaccountable

On one estimate there are over 70,000 public appointments which
now can be made at the discretion of government ministers.
Will Hutton, *The State We're In*, 1995

It is obvious from our polling, as well as from the doorstep, that the
'London Effect' is now very noticeable. The 'loony Labour left' is
taking its toll; the gays and lesbians issue is costing us dear among
the pensioners and fear of higher rates/taxes is particularly prominent in the Greater London Council area.
Patricia Hewitt, 1987

Margaret Thatcher came to power in 1979 dedicated to reducing
the power of government and 'pushing back the frontiers of the
state'. Her chief target in this was local government and regional
administration, particularly in the areas of Labour strength
such as Greater London and the metropolitan counties, and here
a diversity of elected assemblies was replaced by an even greater
diversity of unelected bodies; which may have reduced the role
of government at the periphery but, ironically, greatly increased
government power at the centre. On the eve of the 1996 local
elections a *Guardian* editorial said, 'In any thriving society, local
government will always be the bedrock of meaningful democracy and public service . . . [and yet] . . . the Conservatives have
undermined local government in a way which still shocks many
of their supporters.'[1]

In his retrospective review of the Thatcher years, Hugo Young focused on this aspect of Thatcherism to point out the anomalous effect that ideological actions on the part of government often produce results that are directly opposed to that ideology:

> Despite its protestations, the Thatcher Government was no more immune than any other from the tendency to amass all the power it could. . . . The pieties of modern Conservatism permitted ministers, above all the prime minister, to lay claim to a withdrawal of government from the business of governing. But their certainty that they were right . . . drove them to intervene in many quarters hitherto regarded as independent. Far from reducing the role of government, Margaret Thatcher made it felt wherever she regarded its superior wisdom as a blessing of which no one should be deprived.[2]

Nor was this tendency restricted to the Thatcher years. For all his claims to a greater accountability, John Major proved to be as assiduous as his predecessor in promoting opting-out, privatisation and the growth of quangos. And one trend not exactly sympathetic to democratic principles which flourished under the Major government was a greatly increased use of statutory instruments.

Statutory instruments

Statutory instruments (SIs) are a form of delegated legislation which is intended to make administration easier and more efficient. When laws are made there are many specific details that are too specialised, or too liable to change with time, for them to be written out in full in any act of parliament. But it would not be worthwhile to call parliament and go through all the stages of the full legislative process in order to clarify or change some minor detail, simply because the operation of statute law needs to adapt to changing conditions. Similarly, some event may create an emergency requiring government action on the part of the minister concerned; action so immediate that there would be no time to go through the full process needed to gain parliamentary approval. Statutory instruments are therefore the

means by which ministers can make rules or establish procedures in the shortest possible time, without wasting time by
consulting parliament beforehand.

There are three types of statutory instrument which need
some form of parliamentary supervision.

1 *General instruments.* These are for routine and non-controversial matters that are unlikely to face opposition. They are
   placed before parliament for information only and represent
   less than a hundred of the SIs issued each year.

2 *Affirmative instruments.* These are actions which require
   confirmation by parliament within a certain period – usually
   four weeks. The instrument must be debated by both houses
   and lapses if it does not receive approval within the time
   limit. *Orders in Council,* which are a special type of statutory
   instrument issued with the authority of the Privy Council,
   are usually affirmative instruments requiring parliamentary
   approval. In 1974, after the Birmingham pub bombings,
   anti-terrorist measures were brought into immediate effect
   by the Home Secretary, Roy Jenkins, by means of an Order in
   Council which only later was converted by parliament into
   the Prevention of Terrorism Act.

3 *Negative instruments.* The largest group of statutory instruments come under this heading and are the most contentious in the democratic context. A negative instrument is
   issued by a minister and automatically takes effect unless a
   motion known as *a prayer* is issued by parliament within
   forty days. In theory such instruments are legitimate in a
   democratic sense in that they can be countermanded by
   parliament. This is difficult, however, if parliament is
   unaware of the instrument in question. [3]

In 1978 – the last full year of Labour government – there were
543 statutory instruments issued. By the mid-1980s that
number had risen to an annual average of 1,900; a figure which
remained roughly constant until the 1992 election. In 1994,
however, there were 3,334 such instruments issued by the Major
government and there was a growing feeling that the government was using SIs to impose small but controversial items of

legislation on the public without having to debate the issue in a parliament in which their majority was gradually shrinking. Examples of the type of legislation involved include the privatisation of the Teachers' Pensions Agency, the de-unionisation of concerns with less than twenty employees, and the sale of municipal crematoria. To add to the Opposition's suspicions about these actions, many of the SIs concerned were issued in August when parliament was not sitting, so that MPs only heard about the measures when they had come into force and when it was already too late to debate the matter. It was a Labour MP, David Harrison, who blamed the falling Conservative majority for this growing practice. 'As its majority gets lower,' he said, 'it (the government) is doing this more and more to enact things which it knows it would have difficulty in getting past the Commons.' Of the same practice, Derek Foster, the Labour spokesman on open government, said, 'This sort of thing can undermine British democracy – particularly if it is being used as a smokescreen to smuggle through controversial bits of legislation.'[4]

The democratic nature of SIs is called into question by a number of factors:

- No specific time is made available for the Commons to debate SIs. If they are actually debated, it is usually very late at night, after the majority of MPs have gone home.
- A statutory instrument cannot be amended by either House. It can be accepted or rejected as a whole but partial acceptance, or rejection of just one clause, is not possible.
- In parliament there is a Joint Committee on Statutory Instruments, which serves both Houses and which has a sub-committee – the Commons Select Committee on Statutory Instruments. These committees exist to vet SIs but their powers are limited simply to checking that the SI complies with the original statute to which it is an instrument. If the committee feels that the SI is faulty in some way it can be reported to the House. But neither the House nor the government are required to obey the committee's recommendations.
- Since the 1980s there has been concern expressed as to the

extent to which ministers are not using SIs to enact existing policies but to create new policies that have not been approved by either House.

As statutory instruments normally deal with minor details of legislation that hardly affect the general public; and since such instruments are passed through without debate and with little exposure to the electorate, little attention is paid to them. And yet their impact on political accountability is probably far greater than the spread of unelected bodies, which does attract a great deal of attention. The growth of unelected bodies in recent years, particularly those which have replaced an entire level of local government, has great importance for the question of accountability; although it is not so much their unelected nature that is in question as a major shift in the interpretation of what is meant by accountability.

Restricting local government

At the end of the nineteenth century a system of local government was set up which gathered together, within the framework of democratically elected councils, all the *ad hoc* committees which had heretofore administered the affairs of local areas, particularly within the municipal areas – the towns and cities spawned by the Industrial Revolution. Bodies as diverse as the Poor Law Guardians, the Watch Committee and Parish School Boards, staffed by nominees through political patronage, came together as committees of county or borough councils, their affairs decided by councillors who were directly elected by the people of the area which they served. At the end of the twentieth century it is as though the wheel has come full circle as large sections of local government are removed from the control of elected representatives and given back to quangos and agencies whose members are not elected but appointed through political patronage as they were in the early nineteenth century.

Between 1870 and 1970, local government was established in the British political system as the principal means for delivering government services, such as education; the provision of which was required on a national basis, but which was thought best delivered on a local level. There are basically two reasons for this belief in the importance of local accountability:

1 Councillors who live locally are better able to know the nature of local needs than politicians and civil servants based in London.
2 Making local councils responsible for services brings accountability for administering those services efficiently much closer to the users of those services.

It was in order to supply these services more efficiently that the 1974 reorganisation of local government established a pattern of two-tier authorities, largely financed by a combination of government grants and the local property tax known as the rates. It was this pattern that successive Thatcher governments set out to break down since there was a great deal in local government which offended Thatcherite ideas:

- Two tiers of local government beneath the overall control of national government were far too many for an ideology which believed in reducing the role of government.
- Because electors use local elections as a means of protesting against national government, there were far too many councils in the hands of Opposition parties, making it possible for those responsible for delivering services to thwart national policy on the nature of those policies. For many years the comprehensive versus selective school debate formed a major bone of contention between local and national government: with Labour governments demanding comprehensivisation and Conservative councils resisting, or Conservative governments recommending the use of selective schools but being ignored by Labour councils.
- At a time when central government wanted to cut back on public spending it was felt that local government was spending far too much money. The Conservatives' venom was particularly reserved for those 'loony Left' councils who spent their money on projects of which the Conservatives disapproved such as support groups or facilities for gays, blacks, single mothers and so on.

- The Thatcherite philosophy argued that councils were trying to do things that were better dealt with by private provision. Local government should really not be concerned with running transport systems or leisure centres. Again, there was a key target represented by the in-house 'direct works' departments which the Conservative government largely saw as cosy agreements between Labour councils and the trade unions providing their workforce.

Because of these suspicions of local government held by the Thatcher administrations there was a steady erosion of local powers that could permit a prominent political scientist to say that, 'few changes in the 1980s were more dramatic than the restructuring of the local state . . . We have seen a considerable reduction in the taxing capacity of local government [and we] have also seen a narrowing of local policy autonomy.'[5] Between 1979 and 1994 there were no fewer than 200 parliamentary measures taken to curtail local government powers.

Towards abolition

In the elections of May 1981 Labour gained control of the Metropolitan Counties of Merseyside, Greater Manchester, West Midlands and West Yorkshire. Added to South Yorkshire and Tyne and Wear which they already held, this meant that Labour now controlled all the Metropolitan Counties. They also, by a narrow margin, took control of the Greater London Council (GLC). The government was already in dispute with many local authorities over demands for reductions in spending but the arrival of so many Labour-controlled authorities, mostly inclined towards the high-spending far left, led to increased confrontation.

Most of the government's resentment was directed against the GLC. Ken Livingstone, the council's left wing leader, began to speak out on matters that were not directly the concern of the GLC, such as government policies on Northern Ireland, nuclear disarmament and unemployment. The government tried to counter the activities of the GLC and other left wing councils by ridiculing their more controversial actions. Attention was focused on the policy of grants given to groups such as 'Babies against the Bomb' or 'The Southall Black Sisters'. Newspapers such as the *Daily Mail* made much of the idea that the perfect recipient of a GLC grant would be a disabled, black, lesbian, unmarried mother. Yet the campaign was not successful. The 'fair fares' policy operated by London Transport proved to be popular with Londoners and Ken Livingstone, when interviewed on television, proved to be far from 'loony' but came over as disconcertingly likeable, with a sense of humour.

Having failed to counter the Metropolitan County Councils and GLC the government decided to get rid of them. After the 1983 General Election the government produced its White Paper *Streamlining the Cities*, giving as their reasons for abolition:

- With education and other services in the hands of district councils there were very few services left to be provided by the GLC or Metropolitan Counties, which were seen as 'doing not very much for a great deal of money'.
- There was no clear division between the roles of district and county councils either in London or in the Metropolitan areas, resulting in confusion and the expensive duplication of services.
- The GLC and Metropolitan Counties were too expensive and wasteful. Between 1979 and 1983 the GLC's spending had increased by 185 per cent and the Metropolitan Counties' by 111 per cent, against what should have been an 80 per cent rise if linked to inflation. The accountants Price Waterhouse estimated that abolition would save £20 million.

In reply it was pointed out that the duties exercised by the abolished authorities would have to be passed either to the district councils or to new joint boards. In the case of the GLC for example, the council's functions were divided between a total of fifty-eight different bodies! This was the beginning of the system of quangos and other unelected bodies that has since replaced much of local government provision. Despite considerable opposition which almost led to the bill being thrown out by the House of Lords, the abolition of the GLC and Metropolitan

Counties was made law in 1985 and came into effect on 1 April 1986.

Local government finance

The Conservative government elected in 1979 was determined to cut public spending, and local authority over-spending in particular. In 1980 the Rate Support Grant was replaced by Grant Related Expenditure under which the government set targets for local authority spending and cut grants by the necessary amount. The government publicised the names of those councils it felt were wilfully over-spending and in 1981 introduced the principle of 'claw-back', whereby the government grant was reduced by 3 per cent for every 1 per cent the authority over-spent its government-fixed spending target.

Government action was partially offset by the willingness of some local authorities to raise rates to make up for cuts in government grants. In 1982 the government banned the use of a second rate, issued halfway through the year and known as supplementary rates. However, an all-out attack on the rates problem was promised in the Conservative manifesto for the 1983 general election.

The Rates Bill of December 1983 gave the government the right to decide the level of rates set by local authorities and to penalise 'over-spending' councils by reducing the grant paid to them. In 1983 eighteen councils had a limit imposed on the amount they could levy in rates. By 1986 the use of 'rate-capping' had completely replaced the setting of spending targets.

The process was never entirely successful. The government made no secret of the fact that its policy was aimed at high-spending Labour councils but the mechanism chosen was bound to affect some Conservative authorities. The government felt the electoral cost of this when the Conservative-controlled Portsmouth Council became one of two non-Labour rate-capped authorities in 1983. Soon afterwards, in a by-election for a Portsmouth constituency, a safe Conservative seat was lost to the

SDP. The government thereafter was accused of indulging in a variety of suspect devices, with special grants and transferred funds, in order to protect Conservative authorities from the effects of rate-capping.

In 1984 the rate-capped Labour authorities voted not to comply with making cuts or negotiating spending limits. They chose either not to set a rate or to use deficit budgeting under which they would set a low rate and then deliberately overspend. A total of sixteen councils got the backing of the Labour Party for this action but by April 1985 all had given in to government requests: except for Liverpool, who refused to set a rate but claimed that they would run the council on what resources they had until the money ran out and then they would suspend all services, making the work-force redundant. The whole Labour movement turned against them and the city was rescued by borrowing from Swiss banks. By March 1987, the rebel Labour councillors, under the leadership of Derek Hatton, had been surcharged, made bankrupt, lost their seats on the council and were purged from the Labour Party.

By 1987 it was clear that rate-capping would not control council spending, nor would it discriminate against high-spending Labour authorities. The government changed its approach by introducing the poll tax. It was clear from the start that the government's policy on local government finance was being dictated by an unvoiced political agenda. The government believed the flat rate tax to be ideal for local authorities, especially since so many more would be paying than had paid rates. The two political benefits were thought to be:

1 Since everyone would pay the local tax everyone would be interested in how the council conducted itself. Under the rates large numbers of people had used local services without paying for them.

2 It would make councils more accountable. If the tax was too high the local residents would be critical of the council that had set them so high and would vote them out of office. It was another attempt by the Conservative government to curb what it saw as the profligacy of certain Labour councils.

The government had intended the poll tax to work against the interests of the high-spending Labour councils but it was soon clear that Conservative constituencies were equally as hard-hit. Conservative backbenchers, especially those with small majorities, began to get nervous and there were increasing calls for the poll tax to be scrapped or changed. For example, one of the hardest hit areas was north-east Lancashire where a large proportion of the population lived in Victorian terraced housing that used to pay very low rates. In March 1991 the MP for Ribble Valley, David Waddington, was elevated to the House of Lords and a by-election held in his constituency. A large Conservative majority was turned into a huge Liberal Democrat majority. It was the final straw that convinced Conservatives that the poll tax could well lose them the next election.

While Margaret Thatcher remained Conservative leader the poll tax remained. When she was challenged for the leadership in November 1990, her challenger, Michael Heseltine, made repeal of the poll tax one of the main points of his campaign: and when John Major became leader he appointed Heseltine as Secretary of State for the Environment with special responsibility for devising an alternative to the poll tax. That alternative, the council tax, did not have the same hidden agenda as did the poll tax but by that time changes elsewhere in the provision of local government services meant that the share of public expenditure taken by local government was either reduced or under new accounting procedures. Local government was no longer a financial problem because provision had been subjected to market forces exactly as had the civil service. The democratic concern was no longer the conflict between central and local authority but the removal of local services from democratic control.[6]

The attempt to weaken local government through direct central government control over finance had failed. 'There were signs after the 1995 budgets that this had been achieved at a cost not merely to the freedom of local authorities to set their own level of taxation, but at a cost to central government, which was increasingly seen to be responsible for cuts in services.'[7]

From council to quango

During the 1980s a series of privatisations, de-regulations and transfers of power has reduced the part played by local government in the provision of local services. Some enthusiastic privatisers such as Wandsworth Borough Council have probably made the role of local government as providers redundant.

Sale of council houses

When the Conservatives took power in 1979 they introduced legislation enabling council tenants to buy their homes at advantageous prices. Some authorities protested that this diminished the housing stock available to those who could not afford to buy, but their protests were ignored. When one Labour authority, Norwich City Council, refused to sell its council houses, the government sent in a team of commissioners to enforce the law. Despite Labour's criticisms the policy proved very popular with the electorate and was a major factor in the Conservative victory in the 1983 General Election.

Privatisation of services

The provision of services such as building, street-cleaning, dustbin collection, provision of school meals and office cleaning have increasingly been contracted out to private firms. Legislation in 1988 required councils to offer contracts for such services for competitive tender. In certain instances the council's own work-force has submitted the most competitive tender and the service has continued unaltered but in many parts of the country such services have passed into private hands. Those who argue for this case claim that private contractors are more efficient and cost effective. Those who argue against would say that the private contractors are only lower in cost because they pay low wages and skimp on services. In any case, they argue, once they have got into providing local services through cheap tendering they will increase charges in the future. Further legislation in 1992 extended compulsory competitive tendering beyond manual work to include professional services such as accounting, computers, legal services and so on.

Deregulation
This means the introduction of competition where there had previously been a monopoly. The most obvious example is the deregulation of bus services which permits any operator who meets safety and other standards to compete against the council's transport services.

Schools and education
In its education legislation the Conservative government has produced many measures which effectively reduce the role of local authorities in the running of schools.

(1) *Local management of schools.* The responsibility for controlling the budget of a school has been given to the governors of the school. As a result the Local Education Authority (LEA) no longer deals with such matters as the employment and promotion of teachers, allocation of resources, etc. Critics say that this has increased instability in schools because the need to save money has over-ridden educational needs. Many schools have shed skilled and experienced teachers in favour of young and inexperienced staff who are so much cheaper.

(2) *Opting-out.* The machinery exists for schools that wish to do so to become self-governing, grant-maintained establishments. As such they are funded directly by the central government and no longer have to obey education policy decisions of the LEA. At first schools responded to the call to opt-out because the scheme was very well funded and schools could get a great deal more money from central government than they were able to obtain from the LEA. However, despite the government claiming that ultimately all schools would opt-out, the take up rate was very small. Also, with time, the amount of money available as sweeteners to opting-out schools grew much less, until there was very little financial advantage in doing so.

Local authorities as enablers
A review of local government, published as a Consultation Document by the government in April 1991, sees this process of opting-out and contracting-out continuing. The review states:

> Local authorities are undergoing a fundamental transformation
> from being the main providers of services to having responsibility
> for securing their provision. . . . As enablers, local authorities have
> greater opportunities to choose the best source of service. . . . The
> aim should be to secure the best services at least cost. The private
> and voluntary sectors should be used to provide services where
> this is more cost-effective than direct provision.[8]

The late Nicholas Ridley, when he was Secretary of State for the
Environment, was known to have said that the ideal form of local
government was a body that met once a year in order to hand out
contracts to those organisations providing the services.

When Margaret Thatcher came to power in 1979 she was
pledged to end the system of quangos established by the Labour
government in the 1970s. In fact, rather than ending the
quangos, she multiplied their number many times by abolishing whole sections of local government and setting up
unelected bodies to run services previously provided by local
councils.

Quangos

The term 'quango', first coined in the 1970s for the organ-
istional structure created by the Labour government, originally meant *quasi-non-governmental*, or alternatively *quasi-
autonomous non-governmental organisation*. It is, however, a
vague definition and very different things can be meant when
the term is used. The bodies referred to were set up for a wide
variety of reasons – administrative, managerial or political –
and this has resulted in a very mixed group of bodies, vastly dif-
fering in size and nature.

This accounts for the dispute between the government and its
critics as to the actual number of quangos that are in existence;
the government claiming that there are far fewer than is claimed
by those opposed to what they call a 'quangocracy'.[9] Closer
examination shows that this discrepancy results from the two
sides arguing on the basis of two very different definitions of
what is meant by a non-governmental body.

Government definition

The government, in an official publication,[10] defines quangos as non-departmental public bodies (NDPBs) and divides them into three types, plus one other specific category:

1. *Executive NDPBs* – which carry out a range of operational and regulatory functions. Examples are the Arts Council, the Countryside Commission or the Commission for Racial Equality.

2. *Advisory NDPBs* – which obviously advise government on the application of policy in certain specific areas. Examples are the Police Advisory Council or the Parliamentary Boundary Commission.

3. *Tribunals* – with a judicial or quasi-judicial function, and often providing an appeals procedure for the adjudication of public grievances, as with rents tribunals or the supplementary benefits appeals tribunal.

4. *NHS bodies* – In addition to the three types of NDPBs, the government also recognises public bodies within the National Health Service.

These government-defined quangos all fall within the remit of national government and here government action since 1979 has indeed reduced the number of quangos according to their own definition. William Waldegrave, when Minister of Public Services, could claim that the number of quangos had dropped from 2,167 in 1979 to 1,389 in 1994.

Opposition definitions

Opposed to these government definitions of quangos is the view presented by Weir and Hall in a survey carried out for Democratic Audit in 1994,[11] which saw an entire 'new wave' of unelected bodies being created, largely as a result of the erosion in local democratric controls over local authorities and the health service. 'Since 1987 responsibility for the delivery of a wide range of local services has been given to a number of unelected "local public spending bodies" as a result of changes in education, training, housing and health fields instituted by the government.'[12]

Added to the central government NDPBs accepted by the government, many bodies once entirely controlled by elected local authorities were forced or encouraged to opt out of local authority control to be run by unelected bodies or agencies directly appointed, financed and controlled by national government:

- opted-out grant maintained schools (GMS) and colleges;
- health authorities, trust hospitals, family health services;
- training and education councils (TECs);
- urban development corporations;
- housing action trusts.

All these various and diverse bodies are defined by Weir and Hall as extra-governmental organisations (EGOs) and stigmatised by Stewart as a 'new magistracy – a non-elected elite of appointed individuals'.[13] 'This is hidden government, run by bodies unknown to the public . . . their members may not even live or work locally . . . they may ignore local wishes and there is nothing local people can do about it . . . instead of giving power to individual citizens the government . . . has set up government quasi-markets in which individuals have little or no power.'[14]

To quote Stott from his article in *Talking Politics*, 'the question of quangos and their use has become the subject of a political game in which both Labour and Conservative politicians engage in attacking quangos when in opposition and using them as instruments for carrying out their policies when in government.' Nevertheless, there is an overwhelming body of evidence which seems to suggest that quangos and other EGOs encroach upon the spirit of true democracy insofar as there are questions about the groups which refer to:

- the extent and number of unelected bodies;
- their cost and cost-effectiveness;
- their power of patronage;
- their accountability and other checks on their probity.

Democratic deficit?

The 'EGO Trip' report,[15] which looked at the declining accountability of local and central government, produced some quite disturbing findings for those who believe that quangos are incompatible with democracy:

1 The audit found that at the start of 1994 there were in fact 5,521 executive quangos, and 6,708 quangos overall; as against the 1,389 admitted by government.

2 In the financial year 1992/93, quangos were responsible for spending £46.6 billion, about one third of all public expenditure, and that was expected to rise to £60 billion over the next few years.

3 Most quangos are extremely secretive. Only 14 per cent of the executive quangos are subject to examination by an ombudsman, only 2 per cent subscribed to the government's Open Government Code and only one third were required to submit their accounts to public audit.

4 The ability to appoint executives to the quangos opens up a whole new area of political patronage to ministers. In October 1994 the Labour MP, George Howarth, speaking to his constituency party,[16] highlighted the extent to which Conservative ministers appointed friends of the Tory Party to these positions. Heads of quangos were often Tory councillors, MPs or party workers but even more significant was the failure to appoint known supporters of the Labour or Liberal Democrat Parties. The Conservatives, in their turn, accused Howarth of hypocrisy, pointing out the numbers of trade unionists and left-wing academics who staffed quangos during the Labour government of 1974–79.

5 In Scotland and Wales, where there are very few Conservatives elected, the administration of public life is nevertheless often in the hands of Conservatives appointed by Conservative Secretaries of State.

In the autumn of 1993 the then Secretary of State for Wales, John Redwood, created a sensation in the principality by freezing any new appointments to managerial positions in the NHS. The action was controversial but it served to highlight the major anomaly present in all the government's plans to liberalise the public services. Whether we are talking about consumer choice, market forces or privatisation, the government's case has always been that its reforms are intended to increase efficiency and reduce red tape. Now it appears that all these reforms have resulted in massive increases in the layers of bureaucracy.

- According to the figures quoted by Redwood, NHS reforms in Wales have added 1,500 new managers to the service, compared with only twenty new doctors. In the NHS as a whole 13,000 managers were employed in 1993 in posts which just did not exist twenty years ago. In the same period just 7,000 new doctors have been appointed. The cost to the NHS of the 13,000 managers was £345 million.
- The league tables for schools produced as a result of education reforms meant a massive increase in the numbers of clerical staff needed to handle the vast amount of data and statistics received. There also had to be an equally massive investment in information technology to process this data.
- The transfer of financial control in such services as Health and Education has meant a massive increase in the numbers of auditors and accountants employed by the public services. Money given to locally-managed schools and trust hospitals has to have a proportion ploughed back in order to pay for those now responsible for the financial management of these institutions. As an example, running costs of the education service increased by 45 per cent in the four years between 1989 and 1993.

On 27 January 1994, the Public Accounts Committee of the House of Commons produced a report on the running of the 1,400 quangos, agencies and trusts that were then controlling state services. In a damning review, the report stated that standards in running public services had declined significantly over the previous two years and cited more than twenty instances of massive waste, corruption or fraud. Among the examples quoted were:

- The Wessex Health Authority was accused of 'concealing information, waste and mis-management.' Most serious was the waste of £20 million on a faulty computer system and the payment of a £112,000 'golden handshake' to a director sacked for incompetence.
- A loss of £65.6 million by the Property Services Agency –

estate management for Whitehall. A total breakdown in their invoice system was to blame.
- The Welsh Development Agency employed a criminal to run its international division. The man got his job with the help of forged references.
- Some £55 million of 'dubious' payments made by the Department of Employment.
- Over £1 million spent on over-luxurious offices by the National Rivers Authority.

Quangos, accountability and the Nolan Committee

Naturally enough the Conservative government denied any loss of accountability in the system of EGOs which replaced elected local authorities. The Major government claimed rather that the nature of accountability has changed. In Chapter 8, in connection with the Next Steps reforms of the civil service, mention was made of the Citizen's Charter and accountability to the consumer rather than accountability to the citizen.

In 1993, when he was Minister for the Public Services and responsible for the Citizen's Charter, William Waldegrave gave a lecture in which he claimed that a consumer oriented view of accountability, as exhibited by the NDPBs and EGOs, was a democratic gain rather than a democratic deficit. In answer to those who complained about the undemocratic nature of these unelected groups, he replied that the crucial issue was not, 'whether those who run our public services are elected, but whether they are producer-responsive or consumer-responsive.'[17]

According to Waldegrave, accountability in the public services means:
- Establishing standards of public service so that provision can be judged by the degree of consumer satisfaction.
- Citizens have been given the power of the consumer, so that complaints over public service and redress for failure must be dealt with in the same way as any business deals with complaints from its customers.
- Public services must be more responsive because they are

subject to ever-present market forces rather than the ballot box at four-yearly intervals.

Whether or not quangos represent a democratic gain or deficit, the issue of their accountability was one of the matters investigated by the Nolan Committee's enquiry into standards in public life. The committee was not really concerned with accountability as such but a fair measure of concern was expressed at the way in which quango members are appointed rather than elected, and at the extent to which appointments to quangos are the result of political party patronage. In the Nolan Committee's first report, published in May 1994, there were five recommendations relating to quangos arising from these issues, most of these recommendations accepted by the government, although without a timetable for their implementation:[18]

1 All appointments to NDPBs and NHS bodies should be made solely on merit, and should be with the advice of an independent panel.
2 There should be a Commissioner for Public Appointments who would vet all recruitment procedures.
3 Candidates for membership of quangos should declare any close party interests such as active party membership or candidacy for election.
4 There should be a mandatory code of conduct for quango staff similar to that imposed on the civil service.
5 There should be an urgent government review of the legal framework governing the conduct and accountability of quangos, given their changing nature in recent years.

Conclusion

There has been a decline in recent years in the degree of political accountability, as policy and administrative decisions are increasingly made by unelected bodies which are not answerable to the public at large through the democratic process. On the other hand, these changes may be part of a wider process of change which assumes accountability to the individual as consumer rather than to the individual as citizen. It is a change that is in line with the Conservatives' view of a society based on market forces, or on New Labour's concept of a stakeholder's society.

Notes

1 'A mock general election', editorial in the *Guardian*, 2 May 1996, page 14.
2 Hugo Young, *One of Us*, Macmillan, London, 1989, page 538.
3 The issue of statutory instruments is fully discussed in Andrew Adonis, *Parliament Today*, Manchester University Press, Mancheseter, 1993, pages 113–15.
4 Reported by Andy McSmith in the *Observer*, 7 April 1996.
5 Michael Moran, 'Reshaping the British State', *Talking Politics*, Spring 1995, page 175.
6 Colin Pilkington, *Local Government in England & Wales*, Econ-o-Text, Warwick, 1992.
7 John Stewart, 'Change in local government', *Politics Review*, November 1995, pages 17–19.
8 Department of the Environment, *The Internal Management of the Local Authorities in England, A Consultation Paper*, DoE, April 1991.
9 'The quango explosion', the *Guardian*, 19 November 1993.
10 *Public Bodies, 1993*, HMSO, London, 1994.
11 Stuart Weir and Wendy Hall, *EGO Trip: Extra-governmental Organisations in the UK and their Accountability*, Democratic Audit and Charter 88, May 1994.
12 Tony Stott, 'Evaluating the quango debate', *Talking Politics*, Winter 1995–96, pages 122–7.
13 Stewart, 'Change in local government'.
14 G. W. Jones and J. Stewart, 'A law unto themselves', *Local Government Chronicle*, 14 May 1993.
15 Weir and Hall, *EGO Trip*.
16 George Howarth MP, 'Quangos and political donations to the Tory Party', an address to Knowsley North Constituency Labour Party, October 1994.
17 William Waldegrave, 'The reality of reform and accountability in today's public service', Lecture for the Public Finance Foundation, 5 July 1993.
18 Rob Baggott, 'Putting the squeeze on sleaze?: The Nolan Committee and standards in public life', *Talking Politics*, Autumn 1995, pages 33–8.

V

Democratic deficit

11

Power without responsibility

I see. Power without responsibility: the prerogative of the harlot throughout the ages.

Stanley Baldwin, repeating the words of Kipling
to describe the press

The House of Lords, an illusion to which I have never been able to subscribe – responsibility without power, the prerogative of the eunuch throughout the ages.

Tom Stoppard, *Lord Malquist and Mr Moon*

The expression 'power without responsibility' was originally used about the press, particularly as it referred to the newspaper magnates; such as Beaverbrook in his day, or Rupert Murdoch in the latter part of the twentieth century. Later the statement was inverted by Tom Stoppard in order to describe the House of Lords; although it did not need inversion to be equally relevant. In both these instances we are talking about institutions which have considerable influence on the political life of the country but which are neither democratically elected to their position nor democratically accountable for their influence. To the former, unelected group belongs not only the House of Lords but also the monarchy: both institutions which draw their legitimacy from heredity rather than merit. In the latter group, alongside the media, we can place decisions of the Commission and Council of

Ministers of the European Union, which are legally binding on the citizens of the EU without any real democratic scrutiny or accountability.

The monarchy

Like that other hereditary body, the House of Lords, the monarchy is the subject of much earnest discussion at the close of the twentieth century, as commentators try to evolve a *raison d'être* for what are often seen as anachronisms in this period of our history. In both cases the choice is not, as it once was, between retention and abolition. It is also possible to retain a reformed institution by stripping it of some of its more traditional trappings in order to make it relevant to the age. This is particularly the case as it concerns the present members of the royal family, where criticisms of the constitutional role of the heir to the throne and his brothers have become confused with personal criticisms of the behaviour and marital misfortunes of those same people. The personal behaviour or misbehaviour of the current holder of an office is not an argument for dispensing with that office. Nevertheless, there is an argument for saying that it is worth retaining the monarchy yet at the same time withholding the succession from the present representatives of the House of Windsor.

It is worth bearing in mind that it is not just the monarch herself, nor the royal family as such, that is subject to critical examination. In the second chapter of this book a lot of attention was paid to the antiquity of so many political structures in Britain. The monarchy is very much a part of that tradition and, as such, dignifies and props up the interwoven elitist core that lies at the heart of public life. The select few who form what has been called 'The Establishment' dominate the political life of Britain within a conservative – and Conservative – framework that has been called 'the gentlemanly ideal' by Will Hutton. 'This self-reinforcing network – monarch, church, the law, the City, the army and the landed aristocracy – came to represent the gentlemanly ideal and thus England itself.'[1]

It is not merely this underpinning of élitism that is anti-democratic in the monarchy. There is also the Royal Prerogative, which represents powers possessed by the Prime Minister and government, including the appointment of ministers, patronage, the summoning and dissolution of parliament, the declaration of war and the signing of treaties. These powers are exercised by the government in the name of the monarch but without having to consult or inform parliament before so exercising them! The monarch becomes a symbol behind which a government can hide when over-riding the wishes of the people's representatives.

The last monarch to attempt playing a role in political life was Queen Victoria who was encouraged in this, by her husband Prince Albert at first, and later by her favourite Prime Minister, Benjamin Disraeli. Yet Victoria, during the course of her long reign, came increasingly to support the concept of a constitutional monarch, and indeed came to symbolise the constitutional ideal, not least in the eyes of nineteenth-century nationalists who were attempting to impose constitutions on the old absolute monarchies of Europe. This change in monarchical attitude was encouraged by Gladstone, who, although she heartily disliked him, tutored the queen on the purely symbolic nature of the monarchy within the constitution, and stressed the added legitimacy that had been granted to parliament after the Reform Act of 1832 through the fact of popular election.

In 1867, the constitutionalist, Walter Bagehot, divided the constitution into what he called its '*efficient*' and '*dignified*' elements; the former covering the work done by Prime Minister, government and parliament in actually running the country; the latter referring to institutions like the monarchy which lend legitimacy to the efficient elements by gratifying the need of the masses for an element of pomp and circumstance to act as a focus for their loyalty. It was Bagehot who first coined the definition of a constitutional monarch as someone 'who reigns but does not rule'.

As part of the dignified constitution the monarch has two roles:

1 To act as a symbol of the nation, representing the person-
   ification of that country in the eyes of the nation's own citizens, and also personifying an image of the nation which
   can be presented to other countries. In this the monarch is
   almost an abstract construction, like the flag or national
   anthem, and is necessarily divorced and remote from political partisanship.

2 To carry out, or legitimise, certain largely ceremonial functions to symbolise the British definition of government as
   being by 'the Crown in Parliament'. The State Opening of
   Parliament is a prime example of the purely symbolic nature
   of this ceremonial, typified by the Queen's Speech delivered
   on that occasion, which is presented as though it were the
   monarch addressing her parliament but which is in fact a
   declaration of intent from the government, and written by
   the Prime Minister and the Prime Minister's advisers.

The monarch as figurehead

Criticism of the institution of monarchy in a representative
democracy is centred on the non-elected and hereditary nature
of that institution.[2] A democracy chooses its own representatives to act on behalf of the many; but whom does the
monarch represent, except the abstract idea of the monarchy
itself? If the monarch is given any power, can it be right that that
power is exercised by someone who was chosen not on merit but
by an accident of birth. Beyond these criticisms the monarch is
also said to be undemocratic in a social sense, in that the royal
family can hardly represent the people of this country when
their wealth and their way of life is so very different from the
social norm.

   On the other hand there are those who would claim that these
very factors reinforce the suitability of the monarch to act as a
symbol of national unity. If it is true that the monarch represents
no one in particular then it is equally true that the monarch is
unable to represent any faction that would be unpopular or
alienating to other sections of the community. In countries that

have an elected head of state the situation can be very different. In America, for example, Bill Clinton was elected President, and as such became a symbol of unity for the United States. But Clinton is a Democrat and there are a lot of Republicans who did not vote for him, quite a number of whom worked actively to prevent his election in 1992 and quite as many who, while supposedly loyal to the elected president, continued to work hard to prevent his re-election in 1996. Can someone who is bound up in partisan politics be said to be a unifying force for a nation? If Britain had had an elected president and Margaret Thatcher had been elected, we can be certain that there would have been a sizeable proportion of the British people who could not have given anything like the same degree of loyalty to Margaret Thatcher as they could give to a politically neutral figure such as the Queen.

It is for this reason that the monarch and royal family keep at a safe distance from appearing to take sides in party politics. In the 1930s the Prince of Wales (later Edward VIII) was heard to say 'Something ought to be done about it' when being shown the social conditions in the South Wales Valleys. This simple, and essentially meaningless, expression of sympathy was interpreted as criticism of the government of the day and a constitutional crisis erupted over what was claimed to be royal involvement in politics. There have been incidents since then: the Queen was known to be opposed to Margaret Thatcher's approach to the Commonwealth, particularly her acceptance of the American invasion of Grenada, while Prince Charles was accused by Norman Tebbit in 1988 of being too sympathetic to the unemployed. But, on the whole, the British monarch remains free of the taint of political involvement.

As Lord Plant has said, there is something to be said for the hereditary principle in producing a head of state who is above politics. Unfortunately, as Lord Plant goes on to say, 'the point about hereditary monarchy is that you have to put up with what the accidents of birth produce . . . and there is absolutely no guarantee that the hereditary principle will produce a monarch who is capable of symbolising the nation and its values.'[3] The importance of the tabloid debate about the behaviour of the young royals and their marital problems is that this behaviour detracts from the standards we are ready to accept from people who are supposed to symbolise all that is good about the British way of life. Arguments about behaviour, elitism and wealth in the royal family arise largely from attempts that the royal family have made to change themselves since the 1960s.

As Shirley Williams has said, 'The royal family has made an attempt to change but it has gone in the wrong direction. It has become soap opera.'[4] In the 1960s the BBC made a film about the royal family that allowed the public an insight into the private life of the Queen and her family for the first time. It was a first crack in the dam which ultimately released the intrusive journalism of the tabloids in full flood, with their pursuit of 'Di', 'Fergie' and other royal adulterous affairs. In permitting the BBC to film their documentary the original intention had been to make the royal family less remote by removing some of the mystique surrounding an elitist royalty which was felt to be out of touch with the times, thereby helping to create a 'citizen monarchy' along the lines of the Scandinavian model. It was only after the private lives of the royal family had been opened up to public scrutiny in sordid detail that anyone realised that for the monarchy to work as an abstract symbol of the nation there has to be deference towards the source of that symbolism. And that deference is only possible if the symbolic head is shrouded in a degree of reserve and some mystique is preserved.

The constitutional role of the monarch

Criticisms of the royal family which have led to calls that Prince Charles should be barred from the succession, only have an importance if royalty's behaviour has a political content. For example, the fact that the heir to the throne is about to divorce his wife is largely irrelevant except for the facts that the Church of England does not approve of divorce, that the Church of England is the established church and that Prince Charles will ultimately inherit the title of Head of the Church. It was that aspect which forced Edward VIII to abdicate in order to marry a divorcee, triggering a debate on the future of the monarchy very similar to that surrounding the succession of Prince Charles. Yet Edward VIII's grandfather, Edward VII, was notorious for his love affairs without this noticeably bringing the monarchy into disrepute. Indeed, the king's affairs seemed to contribute to his popularity with the people. Of Edward VII's popularity despite his infidelities we may say the same as Anthony Barnett says of George III's popularity despite his madness, 'Being mad didn't matter. It just showed that he was human – the more human, the more lovable.'[5]

The point being made by Barnett in his article – a point reinforced by the 1993 conference on the monarchy organised by Charter 88 – is that the Edwardian age was still one where the royal prerogative could be seen as a safeguard against the abuse of power and political office; just as had been described by Victorian constitutionalists like Dicey and Bagehot. By the end of the twentieth century on the other hand the royal prerogative is seen as a way by which over-powerful governments can legitimise their actions and cloak them in secrecy. As Shirley Williams says, 'The executive in Britain has something very close to absolute power. It hides behind the crown as a way of hiding from us the extent of that power.'[6] In his inaugural professorial address, Peter Hennessy speaks of having asked a very senior civil servant to define the British constitution and being told that the constitution is 'something we make up as we go along'. It is through the royal prerogative that the senior ranks of the civil service justify their invention of constitutional rules.

Those who are opposed to the hereditary system in principle will only be satisfied with the abolition of the monarchy and the creation of a republic, but there are still those who argue that a hereditary monarchy with its traditions and ceremonial can serve a useful purpose as a figurehead symbol of the state; even if it is merely in its contribution to the tourist trade. For this to work, however, there has to be reform of the institution as part of a wider constitutional reform, which will give a new and different legitimacy to the monarchy.

Without a set of written constitutional obligations or democratic legitimacy, the royal family has to rely on its unimpeachable behaviour for its continuing legitimacy – and this is beyond the capacity of any human family to guarantee.[7]

As is fairly obvious, the abolition of the monarchy would demand a written constitution in order to define the duties and function of an elected president. What is perhaps less obvious is that reform of the monarchy would not only demand a written constitution but would in fact be an inevitable by-product of the writing of a constitution. This is particularly true for the two areas where the monarchy could be said still to have a political role in the governance of the country.

(1) As a protector of the country's liberties, so as to safeguard us against dictatorship or absolutist government. Although there is a statute limiting the life of a parliament to five years, there is nothing constitutionally to prevent a government from passing an act of parliament in order to prolong its own life. Because of two world wars this has happened twice in this century, the parliament elected in 1910 surviving until 1918, and that of 1936 lasting until 1945. The only safeguard against this happening for a less democratic reason is that the monarch has the right to dissolve parliament and invalidate the acts of that parliament, with the ability to call on the army and police to support the monarch's actions. Such an emergency has never arisen in this country but it has happened elsewhere.

- In 1943 the Italian king, Victor Emmanuel III, dismissed Mussolini as his prime minister and had him arrested and imprisoned, thus causing the fall of Fascism.
- In Spain, King Juan Carlos resisted a pro-Franco faction of the Civil Guard when they attempted an armed coup against the Spanish parliament.

(2) As the person who appoints the Prime Minister and government ministers. Mostly this is settled by convention and the leader of the party which has the largest number of parliamentary seats after a general election is asked to form a government. The possibility does exist, however, that a situation could arise where there is no obvious candidate and the monarch

would actually have to choose who should become Prime Minister. This has in fact twice faced the present monarch, in 1957 and 1963, when Anthony Eden and Harold Macmillan resigned while still serving Prime Ministers; at a time when the Conservative Party did not have a mechanism for the election of a leader. The confusion of the events, especially the 1963 choice of Sir Alec Douglas-Home, conducted in the glare of the television cameras, hastened the development of a leadership election process for the Conservative Party so that the situation would not rise again. In the mid-1980s, however, at the height of the Alliance's popularity, there was a great deal of speculation over a general election resulting in a hung parliament, with the very real prospect of there being no clear majority party. This would mean that the Queen would have had the equivalent of a casting vote in deciding which of the various party leaders should be asked to form a government, with the very real risk of a constitutional crisis as the monarch made a political decision.

The House of Lords

Very much the same arguments centre on the House of Lords as surround the monarchy but with an added importance in that the Lords is part of the efficient element of the constitution, as well as the dignified. Again, as with the monarchy, there are three perceived responses to the House of Lords – it could be retained as it is, it could be abolished completely or it could be reformed. Attitudes to the Lords as compared to the monarchy do result in the position that there are far fewer supporters for the extremes of retention or abolition, and a significant majority who are for some form of reform.

Criticisms of the House of Lords are obviously based on its unrepresentative nature:
- Out of a total 1,200 accredited peers, 775 are hereditary peers. Only 15 of these are peers of first creation, which means that they themselves were awarded the title on merit; the remaining 760 have all inherited their titles.
- There are only 79 women in the Lords and, since succession

in Britain is based on male primogeniture, 62 of these are life peers.

- The Lords is an overwhelmingly Conservative body, with 480 accepting the Tory whip as against 116 for Labour and 58 for the Liberal Democrats. Many of the 278 peers who do not accept a party whip but sit on the cross-benches are conservatively inclined even if not actual Conservatives.

- Only a minority of peers are active in the House of Lords. About 300 attend on a daily basis but no more than 800 attend at least once a year.[8]

Despite these criticisms there are still arguments in favour of the House of Lords, even as presently constituted. Indeed, given the present demands on the House of Commons, there would seem to be overwhelming arguments for the retention of a second chamber of some kind.

- The Lords has an important function as a revising chamber since it has the time to look at the detail rather than the principle of proposed legislation. The Lords is particularly good at picking up and amending errors that have crept into government bills through faulty drafting: in the 1992–93 parliamentary session the House of Lords passed a total of 1,674 amendments to 28 government bills.[9]

- The Lords is able to ease the strain on the parliamentary workload by taking the lion's share of routine and non-controversial bills from the Commons. This is particularly true of the largely technical and formalised private bills.

- Since life peerages in particular are awarded for achievements in fields other than politics, there is an authority based on wide experience in the Lords. The scientists, academics, industrialists, etc. who are given life peerages all contribute what David McKie has called 'influence based on expertise'.[10]

- That same expertise lends considerable authority to the growing number of select committees which the Lords has created in recent years. This is particularly true of the scrutiny of matters relating to Europe, where the Lords has five sub-committees where the Commons has only two.

- In parliaments where the Commons is dominated by a heavily whipped party system, the Lords manages to retain sufficient independence as to represent a serious agent for the scrutiny of government legislation. Ironically, despite the natural Conservative bias of the Lords, there were times during the years of large Tory majorities between 1979 and 1992 that the Lords represented what Simon Hoggart called, 'the only true opposition to the Thatcher government'. 'In the period from 1979 to 1991, the government suffered no less than 173 defeats at the hands of their Lordships.'[11]

Despite these very strong arguments in favour of the *status quo* there remains the problem of accountability and non-representation which leaves the argument divided between retention, abolition and reform.

Retention

Only a very few die-hard traditionalists still wish to keep the House of Lords as it is and they are either High Tories or rigid parliamentarians in the mould of Enoch Powell. They argue that the nature of the Lords ensures that it can take decisions without fear or favour and without being subject to the demands of party or special interest group.

Abolition

This was once the position adopted by the Labour Party, as exemplified by Michael Foot. Indeed, it was official party policy after 1977, when the party demanded a unicameral parliament on the New Zealand model, with all the work of parliament handled by a reformed House of Commons. The Labour abolitionist argument was expressed by Lord Wedderburn,[12] 'Either the second chamber is less democratic than the Commons, in which case it should not be able to delay legislation, or it is just as democratic, when there is no point in having two chambers'. However, as part of Neil Kinnock's re-positioning of the Labour Party prior to the 1987 election, the party shed its abolitionist stance in recognising the value of a second chamber.

Reform

An overwhelming number of politicians, from all parties, are in favour of reform. Unfortunately no one can agree on the nature of that reform. Most people would recognise the case for phasing-out the hereditary element in the Upper House and a move to replace the hereditary lords has been on the table since it was adopted as Liberal Party policy in 1891. The last serious attempt to reform the Lords was made by the Wilson government of 1969, by which hereditary peers would have remained solely as non-voting members; only an enlarged number of life peers having the right to vote on legislation. That move was defeated by the unlikely alliance of Enoch Powell and Michael Foot, since reform was neither the retention nor the abolition they respectively wanted. Between 1977 and 1979, in response to Labour's abolitionist stance, the Conservatives proposed that hereditary peers should be removed and replaced by a second chamber that was one-third appointed and two-thirds elected. The plan did not survive the Tory victory of 1979. The problem with reform is an inability to decide between the rival merits of appointment or election as a means of choosing members for the second chamber.

(1) Appointment would enable the Lords to continue possessing the virtues of experience and expertise since appointments would be on the grounds of merit and judgement of the contribution they could make to the work of parliament. The suggestion has been made that a second chamber should be representative of interest groups, enabling trade unions, environmental groups and the professions among others to have a direct input into the political process. On the other hand, appointment is not much more democratic than heredity, it would increase the prime ministerial power of patronage and would open up the prospect of purely political appointments.

(2) Election of members, as is now favoured by the Labour Party, would be democratic. But, if a reformed Lords were merely elected on the same lines as the Commons, even if at different times or by a different electoral system, the risk is that the two chambers would either be carbon copies of one another or they

would be in perpetual conflict with each other. One possible suggestion has been that, if plans for devolution go ahead, an elected second chamber could represent Scotland, Wales, Northern Ireland and the English regions, in the same way as the Senate represents States' Rights in the American Congress.

Europe

The expression 'democratic deficit', as it is used to refer to a lack of public accountability in the making of important political decisions, was originally so used in association with the European Community (EC). In particular it refers to the unelected powers of the European Commission, the fact that an unaccountable Council of Ministers forms the legislature of the EU and the impotence of a European parliament which has no control over legislation and no ability to curb the Commission or Council.

In 1972, by signing the Treaty of Accession, the British government tacitly accepted as part of British law some 43 volumes of European legislation, made up of more than 2,900 regulations and 410 directives; the sum total of legislation agreed by the Community over the 20 years since its formation. Admittedly, much of this legislation was trivial: most regulations or directives from Brussels dealing with small points of detail such as intervention prices for commodities within the Common Agricultural Policy. Nevertheless, there were some major issues involved and, in any case, the triviality of certain details is unimportant compared to the basic principle that here was a solid *corpus* of law that became binding upon the peoples of the United Kingdom, despite that law never having been scrutinised or debated by the British parliament. It was a massive breach of the constitutional convention which holds that parliament is the supreme, and indeed only, law-making body in the United Kingdom.

Euro-sceptics, in their criticism of Europe, often use the terms 'unelected' and 'undemocratic' in talking about the institutions of the Community. Britain needs to defend its parliamentary sovereignty, they suggest, because at least the British parliament can claim to speak for the British people since it was the British electorate which elected that parliament. For whom can the European Commission claim to speak when its members are appointed rather than elected and to whom is the Commission accountable?

There is, however, an anomaly in the situation when national parliamentarians criticise the Community for its lack of democratic institutions; the so-called 'democratic deficit'. There are three simple solutions to accusations of non-accountability and they are:

1 strengthen the powers of the EP;
2 make more European institutions, and their officials, answerable to the EP;
3 open up even more European legislation to scrutiny by MEPs.

The anomalous situation, however, arises because proposals to democratise the Community through strengthening the EP are bitterly opposed by national parliaments.

1 To increase the democratic nature of the EP would be to legitimise its activities, whereas now its actions can be contemptuously dismissed as being 'unrepresentative'.
2 To legitimise the EP is to strengthen it in relation to national parliaments to the extent that national parliaments could become irrelevant in time.

So we end with the ironic situation that the very ministers who can criticise the Community for being 'undemocratic' are the same people who, as members of the Council of Ministers, refuse to legislate for democracy within the Community.

The scrutiny of European legislation

By accepting the terms of the Accession Treaty the British Parliament accepted the primacy of EC legislation within the United Kingdom, with the exception of the need for some UK legislation to supplement Regulations and implement Directives. The House of Commons seeks to overcome this breach with parliamentary sovereignty by insisting that when a proposal goes from the Commission to the Council, the British minister concerned will not approve the measure until it has been scrutinised by the relevant parliamentary committee. This reservation has been expressed in a series of resolutions by the House, most recently in a Resolution of 24 October 1990:

> In the opinion of this House:
> 1 No Minister of the Crown should give agreement in the Council of Ministers to any proposal for European Community legislation
>   (a) which is still subject to scrutiny (that is, on which the Select Committee on European 'egislation has not completed its scrutiny); or
>   (b) which is awaiting consideration by the House.
> 2 In this Resolution, any reference to agreement to a proposal includes, in the case of a proposal on which the Council acts in co-operation with the European Parliament, agreement to a common position.[13]

It has to be said that the scrutiny process can do nothing to prevent the implementation of Community legislation; the committees involved can only concern themselves with *prospective* legislation. Parliament can advise ministers on the line to take in negotiation, they cannot amend or revise legislation that has been through either of the European legislative procedures. However, parliament obviously believes in the need for national scrutiny of European legislation and Select Committees for both Houses of Parliament to investigate the scrutiny process were set up even before the United Kingdom formally became a member of the EC.[14]

The media

In countries other than England where parliament did not develop as a representative body, the deliberative body of the feudal state was a meeting of the Estates of the Realm. There were traditionally three estates representing the classes or orders of society which had a recognised share in the running of the body politic: the three estates being the nobility, the clergy and the commons. In 1828 Lord Macaulay wrote about parliament, echoing words originally said by Burke, 'The gallery where the reporters sit has become a fourth estate of the realm.' In the best part of two centuries since then the nickname of 'the fourth estate' has been firmly attached to the press in recognition of the influence wielded by them on political life. Even the BBC has been referred to jokingly as 'the fifth estate', extending a recognition of its importance from the press to the broadcasting media, and acknowledging that the media as a whole are as much an institution of political life as parliament and the government.

Most of the political debate about the media has tended to centre on the intrusive behaviour of the press, typified by the scandal-mongering and invasions of privacy associated with the events of 1992–93, when a succession of figures in public life, from royalty to cabinet ministers, found the secrets of their private lives exposed in the tabloid press. At that time there had already been a review of press activities chaired by Sir David Calcutt, as a result of which the old Press Council had been replaced by the Press Complaints Commission (PCC). The first Calcutt Report had argued against statutory controls over the press, trusting in self-regulation under the guidance of the PCC to curb the excesses of the tabloids. Embarrassingly for the government, the minister responsible, David Mellor, had just announced stricter measures and a second Calcutt review in August 1992, when he himself was plastered across all the tabloid front pages because of his affair with Antonia da Sancha. There were suggestions that the minister had been deliberately targeted by the press to defuse the threat he posed to their freedom of action.

The second Calcutt Report in January 1993 led in March to proposals for:
- legislation to prevent press invasions of privacy;
- possible compensation for victims of press intrusion;
- a government-appointed press ombudsman.

Two years later the government published its white paper on the subject, which back-tracked very substantially on what had been proposed.[15] Measures intended to strengthen self-regulation were introduced but legislation was ruled out. Main proposals were:

- the PCC would pay compensation to victims of intrusion;
- there should be a clearer definition of privacy;
- there should not be any criminal offence of intrusion;
- there would not be a government bill for the protection of privacy.

The debate about control of media excesses is central to the debate on democracy because, for all that much of the activity of the press is indefensible, too much control of the press would smack of censorship. Investigative reporting might be intrusive where the private lives of citizens are concerned but to prevent that investigation is to permit the government to keep secret those things it wants to keep secret from the public; not always for the most laudable of reasons. 'Pursuit of sex-and-politics stories by the tabloids may be objectionable but attempts to discourage a culture of investigation, is to offer governments even more secrecy and power than they currently have.'[16]

The main political thrust of the media debate is therefore over the delicate balance between a citizen's right to privacy and a citizen's right to know what the government is doing. There are, however, two other areas of political concern:

1 The first, largely relevant to television, is the trivialisation of politics and the debasing effect of the media on the status of politicians.
2 The second, largely concerning the tabloid press, is the manipulation of public opinion for the benefit of one party (usually the Conservatives).[17]

Television and the election campaign

The first general election campaign really to use television was that of 1959 and the winner of that election, Harold Macmillan, was the first Prime Minister who deliberately cultivated a television image. Since then matters have advanced to the point where it is now not so much that television reports the course of an election campaign but more that an election campaign is tailored to fit the demands of television reporting and the leaders of political parties are chosen more for the image they can project on television than for their political skills. From the 1960s onwards the main political parties invested in centres which trained leading politicians in the use and exploitation of television. The ultimate exponent of this was Margaret Thatcher whose television image, from her hairstyle to the tone of her voice, was created in 1974 by the former television producer turned media consultant, Gordon Reece.

During the 1980s the broadcast media helped to change the nature of British politics. The introduction of first radio and then television into the House of Commons made a much wider public aware of what went on in parliament. It also, through exposing the rowdy behaviour of many MPs and the often meaningless confrontations of Prime Minister's Question Time, contributed to a disillusionment with politicians that increased feelings of alienation on the part of the electorate. The growing television presence also created new factors in the political process such as *sound-bites*, which are short political statements just long enough to fit neatly into a television news bulletin; or *photo-opportunities*, which means leading politicians doing something – not necessarily political – that will look interesting to the cameras of the press or television; or the *spin-doctors*, who are the press secretaries and media consultants, the successors of Gordon Reece, whose job it is to present the politicians to the media in the best possible light.

By the time of the 1987 general election, television was dictating the shape of the election campaign:

- Each day began with press conferences, carefully timed so that the media could take in all three major parties in turn.
- Each press conference would summarise the events of the day before and then a frontbench spokesperson would be produced to set the agenda for that day's policy issues.
- Leading politicians would disperse through the country for a series of photo-opportunities, the most famous of which came in 1983 when Margaret Thatcher was photographed in the middle of a field holding up a calf. There was no political message in the photograph but it got Margaret Thatcher onto

the front page of every paper and into news bulletins on every TV channel.

- Campaign speeches from the party leaders would be made from a party rally for the faithful, at which there would be music, a light-show and a host of showbiz and sporting celebrities on stage. A copy of the proposed speech, with the key passages highlighted, would be given to the broadcasters beforehand; the highlighted passages enabling the news teams to have lights and cameras active for the key moments.

The impact of all this on the political process would seem to be two-fold.

(1) The medium now seems to be more important than the message. Getting good television coverage of the leader's activities is now seen as more important than winning the argument on policy, making a spin-doctor as important to the party as any policy adviser. Instead of the broadcasters simply reporting political events the parties are now trying to influence the way in which events are recorded, as when Tony Blair's press secretary, Alastair Campbell, caused a sensation during the 1995 Labour Conference by attempting to influence the running order of a BBC news broadcast. Campbell's faxed letter, urging the news team to use Tony Blair's speech ahead of the O. J. Simpson verdict, was dismissed by John Birt, the Director-General, as 'crass and inappropriate' but the Nine O'clock News did lead with the Blair speech.

(2) Using these techniques to promote politicians has devalued their political currency, in that the public has come to view the politicians as no more important than the stars of show business with whom they share the television screen. The same effect is seen in the televising of parliament in that the one parliamentary occasion to be broadcast regularly is Prime Minister's Question Time, and that is seen as the equivalent of a gladiatorial contest and a sort of spectator sport. It is a similar situation to that faced by the royal family in that television may be able to make politicians more accessible to the public but it also removes much of their mystique, their credibility and much of the respect which used to be their due.

'It's the *Sun* wot won it'

The broadcasting media have to remain impartial in the political debate, being required by law to preserve a balance between party viewpoints in covering controversial matters. No such constraints, however, exist for the newspapers.

The press has always been used for political propaganda. Newspaper magnates like the Lords Rothermere, Northcliffe or Beaverbrook acquired and launched newspapers with a particular political purpose in mind. Beaverbrook is a clear example of this in the way he used the *Express* newspapers to promote his obsessional interest in the Empire and imperial preference; going so far as to forbid any mention of Lord Mountbatten in the pages of either the *Daily Express* or *Sunday Express*, because Mountbatten had been the last Viceroy of India at the time of independence and therefore became, in Beaverbrook's eyes, the man who gave India away. From the beginning it was seen that the proprietors of the popular press would attempt to bring political influence to bear on the voting intentions of their readers and over the years that has meant that newspapers read by a significant majority of the British people are biased in favour of the Conservatives and opposed to Labour.

The anti-Labour bias of most newspapers received a new edge after 1974 when the *Sun* newspaper was taken over by Rupert Murdoch and turned into a mass circulation tabloid. There were certain points about the Murdoch-owned *Sun* that proved very significant:
- The *Sun* supported the Conservatives, but it was a working class populist form of Conservatism that was as hostile to High Toryism as it was to Labour.
- The majority of *Sun* readers were previously Labour voters and many of them actually believed that the *Sun* was a Labour paper.
- The Tory press was always ready to use dirty tricks against Labour ever since the *Daily Mail* published the fake Zinoviev Letter and helped defeat the Labour government of 1924. The rise of the *Sun*, however, coincided with an increase in the use

of 'negative campaigning' in which the use of smears and unsubstantiated rumours are used to blacken the opposition. In 1996 both the *Daily Mail* and the *Daily Express* were shown to be trying to rake up dirt in the past lives of John Prescott and Cheri Blair respectively.

In 1992 everyone was convinced that Labour would either win the general election, or would run the Tories very close. Yet a last minute swing gave the Conservatives enough of a lead as to give them a twenty-one seat majority in the Commons. When the election was over, amid recriminations in the Conservative Party as to the quality of party organisation, the ex-treasurer of the party, Alastair McAlpine, said that the party's propaganda machine had nothing to do with the election victory, the real 'heroes' were the editors of the *Sun, Daily Mail* and *Daily Express*. During the campaign the tabloid newspapers had led a continuous attack on Labour policies – on immigration, proportional representation, taxes and Europe. Personal attacks on Neil Kinnock culminated in the famous *Sun* headline on election day, 'If Kinnock wins today will the last person to leave Britain please turn out the lights.' On the Saturday after the election the *Sun* led with its famous headline 'It's the Sun wot won it'. Yet, by Monday, when Neil Kinnock was also blaming the tabloids for Labour's defeat, the tabloids were having second thoughts; a *Sun* spokesman saying that it was flattering that the Labour leader should suggest that the press had so much power but he was exaggerating.

In October 1995, Martin Linton of the *Guardian* published the results of intensive research he had carried out into press influence on the 1992 election.[18] His findings, supported by research done by the ICM and MORI polling organisations, show just how great the influence of the tabloids was, and that of the *Sun* in particular. The *Sun*'s readers are normally Labour supporters, often by quite a large margin, but in just one three-month period in the five years from 1990 to 1995 an 8 per cent swing to the Conservatives produced a Tory majority among *Sun* readers. That period was between April and September 1992 and included the date of the general election.

Linton produces the concept of the 'press deficit' to represent the difference in readership between newspapers supporting the Conservatives and those supporting Labour. Thanks to true Tory papers such as the *Telegraph*, *Daily Mail* and *Daily Express*, Labour has always had a 'press deficit' but, between 1945 and October 1974, that deficit varied between 10 and 18 per cent and Labour managed to win five elections. Since that time, however, the growth of Murdoch control of the press has vastly increased the numbers of newspapers sold which support the Tories. In 1992 70 per cent of all national daily newspapers supported the Conservatives, as against 27 per cent for Labour – a Labour 'press deficit' of 43 per cent. Labour has never won an election with a 'press deficit' greater than 18 per cent.

That 'press deficit' is not only in numbers but in the type and nature of voters delivered by the tabloid press. In the 1970s private research on behalf of the Conservative Party identified the type of voters the party needed to attract; the ideal being the skilled working class known as the C2 socio-economic group. The target voter was 'fairly young, slightly inclined to Labour and not highly educated'. It was almost a perfect description of a *Sun* reader and Margaret Thatcher began to woo the editor of the *Sun*, Larry Lamb, who in return helped to write the Thatcher speeches and contributed to the writing team creating the Tory manifesto, bringing the concerns expressed by Margaret Thatcher into line with the concerns of the *Sun* readership. In the 1979 election the country-wide swing to the Tories was 5 per cent, but the C2s swung by 9 per cent and the *Sun*-C2 heartland of Essex swung by 13 per cent, turning Basildon into the symbol of Thatcherite Britain. Larry Lamb acquired a knighthood and the Murdoch organisation extended its control over the British press and Sky television without any interference from the Monopolies Commission.

The story of the 1992 election can show how much influence the press can have over the democratic process. But there is a difference in the 1990s compared with previous periods. The Northcliffes and Beaverbrooks who made the British press so Conservative were die-hard Tories who would never have thought of considering any other party. Murdoch has shown that he is far more flexible. In 1992 the *Sun* may have been totally behind the Tories in England and Wales but Scottish editions of the paper supported the Scottish National Party. Since 1992 Murdoch has had long talks with Tony Blair, his papers have criticised John Major and the columns of the *Sun* have been opened to Labour politicians. This is not to say that Murdoch is likely to throw the weight of his papers behind Labour but it does mean that the relationship between politicians and the press has changed. 'Profits have become the motivation for ownership, rather than propaganda.'[19]

The press is in pursuit of a commercial profit and it will support any party or viewpoint which it feels will maximise readership. And the propaganda value of the press is a commercial asset like any other. If a party wants a newspaper to support it then the newspaper is in need of rewards, just as the Murdoch press was rewarded in the 1980s. It is a new dimension in the development of popular democracy.

Notes

1 Will Hutton, *The State We're In*, Jonathan Cape, London, 1995, pages 42–5.

2 The future of the monarchy was discussed at a conference jointly organised by Charter 88 and *The Times* on 22 May 1993. The substance of what was said was later published in book form, edited by Anthony Barnett, *Power and the Throne: The Monarchy Debate*, Vintage, London, 1994. The main points made by three contributors – Charles Moore for retention, Shirley Williams for reform, and Sue Townsend for abolition – appeared in *Politics Review*, September 1995, pages 5–7.

3 Raymond, Lord Plant of Highfield, is the Labour Party's constitutional expert who chaired the Labour enquiry into electoral systems. His thoughts on the monarchy are contained in an article 'Royal flush-out', which appeared in the *Guardian*, April 1996.

4 Shirley, Baroness Williams of Crosby, 'The case for reform', *Politics Review*, September 1995, page 6.

5 Anthony Barnett, 'The constitutional crisis and the monarchy', *Politics Review*, September 1995, pages 2–4.

6 Williams, 'The case for reform'.

7 Hutton, *The State We're In*, page 323.

8 Statistics concerning the House of Lords were provided by the Journal and Information Office of the House of Lords and are true for November 1993. Figures quoted in D. Shell and D. R. Beamish (eds), *The House of Lords at Work*, Clarendon Press, Oxford, 1993.

9 Donald Shell, 'The House of Lords', *Politics Review*, September 1995, pages 21–4.

10 David McKie, 'In praise of spooks and eunuchs', the *Guardian*, 18 March 1996, page 13.

11 Philip Norton, chapter eighteen of *Politics UK*, (2nd edition), Harvester Wheatsheaf, Hemel Hempstead, 1994, page 352.

12 Quoted by Philip Norton, 'The constitution in question', *Politics Review*, April 1994, pages 6–11

13 Factsheet no. 56, *The House of Commons and European Communities Legislation*, Public Information Office of the House of Commons, 1991.

14 Colin Pilkington, *Britain in the European Union Today*, Manchester University Press, Manchester, 1995, chapter 4.

15 Government White Paper, *Privacy and Media Intrusion: The Government's Response*, HMSO, London, 17 July 1995.

16 Alex Doig, 'Scandal, politics and the media', *Politics Review*, November 1994, pages 2–6.

17 The reader who is interested in the long-term interaction between media and politics, is recommended to two excellent non-academic books, which treat the subject from the inside. Michael Cockerell, reporter on BBC's *Panorama*, wrote *Live from Number 10* (Faber, London, 1988) to trace the history of television's involvement in politics, from Churchill's first experiments in 1953 to Margaret Thatcher's election victory in 1987. John Cole in *As It Seemed to Me* (revised paperback edition, Phoenix, London, 1996) presents the viewpoint of someone who has been in turn Labour Editor of the *Guardian*, Deputy Editor of the *Observer*, and Political Editor of the BBC.

18 Martin Linton delivered the seventh Guardian Lecture at Nuffield College, Oxford, on 30 October 1995, with a summary of his findings published in the *Guardian* of that day's date.

19 Roy Greenslade, 'Contempt bred of freedom', the *Observer*, 5 May 1996.

12

Power to the people!

Let's see it. Why is it that the Pope is supposed to have seen this document? Clinton is supposed to have seen these proposals. And I am a voter and a member of parliament and I am not allowed to see them. Yet they are deciding my future. Is that democracy?

Ian Paisley, 1993

A whole raft of constitutional doodling.

John Major's view of Labour's reform programme, May 1996

Virtually everyone is willing to concede that the unwritten British constitution is flawed and that the British vision of democracy is far from perfect. Yet this concession usually results in suggestions that one part of the process should be reformed: we should introduce proportional representation or toughen up parliamentary scrutiny. There are those, however, who recognise that the faults in the system go beyond what can be put right by mere tinkerings with the details. In their view there is need for a root and branch reform of the entire system, as has been recognised by groups like Charter 88. Changing the electoral system or making ministers more accountable would change the structure but leave the process basically unchanged, unless the relationship between government and people were also reviewed and altered. In 1995 the General Secretary of Liberty, the pressure group formerly known as the National Council for Civil Liberties, traced the problem back to the Bill of Rights of 1689, which originally transferred power from the monarch to parliament only to have parliamentary sovereignty become government sovereignty in time.

> Now government domination of parliament is extremely effective. One third of all MPs of the majority party are on the government payroll. The Prime Minister possesses considerable powers of patronage . . . Government whips, who attend every debate, can [discipline] any MP who fails to support the government . . . and can apply pressure on constituency associations. The government can exercise powers of the Royal Prerogative . . . In recent years governments have also resorted to the creation of large numbers of QUANGOs – bodies whose nominees can be controlled by the government.[1]

At the heart of this critique of British democracy today, which repeats briefly what we have already discussed in this book, is the fact that government maintains its control through being secretive, restrictive and remote. To combat those problems, reformers such as Liberty and Charter 88 would say that the very least that we need is a Freedom of Information Act, a Bill of Rights and some form of subsidiarity or devolution of power.

Freedom of information

'The extent to which information is freely available in a form to inform decisions, accountability or redress, will determine the extent to which the administrative process can function effectively.'[2] Yet the British governmental system is almost pathologically secretive, as exemplified in the Official Secrets Act which still has to be signed and observed by an army of public servants – by whom almost anyone in public service is meant. Originally drawn up in 1911 to tighten security in the lead up to the First World War, the main purpose of the Act was to combat espionage, but Section 2 of the Act merely stated that public servants must not disclose any information they had learned in the course of their work to any unauthorised persons. This would sound reasonable enough if it were intended to penalise those who might be guilty of passing state secrets to a hostile power. But

Section 2 is a catch-all provision which, if carried to a logical conclusion, makes a public servant liable to prosecution for divulging anything whatsoever learned at work. Carried to ridiculous extremes it would be possible to prosecute an official messenger for telling his wife the price of biscuits in the Ministry of Defence canteen.

That is a ludicrous example, and not seriously intended, but it is not too far from some of the decisions that have been made in the past to prosecute under the Official Secrets Act. The problem in democratic terms is that so many of the secrecy rules surrounding government are concerned with political problems rather than issues of state security. There are a number of factors in the British political system that encourage a culture of secrecy:

- The adversarial nature of the two-party system which encourages the government to keep secret all its workings in case the opposition might find out too much.
- The doctrine of collective responsibility and the need for the government to present a united face to the world means that disagreements within Cabinet or between ministers have to be kept from the outside world.
- The doctrine of ministerial responsibility and the anonymity of civil servants conspire to make it necessary that the workings of government be kept concealed.
- The link in the British system between executive and legislature, with the need of government ministers to be elected, creates a desire on the part of ministers that their errors and misjudgements should never be known to the voters who must re-elect them.

During the 1980s there were a number of famous court cases where individuals were prosecuted under the Official Secrets Act, not for betraying the national interest, but for embarrassing the government. Probably the most famous case was that of Clive Ponting, a senior civil servant in the Defence Ministry. During the Falklands War of 1982 there was a great deal of concern expressed about the circumstances surrounding the sinking of the Argentinian battleship, the *General Belgrano*, criticisms of government action being led by the Scottish Labour MP, Tam Dalyell. Ponting became convinced that Dalyell and the House of Commons were being misled by ministerial disinformation and, to clarify matters, sent Dalyell two documents relating to the affair, only one of which was marginally confidential. In 1985 Ponting was prosecuted for leaking official information under Section 2 of the Official Secrets Act; the case hinging on two different interpretations of the expression 'national interest'.

1 For Clive Ponting it was in the national interest for the public to know the truth and, by releasing this information he was serving the national interest.

2 For the government and prosecution (and indeed the judge, in his summing up) the national interest equates with the policy of the government of the day and a civil servant has a primary duty to uphold government policy, including the concealment of information, if that is the wish of the government.

To the government's consternation the jury in the Ponting case found the civil servant not guilty and sent a clear message to the government that a civil servant should place his or her duty to the community at large before any loyalty to a partisan administration. This verdict, together with other cases such as the *Spycatcher* affair, led to calls for a reform of the Official Secrets Act, even senior judges joining in the demand, 'For heaven's sake legislate now before our law, our courts and our reputation as a free country become the laughing stock of the world.'[3] At the time when that was written the House of Commons was debating a private member's bill promoted by a Conservative backbencher, Richard Shepherd, which would have reformed the Official Secrets Act by allowing someone accused under the Act the defence of prior publication or public interest. However, the government killed off Shepherd's bill by imposing a three-line whip against the bill on its second reading.

The Official Secrets Act of 1989 was presented by the government as reforming Section 2 of the 1911 Act and thereby satisfying critics such as Richard Shepherd. It does clarify parts of

Section 2 by allowing large quantities of harmless information to be revealed without penalty. But in other respects the Act became even more severe than its predecessor:

- Certain categories of disclosure become criminal without the prosecution having to prove that disclosure is harmful.
- Criminal liability extends not only to those disclosing any secrets but also to those publishing those secrets, such as newspaper editors.
- Neither the fact of the information having been published previously elsewhere, nor the claim that disclosure was in the national interest would be available as an argument for the defence.

The situation as regards the freedom of information is very different from that in other countries. In the United States the first amendment to the constitution lays down that there should be no laws to curtail or limit the freedom of 'speech or of the press'. The United Nations declaration of human rights included the freedom of information as a fundamental right and over a dozen European and Commonwealth countries have Freedom of Information Acts written into their laws. Moves towards a similar act in Britain have resulted in limited access for the public into educational, medical and computerised records. Even the Major government's much-vaunted espousal of 'open government', and the appointment of William Waldegrave as Public Services Minister to promote openness, has not resulted in much more than a voluntary code of practice for government departments as to the amount of material they should make available.

The fundamental difference between British policy on freedom of information and that of other countries is that in other countries the government is required to prove the need to keep something secret: in Britain the person seeking information has to prove why it should not be kept secret. Even more fundamental is the fact that the 'right to know' is nowhere written down for the British people. The 'right to know' is just one of a whole series of rights that are not codified for the British people because the United Kingdom has neither a written constitution nor a Bill of Rights.

Civil rights

Although the American Declaration of Independence began with the stirring message that all citizens had the natural god-given right to 'life, liberty and the pursuit of happiness', there was nothing about citizens' rights in the US Constitution as it was originally drafted in 1787. It was only later that a succession of amendments to the constitution were passed, the first ten amendments being known collectively as 'the Bill of Rights' because they granted rights to freedom of worship, assembly and speech, as well as safeguards against unlawful persecution. Concern over civil rights nevertheless languished in the United States until the 1960s, when the foundation of the National Association for the Advancement of Coloured Peoples and the American Civil Liberties Union, together with the mass protests against segregation by the blacks of America, led to civil rights becoming the main concern of protesters during the student unrest of the 1960s.

In Britain there was no Bill of Rights comparable to that of the United States to give substance to a protest movement. The English 1689 Bill of Rights, granted by William and Mary, was concerned with the rival powers of monarch and parliament rather than the rights of individual citizens. In Britain it was assumed that a wealth of Common Law, dating back to Magna Carta and beyond, guaranteed the rights and liberties of free individuals without the need for them to be written down. The civil rights movement in Britain began through representing the interests of vulnerable minorities who, it was felt, were ignored by a Common Law formulated by the majority population. Protest movements sprang up to help minority groups fight against discrimination. The protesters advocated equal rights and opportunities for ethnic minorities and women; and in Northern Ireland there were marches by the Catholic minority against the Protestant Ascendancy.

A series of Race Relations Acts between 1965 and 1976, together with the foundation of the Commission for Racial Equality, has given a legal and administrative foundation to outlaw both direct and indirect racial discrimination. The Equal Pay Act of 1970 and the Sex Discrimination Act of 1975, together with the Equal Opportunities Commission, have done much the same thing for women's rights. The success of minority groups in winning a number of rights which were then enshrined in law caused a realisation that for the majority of the population there is no legal authority for the rights which it is assumed we possess as citizens. This became even more relevant during the 1980s, as events such as the Ponting trial, the *Spycatcher* affair, the controversy over union membership at GCHQ (Government Communications Headquarters), suspect police powers during the miners' strike, the suspension of rules governing arrest and detention in anti-terrorist legislation, and so on, led people to wonder just how much the supposed rights of freedom of speech, assembly and belief were really worth.

Unlike countries that have a written constitution Britain does not have a codified document which defines the rights possessed by the individual. Instead the British view of civil rights is based on the libertarian philosophies of nineteenth-century thinkers like John Stuart Mill, who desired 'unbounded freedom of individual action in all modes not hurtful to others'. In other words, the individual has the right to do whatever they want, as long as they do no harm to other individuals and there is no law against it. This has resulted in a negative expression of rights for the British citizen, in that there are plenty of laws saying what one *may not* do, but none which lay down guidelines as to what one *can* do.

This liberal or *laissez-faire* approach to rights, which says that you can do whatever you like if there is no law against it, is very attractive and was held up for a long time as evidence of the superiority of 'England's ancient liberties'. Events of the 1970s and 1980s, particularly the draconian suspension of civil rights in anti-terrorist legislation, forced people to realise that if there were only a negative definition of individual freedom there was nothing to stop the government from issuing whatever legislation they liked to curtail that freedom. It is worth remembering that the theory of parliamentary sovereignty states that parliament cannot be bound by any other body and any ruling issued in the name of parliament cannot be resisted, even when exercised by prerogative powers.

> The liberal approach stresses in particular the inability of existing structures to protect the rights of the individual from encroachment by agencies of the state . . . Political power has been centralised in Downing Street and Cabinet, with neither House of Parliament able to stand up effectively to the wishes of the executive. Control of a party majority in the House of Commons is all that is needed to ride roughshod over the rights of the individual.[4]

It is recognition of this flaw in the existing political system that has led increasing numbers of individuals and groups to call for a Bill of Rights. These calls received renewed life because of certain acts by the Major government, and particularly by the Home Secretary, Michael Howard, in his Criminal Justice and Public Order Act of November 1994. This Act contained a number of measures which were seen as constraints on civil liberties.

(1) A new offence of 'aggravated trespass' which makes it illegal for people to assemble on land owned by a private or public body if the assembly is liable to disrupt other people. The legislation was aimed at problems caused by the so-called New Age Travellers but the wording of the Act rendered potentially illegal any meeting of people that might possibly cause disruption and thereby gave the authorities *carte blanche* to ban any form of mass protest; curtailing the civil right of freedom of assembly.

(2) The criminal justice section of the bill abolished the historic right to silence, which has been regarded as a civil right since the seventeenth century, and which is enshrined as a main plank of any Bill of Rights through its existence as the fifth amendment to the US Constitution.

A Bill of Rights

There are a number of reasons put forward to support the idea of a Bill of Rights:

- If civil rights were clearly stated and existed in written form it would help individuals to understand exactly what they were and were not entitled to do. A codified Bill of Rights could be taught in school so that everyone could grow up as an informed citizen.
- Someone whose rights were abused would have the backing of the courts to give redress to individuals against public officials. Officials might be less likely to abuse peoples' rights if they felt they might be taken to court as a result.
- Any legislation passed by parliament would have to observe the Bill of Rights and any proposed laws that infringed the Bill of Rights would be rendered invalid.
- A Bill of Rights would protect the interests of vulnerable minorities such as travellers, gays, certain religious sects and other minorities an elected representative might fear to champion in the face of majority opinion.

Those who are opposed to a Bill of Rights argue from the same basis as those who oppose a written constitution: on the grounds of inflexibility. There is no such thing as an absolute right, argue these critics: the rights of one individual have to be measured against the effect those rights would have on the rights of other individuals. If it came to a legal dispute between conflicting rights, the courts would need to interpret the balance of rights and that judicial decision would mean that, constitutionally, power would be transferred from an elected parliament to an unelected judiciary.

In one respect Britain already has access to a Bill of Rights. In 1950, Britain, as a member of the Council of Europe, was a signatory of the European Convention of Human Rights which, modelled on the United Nations 'Declaration of Human Rights', set out to define those civil and natural freedoms which should belong by rights to the citizens of Europe. Britain ratified the Convention in 1951 and has continued to ratify it each year ever since, but the Convention has never been incorporated into British law. A civil rights issue cannot be tried in a British court but a British citizen can seek redress by direct appeal to the Commission, for referral to the European Court of Human Rights in Strasbourg.[5]

Around 800 complaints from British subjects are laid before the Commission each year. Only a few of these are judged suitable for hearing by the Court but almost a quarter of all cases heard come from Britain and only the Italian government has a higher record of adverse judgments than the British. In cases against the British government the Court has:

- found that the IRA members shot in Gibraltar by the SAS (the *Death on the Rock* incident) were 'killed unlawfully'.
- condemned the use of corporal punishment in schools.
- found for the parents and the *Sunday Times* in the thalidomide case.
- upheld the rights of workers not to join a closed shop.
- allowed *Spycatcher* defendants the defence of 'prior publication'.

It would be very easy for Britain to acquire a 'ready-made' Bill of Rights by fully accepting the European Convention and incorporating it in to British law. But all governments since 1965 have shown themselves to be against such a move. Indeed, recent decisions by the Strasbourg court, especially the Gibraltar shootings case, have angered the British government so much that there is talk of a British withdrawal from the Convention. Michael Howard, as Home Secretary, seemed to have a particular grievance against the Court of Human Rights. The constitutional lawyer, Anthony Lester, listed four occasions on which Howard thwarted attempts to make the European Convention applicable to member governments:

1 He opposed reform of the Convention 'to the point where the United Kingdom and Turkey were in unsplendid isolation from the rest of the Council of Europe, and had to back down'.

2 He opposed Lester's bill that would have enabled British courts to administer aspects of the European Convention.

3 He opposed European Convention rulings on personal privacy, acting alone against all other member governments.

4 He brought pressure to bear on other governments to limit the scope of the European Court of Human Rights in reviewing national laws.[6]

With this attitude to the European Convention on Human Rights, which was supposedly a British conception, it is not surprising that recent British governments have shown no real enthusiasm for the idea of a British Bill of Rights. The attitude is part of the dichotomy in British government thought which, on the one hand, says it wants to allow freedom of choice and independent action to the citizen while, on the other, centralising all power into its own hands. This theoretical dichotomy is nowhere clearer than in the government's use of the term 'subsidiarity', dependent on whether the term is applied to the government's relations with Europe or to the government's relations with the constituent regions of the United Kingdom.

Subsidiarity

As a political concept 'subsidiarity' has been in use for some time but it came to have a specific application in negotiating sessions of the Intergovernmental Conference that led to the Treaty on European Union (Maastricht). A particular interpretation of the concept of subsidiarity was developed in that context, at the wish of John Major's negotiating team, in order to counter British fears of what was seen as the committed pro-federalism of the Maastricht agreement. In Britain, unlike the rest of Europe, federalism was equated with centralism, giving rise to fears of a powerful federal administration in Brussels imposing its will on the Member States, with no regard being paid to the wishes of national parliaments. What was developed at Maastricht was a form of the doctrine of subsidiarity, originally defined in the Treaty itself as being when 'decisions are taken as closely as possible to the citizen'.

> In areas which do not fall within its exclusive competence, the Community should take action, in accordance with the principle of subsidiarity, only in so far as the proposed action cannot sufficiently be achieved by the Member States and can therefore, by reason of the scale or effects of the proposed action, be better achieved by the Community. Any action of the Community shall not go beyond what is necessary to achieve the objectives of this Treaty.[7]

Subsidiarity as a concept was seized on during the period of Britain's presidency of the EU in 1992 and was debated at length at the Edinburgh European Council, being seen by John Major as an anti-federal position that might pacify the anti-Maastricht elements in Britain and those Euro-sceptics in Denmark who had voted 'no' in the Danish referendum of that year. In Major's view, and that of his supporters, subsidiarity was seen as a 'shield protecting the rights of Member States against undue EC interference'.[8] The argument against the centralising powers of the EU is that Brussels is too remote from the people and, for certain critical legislation, decisions need to be taken by competent authorities closer to the people – like national governments. Where the democratic needs of the people are concerned, action by a remote federal government are deemed inappropriate.

It is here that the proponents of subsidiarity have made a rod for their own backs. Simply because a proposal is thought to be inappropriate for Community action does not necessarily mean that action by national governments is any more appropriate. It could well be the case that regional or local action might be even more suitable. Certainly, the Scottish National Party has adopted the concept of subsidiarity with enthusiasm, with its slogan of 'Scotland in Europe', meaning that, in matters of importance to Scotland, there need be no intervening English body between Brussels and a Scottish Assembly or Council. And the anomaly is that, although the Westminster government advocated subsidiarity to prevent centralisation in Brussels, that government remains very ardently centralist in their management of the affairs of the United Kingdom. Yet the British government may find that, in safeguarding the principle of national sovereignty, they have sacrificed the union of the United Kingdom to the greater democratic goal of subsidiarity through devolution.[9]

The sidelining of local government during the Thatcher years, with its consequent intensive centralisation of British politics, allied to the role of centrally-appointed quangos in taking accountability away from local communities, has led to an increased awareness in the regions of the gulf between the decision-makers in London and the general public in the rest of the

United Kingdom – a gulf that is both geographical and ideological. That awareness has re-awakened the devolution issue, not only for Scotland and Wales but as a possibility for the regions of England as well; not to mention its relevance to any settlement of the Northern Ireland situation.

English regionalism

It is ironic that, while the Conservative government under John Major has been continuing to reduce the powers of local government, attempting to replace the old county–district two-tier council structure with a unitary single-tier system, a whole new tier of government is emerging where it did not exist before; in the form of executive regionalism.[10] There are a number of factors which have caused the introduction of this new tier of government, sometimes at the wish of central government, in other cases informally and without recognition from the centre.

(1) In 1994 the government created ten English integrated regional offices (IROs) which have merged the regional offices previously maintained by the Departments of the Environment, Employment, Transport and Trade and Industry. These regional offices, with the population for the area covered by that office, are:

London	6.9 million	South-East	7.7 million
Eastern	5.2 million	South-West	4.8 million
West Midlands	5.3 million	East Midlands	4.1 million
Yorks & Humberside	5.0 million	North-East	2.6 million
North-West	2.6 million	Merseyside	1.5 million

These integrated offices are supposed to serve the same administrative functions for the English regions, as the Northern Irish, Scottish and Welsh Offices do for the national regions.

(2) The replacement of local authority bodies by quangos, and the handover of certain civil service functions to government agencies, has led to networks of semi-autonomous bodies, each of which has a strong regional structure. Taken together with the IROs this means that there is a regional level of government

designed to supervise the regional implementation of government policy. It is, however, wholly subordinate to the central government and is not democratically accountable to the people of the regions concerned.

(3) The EU's structural aid funds are distributed on a regional rather than a national basis and the EU prefers to work directly with regional authorities. In the case of Objective One funding, which is the most generous assistance programme, help is given to areas whose GDP (gross domestic product) is less than 75 per cent of the EU average and originally there were no Objective One regions in England, although Northern Ireland and the Highlands and Islands of Scotland did qualify. The unilateral action of Liverpool in forming the Merseyside Task Force from local authorities in the area, declaring that Merseyside is separate from the rest of the north-west region, and entering into direct negotiations with the EU, has resulted in Merseyside gaining Objective One funding worth £1.28 billion over six years. Merseyside's success has led to other local authorities getting together to form regional action groups to handle negotiations with Brussels.

(4) The Maastricht Treaty created the Committee of the Regions (COR) to act as a body which must be consulted during the EU legislative process on any matter which it is felt has regional implications. In most Member States of the EU there are strong regional governments and administrations which can be represented on the COR. Since no such bodies exist in Britain the United Kingdom is represented on the COR by a representative delegation from regionally grouped local authorities.

(5) The IROs and quango networks are examples of 'executive regionalism' and exist as an arm of central control. As these have grown, from the late 1980s on, they have been countered by regional associations of local authorities made up of nominated members and seconded local government officials. They exist to promote co-operation between local authorities to create regionally integrated policies on matters such as transport, economic development and liaison with the EU. They cover much the same ground as the IROs and act as a defence of local government against encroachment from the centre.

As Jack Straw, the Shadow Home Secretary, said in July 1995: 'the government regional offices, sub-regional and regional quangos, and numerous agency offices form a nascent administrative and governmental infrastructure for England's regions'.[11] If such a framework exists, it suffers from the disadvantage of being largely formed by nominated rather than elected representatives. This aspect caused parliament to inflict an important defeat on the government during ratification of Maastricht Treaty, when ministers wanted to send quango members to the COR but opposition parties demanded that those representatives should all be elected councillors.

For those wishing to curb the centralising imperative of central government, this development of regional structures is considered to be highly desirable. If the logic of the development was accepted, and legitimised by introducing elected regional governments, then the enthusiasts would see this as a key factor in constitutional reform. Most enthusiastic is the Liberal Democrat Party, which would like to see devolution to the English regions just as much as it desires devolution for Scotland and Wales, and, as a logical conclusion, would like to see a federal structure for the whole of Great Britain.

The Conservative Party, while being responsible for the growth of regional bureaucracy, is opposed to any form of devolution which it sees as tending to the break-up of the United Kingdom. Therefore, any proposals for directly elected regional government are rejected on the grounds that:

• regional government would be an additional layer of government in an already over-governed state;
• it would be an additional burden on the taxpayer, being in effect a needless extra expense;
• there is no evidence of any public demand for English devolution.

The Major government has done all that it can to prevent regional representation on the EU's Committee of the Regions, believing that 'the prospect of British representatives in EU politics, acting for regions rather than the British state as a whole, undermines the very sovereignty of the state'.[12]

The Labour Party, on the other hand, has taken a position virtually midway between the Liberal Democrats and the Conservatives. There is a faction within the party which favours regional government, largely because of Labour's concentration of support within certain regions, but also as a by-product of Labour's support for Scottish devolution. However, Labour has recognised that there is not the same public demand for devolved government in the English regions as there is in Scotland or Wales and the idea also meets with not inconsiderable opposition from the Labour-dominated local authorities who would have most to lose in terms of power and influence from the introduction of an additional tier of government. In July 1995, Jack Straw, then Shadow Home Secretary, proposed a gradualist approach to the issue.

Straw's proposal was that the regional associations of local authorities should be given the control of IROs, quangos and agencies in their region and that the regulation of privatised utilities in the region should also be their responsibility. They would be strategic bodies responsible for planning across a range of policy areas, including the implementation of EU policy. Such bodies would be indirectly democratic in that a large proportion of their membership would be composed of elected councillors but, if public opinion demanded it, they could institute direct elections to regional assemblies later, thereby becoming fully devolved bodies. Since this would involve constitutional change, the move to directly-elected assemblies would only be made as the result of a referendum and the transfer of power would only take place when the people so decided. As a result, Straw could foresee a future in which some regions of England would follow Scotland and Wales in accepting devolved power, while other regions might choose not to do so.

Devolution

The arguments for devolution are strongest where the people of a given region feel a sense of common identity: an identity, moreover, that is distinct from that of other regions and from that of the centralising power. This sense of identity is obviously strongest where there is a history of separate development as with Northern Ireland, Wales and Scotland and where rule from London is seen as not only remote but actually alien. Here the options are not confined to regional local government but to the alternatives of devolution of power or outright independence.

It must be recognised that the United Kingdom is neither a unitary state nor a federal state. Like a unitary state it has one sovereign parliament but that parliament has grown from the merger of previously separate assemblies. The UK parliament was formed through the union of the English parliament with the councils, assemblies or parliaments of Wales (1543), Scotland (1707) and Ireland (1800). In contrast to a federal structure, therefore, the component parliaments have surrendered their jurisdiction and sovereignty. Unlike a unitary state, on the other hand, the component nations of the United Kingdom continue to possess pre-union rights and institutions peculiar to themselves which maintain some administrative autonomy.

Northern Ireland

Northern Ireland is the one region of the United Kingdom which has had a devolved assembly in recent times. When the larger part of Ireland gained its independence in the 1920s, the six predominantly protestant counties in the north-east formed a separate province still subordinate to the British Crown and with MPs in the Westminster parliament. The UK government was, however, responsible only for major policy matters such as economics and foreign affairs; most executive and legislative matters concerning the province being dealt with by a Northern Ireland Parliament at Stormont which had its own executive, legislative and administrative powers, including the control of law and order. However, it was long recognised that Stormont was totally dominated by the Ulster Unionist Party and was used as a tool to maintain a protestant supremacy in the province. During the 'troubles' of the 1970s, Stormont was suspended and its executive and legislative powers were transferred in 1972 to the direct rule of Westminster. Northern Ireland continues to have its own institutions, however, and they are administered by the Northern Ireland Office rather than Whitehall departments, so that a form of administrative devolution remains. Devolution in the form of a return of executive powers to Stormont was foreseen by the government when it imposed direct rule and various power-sharing solutions have been proposed, only to founder in the light of the continuing conflict. Nevertheless, some form of devolution is likely to be offered as a solution of the 'Northern Ireland Question'.

Wales

In one respect, Wales has less of a claim to political autonomy than other regions of the United Kingdom, in that it was never a fully independent state in its own right. Under feudal law, unlike Scotland but rather like Ireland, it was not a unified kingdom but merely a collection of small principalities who, more often than not, accepted the overlordship of the English king. Much of the territory we call Wales was in the hands of Anglo-Norman marcher lords by the end of the twelfth century. and it was only the north-western principality of Gwynedd which held out independently of the English Crown until the late thirteenth century. It is this north-western corner of the country which continues to exhibit Wales' strongest argument for separate treatment, which is the existence of a distinctive linguistic and cultural difference in the Welsh language, with its poetry and music. It is no coincidence that the four constituencies which elected Plaid Cymru MPs in 1992 – Caernarfon, Ceredigion, Meirionydd and Ynys Mon – are essentially Welsh-speaking and cover an area which corresponds precisely with the borders of ancient Gwynedd. Wales has had administrative devolution through the Welsh Office since 1964.

Scotland

Constitutionally, Scotland has the strongest case of any region of the United Kingdom for devolution, if not complete independence. Scotland was a separate country with its own monarch, parliament, laws, economy and diplomatic relations until as late as 1707. Even then, the union was achieved through negotiation between equals, rather than through one side imposing its authority on the other: however it may have appeared since! Since the union Scotland has retained its own, very distinctive, legal and education systems, the Presbyterian Church has remained the established Church of Scotland, Scottish banks have been allowed to print their own bank notes and there is an advanced form of administrative devolution in the institutions of the Scottish Office and the Scottish Grand Committee. There has been a movement for Home Rule since 1886 and ten Home Rule bills were presented to parliament between 1886 and 1914. The Scottish National Party was founded in 1927 but made little headway until the 1960s, when a combination of alienation from the unionist parties and the realisation that North Sea oil could give Scotland economic independence, led to an upsurge in interest and support for the nationalist cause. In 1979, the referendum on devolution and a Scottish Assembly actually gained a majority of the votes but, because there were many abstentions, the 'Yes' vote did not receive support from the majority of the Scottish population and the reform failed according to the rules governing the referendum.

Administrative devolution

The Scottish Office was founded in 1885, with a remit totally unlike that of other government departments, in that it was a territorial rather than a functional department, with responsibility for general government activity in Scotland.[13] At the head of the Scottish Office is the Secretary of State for Scotland, a Cabinet Minister, with two Ministers of State and two Under-Secretaries of State in support. Also, since the Scottish legal system is very different from the English, there are two Scottish law officers, the Lord Advocate and the Solicitor-General for Scotland. The Scottish Office took on its present form when it was established at St Andrew's House in Edinburgh in 1939. At that time the Scottish Office was organised into four functional departments, but that has now been extended to five, dealing with agriculture and fisheries, education, environment, home and health, and trade and industry.

Within the Westminster parliament there has been, since 1894, a Scottish Grand Committee, on which all MPs for Scottish constituencies have the right to sit. Two committees within the standing committee structure exist to examine the details of specifically Scottish legislation and, since 1979, there has also been a Scottish Affairs select committee. One difficulty with the last is that in recent years the Conservative Party has not won sufficient Scottish seats to staff the select committee, once Scottish Office ministers had been appointed. The Scottish Affairs Committee was suspended between 1987 and 1992 and was only resumed after the 1992 election by being allowed a Labour chairman and having Conservative numbers made up by English MPs.

Some element of accountability is introduced into Scottish affairs by there being a Question Time in the Commons set aside for Scottish questions. But this is counter-balanced by the fact that party membership of the Scottish select and standing committees is proportional to the composition of the Commons as a whole and does not reflect the party balance in Scotland. This is a significant argument against those, like the Conservative Party, who say that a reformed use of administrative devolution is sufficient to meet the distinctive needs of Scotland. Critics reply that the Scottish Office and Scottish committees are subordinate parts of an overwhelmingly English parliament.

After direct rule was imposed in 1972 the Northern Ireland Office acquired many of the same characteristics of the Scottish Office. A Secretary of State is supported by two Ministers of State and two Under-Secretaries. The Office is responsible for functional departments like education but, of course, routine administration has taken second place in the past twenty-five years or so in the face of the continuing 'troubles' and security situation. Unlike Scotland, Northern Ireland did not have a select committee of the Commons dedicated to it until after the 1992 election, when one was promised by John Major in his bid to win Ulster Unionist support for his government.

The Welsh Office was only established in 1964 with a Secretary of State for Wales and an executive base in Cardiff. The Welsh Office is smaller than the Scottish, with just one Minister of State and one Under-Secretary, and there is less of a departmental function than a remit to oversee the application of national policy to Wales in the areas of agriculture, education, health, labour, planning, trade and transport. There is a Welsh Affairs select committee but, as is the case for Scotland, the Conservatives are so under-represented in Wales that the select committee has a Labour chair and English Conservative MPs in its membership. Indeed, for most of the period of Conservative government after 1979 the Secretary of State for Wales was either English, or a member for an English constituency, or both.

The democratic deficit for the people of Scotland, Wales, Northern Ireland and some English regions, particularly in the north and south-west, is that there is no direct democratic accountability in the administrative services that are devolved to their region. This has been particularly true since 1979 for Scotland, Wales and large areas of northern England where there is a natural majority for the Labour Party but where they have been subjected to the rule of a Conservative government largely elected by south-eastern England.

Devolution or independence?

Generally speaking, there seem to be three possible solutions for the future governance of Scotland; and, by inference, for Wales, Northern Ireland and perhaps the English regions as well:

1 Things could go on as they are, but with increased and improved administrative devolution. This is largely the position of the Conservative Party.

2 There could be executive and legislative devolution, as advocated by the Labour and Liberal Democrat parties.

3 There could be full sovereign independence within Europe, as desired by the SNP in Scotland and Plaid Cymru in Wales.

The Scottish local election results of 1995, which saw the Conservative Party virtually eliminated north of the border, awoke renewed interest in the plans being made by the various parties for the future governance of Scotland. For some time a special committee, the Scottish Constitutional Convention, had been meeting to discuss these matters in an unusually wide alliance of the Labour and Liberal Democrat Parties, the Scottish churches, the Scottish TUC and various civic bodies. On 30 November 1995, St Andrew's Day, the Convention was due to hold a celebratory meeting to mark the publication of their findings. Two days before this the Scottish Secretary, Michael Forsyth, made a series of declarations to outline government proposals for changes in how Scotland is governed. And, so as not to be left out, while the Convention was meeting in the Assembly Hall of the Church of Scotland, the SNP was at the Edinburgh City Chambers to outline the Nationalists' proposals for an independent Scotland. Within the term of one week therefore, three alternative proposals for the future of Scotland had been announced:

Scottish Constitutional Convention (Labour/Liberal Democrat)
- There would be a Scottish parliament of 129 members, 73 of them elected according to first-past-the-post in Westminster-like constituencies, but with 56 top-up members elected proportionately from Scottish Euro-constituencies.
- Parliaments would be for a fixed term.
- Both parties would ensure that at least half the candidates in winnable seats would be women.
- The Scottish parliament would have powers over all decisions currently taken by the Scottish Office. The SMPs (Scottish MPs) together would elect a Chief Minister who would take the place of the present Scottish Secretary.
- The Scottish parliament would have tax-raising powers to pay for services and legislation peculiar to Scotland. Those tax-raising powers would include the ability to vary the rate of income tax from the UK level by plus or minus three pence.

Independent Scotland (Scottish National Party)
- The Queen would remain as Queen of Scots and Head of State.

- There would be a single chamber parliament of 200 members. Of these 144 would be elected for constituencies by the existing first-past-the-post system. These constituency members would be augmented by 56 members chosen by a list system of proportional representation.
- A Chancellor would be elected to preside over parliaments.
- There would be no place for peers except as elected members.
- There would be a written constitution and Bill of Rights. Gaelic would be recognised as an official language.
- Links with England, Ireland and Wales would be maintained through a loose confederation known as the 'Associated States of the British Isles'.

The Scottish Grand Committee (Conservative and Unionist Party)
- The existing Grand Committee of 72 Scottish MPs would be given the right to scrutinise Scottish legislation through the second and third readings being heard in Committee rather than the full Commons.
- The Grand Committee would sit in Scotland rather than at Westminster. Scottish towns and cities would bid for the honour of hosting the Committee.
- Many Scottish powers currently administered by the Scottish Office, such as education, roads and social services, would be devolved to local authorities in an enhancement of administrative devolution, subject to some elected accountability in the person of local councillors.
- A special standing committee at Westminster would consider the content of all Scottish bills before they began the legislative process.
- The Prime Minister, Chancellor and other ministers could be asked to debate legislation with the Grand Committee.

The West Lothian Question

For how long will English constituencies and English Honourable Members tolerate not just 71 Scots, 36 Welsh and a number of Ulstermen but at least 119 Honourable Members from

Scotland, Wales and Northern Ireland exercising an important, and probably often decisive, effect on English politics while they themselves have no say in the same matters in Scotland, Wales and Ireland?[14]

The question set out above was asked by Tam Dalyell, MP for the Scottish constituency of West Lothian, during the second reading of Labour's Scottish devolution legislation in 1977, and has become famous since then as the 'West Lothian Question'. It recognises the point that any devolution of power from Westminster would lead to a disproportionate presence of MPs from the devolved regions in the Westminster parliament.

Scotland has always had more representatives at Westminster than the size of the country would seem to warrant. In the 1707 Act of Union, Scotland was granted forty-five MPs and sixteen representative peers in the parliament of Great Britain, the over-representation being said to compensate Scotland for the loss of an independent parliament and to prevent the Scottish voice being swamped beneath the English majority. By the time of the 1992 election, Scotland contained 9 per cent of the UK population but its seventy-two MPs represented 11 per cent of Commons membership. The same picture is reflected for Wales, where 5 per cent of the population are represented by 6 per cent of MPs.[15]

This disproportionality, if it continued after the introduction of devolution for Scotland or Wales, leads directly to the West Lothian Question, or rather to two related questions:

1 If Scotland had its own parliament and Wales its own assembly, each dealing with Scottish or Welsh legislation, would either country need so many Westminster MPs? Would it not be the case that Scottish and Welsh electors would be twice as well represented as the electors of England?

2 Would it be right for English MPs to have no say on legislation that was specifically Scottish or Welsh, when Scottish and Welsh MPs would be able to speak and vote on legislation that was specifically English in nature? This is, of course, the real West Lothian Question.

The obvious answer is that the number of Westminster constituencies would have to be reduced for any part of the United

Kingdom which became subject to a devolved assembly. The reverse was shown in 1972 when Stormont was suppressed. Before that time, while the Stormont parliament existed, Northern Ireland had twelve Westminster MPs; after the abolition of Stormont the number of Northern Irish constituencies was increased to seventeen.

There is one fly in this ointment and that is the heavy reliance of Labour on Scottish and Welsh seats for the party's representation in parliament. The party easily predominates in both countries: half the votes cast in Wales are for the Labour Party, while almost a fifth of all Labour MPs sit for Scottish constituencies. The dilemma for Labour is that they are a party committed to some form of devolution for Scotland, and yet to re-distribute and reduce the number of Scottish seats in the wake of devolution could well remove any Labour majority in the Westminster parliament.

Conclusion

Within the concept of liberal democracy there are overwhelming arguments in favour of a Bill of Rights, a Freedom of Information Act and devolution for the constituent countries of the United Kingdom. As with other aspects of democratic reform along liberal democratic lines, such as electoral reform, these ideas are enthusiastically adopted by political parties while in opposition but could well be forgotten when those parties come into power. The position can be summed up in Professor Norton's words on 'the constitution in question'.[16]

> The chances of a new constitutional settlement are remote. Such a settlement must await the time when those who are currently the 'outs' in British politics become the 'ins'. However, becoming the 'ins' in British politics can affect previously held perceptions about the need for change.

Notes

1 Andrew Puddephatt, General Secretary of Liberty, 'The Criminal Justice and Public Order Act and the need for a Bill of Rights', *Talking Politics*, Autumn 1995, pages 59–62.

2 Andrew Gray and Bill Jenkins, 'Ministers, departments and civil servants', chapter 20 of *Politics UK* (2nd edition), Harvester Wheatsheaf, Hemel Hempstead, 1994, page 421.

3 Lord Scarman, letter to *The Times*, 7 January 1988.

4 Philip Norton, 'The constitution in question', *Politics Review*, April 1994, pages 6–11.

5 It is stressed that the European Court of Human Rights is administered by the Council of Europe and is located in Strasbourg. It is not to be confused with the European Court of Justice, which is an institution of the EU and is located in Luxembourg.

6 Anthony, Lord Lester of Herne Hill QC, contributing to a symposium on Michael Howard, 'Is this man the worst Home Secretary ever?' in the *Observer*, 19 May 1996, page 7.

7 *Treaty on European Union*, Title II (Amendments to the Treaty of Rome), article 3b.

8 Marc-Philippe Cooper, 'Understanding subsidiarity as a political issue in the European Community', *Talking Politics*, Spring 1995, pages 178–83.

9 Colin Pilkington, *Britain in the European Union Today*, Manchester University Press, Manchester, 1995, pages 112–13.

10 The issues involved in regionalism – especially English regionalism – were discussed in two articles which appeared at around the same time, Jonathan Bradbury, 'English regional government', in *Politics Review*, April 1996, pages 16–19, and Gerry Stokes, Brian Hopwood and Udo Bullman, 'Do we need regional government?', in *Talking Politics*, Spring 1996, pages 191–5.

11 Jack Straw, speech of July 1995, quoted by Stokes, Hopwood and Bulman, 'Do we need regional government?'.

12 Bradbury, 'English regional government'.

13 A great deal of interesting information on devolution in Scotland can be found in James Mitchell, 'Reviving the Union State?' *Politics Review*, February 1996, pages 16–18.

14 *Hansard*, Vol. 939, Cols. 122–3, 14 November 1977. Quoted by Mitchell, 'Reviving the Union State?', page 18.

15 Figures taken from Andrew Adonis, *Parliament Today*, Manchester University Press, Manchester, 1993, page 8.

16 Norton, 'The constitution in question'.

Index

A number of politicians have now received peerages (e.g. Lady Thatcher, Baroness Williams) but they are listed here under the names by which they were known when active in the Commons (i.e. Thatcher, Margaret; Williams, Shirley).